WRITING OFF IDEAS

Independent Studies in Political Economy

WRITING OFF IDEAS

*Taxation,
Foundations, and
Philanthropy in America*

Randall G. Holcombe

Transaction Publishers
New Brunswick (U.S.A.) and London (U.K.)

Copyright © 2000 by The Independent Institute, Oakland, Calif..

This book is printed on acid-free paper that meets the American National Standard for Permanence of Paper for Printed Library Materials.

Library of Congress Catalog Number: 00-020660
ISBN: 0-7658-0680-0 (paper); 0-7658-0013-6 (cloth)
Printed in the United States of America

Library of Congress Cataloging-in-Publication Data

Holcombe, Randall G.
    Writings off ideas : taxation, foundations, and philanthropy in America / Randall G. Holcombe.
        p.   cm.
    Includes bibliographical references and index.
    ISBN 0-7658-0013-6 (alk. paper) — ISBN 0-7658-0680-0
    1. Endowments—United States.   2. Endowments—Taxation—United States.   3. Nonprofit organizations—Taxation—United States.   4. Tax exemption—United States.   I. Title. II.

HV91 .H57 2000
361.7'632'0973—dc21   00-020660

The INDEPENDENT INSTITUTE

The Independent Institute is a non-profit, non-partisan, scholarly research and educational organization that sponsors comprehensive studies on the political economy of critical social and economic problems.

The politicization of decision making in society has largely confined public debate to the narrow reconsideration of existing policies. Given the prevailing influence of partisan interests, little social innovation has occurred. In order to understand both the nature of and possible solutions to major public issues, The Independent Institute's program adheres to the highest standards of independent inquiry and is pursued regardless of prevailing political or social biases and conventions. The resulting studies are widely distributed as books and other publications, and publicly debated through numerous conference and media programs.

Through this uncommon independence, depth, and clarity, the Independent Institute pushes at the frontiers of our knowledge, redefines the debate over public issues, and fosters new and effective directions for government reform.

THE INDEPENDENT INSTITUTE
100 Swan Way, Oakland, CA 94621-1428, U.S.A.
Telephone: 510-632-1366 • Fax 510-568-6040
E-mail: info@independent.org • Website: http://www.independent.org

Contents

Preface

In the early twentieth century, America's nonprofit foundations were few in number, and dedicated their resources toward clearly defined ends, mostly having to do with improving the well-being of the less fortunate members of society. At the close of the twentieth century there are more foundations with more resources attacking problems that are much less clearly defined. Rather than help people after they run into problems, foundations have increasingly devoted their resources toward preventing problems from occurring in the first place. This line of reasoning has led foundations to devote considerable resources toward developing social science, and toward analyzing public policy issues. Foundations have expanded from charity, narrowly defined, into the world of ideas. By nurturing the ideas that can make the world a better place, everybody can benefit.

It is more difficult to evaluate the efficacy of ideas than the efficacy of charitable giving, which raises the question of the degree to which foundation funding of ideas actually makes the world a better place. Critics argue that in some cases foundations have funded projects that have worked against the public interest. In many cases it is obvious that the donors who created foundations would be appalled by the activities that foundations are undertaking with their fortunes. Fortunes made through the productivity of the market economy have established foundations that have used those fortunes to oppose the capitalist system that created them. Yes, it is difficult for people to continue to control their fortunes from the grave, but not only are those who run America's nonprofit foundations not accountable to the original donors, they are, in truth, accountable to nobody.

The issue is complicated by the fact that tax law affects every facet of foundations, from their creation to their day-to-day operation. Thus, the ideas promoted by foundations are, in part, a product of the tax system that provides tax advantages for creating foundations and that imposes regulations on foundation activities as a condition of their maintaining tax-preferred status. One must evaluate the products of foundations, and especially the ideas they promote, as, in part, a product of the tax system. This study examines the relationship between tax laws and America's nonprofit foundations.

My work on this project began in 1995, when David Theroux of the Independent Institute asked me if I would be interested in doing a study of the public policy impact of projects funded by nonprofit foundations. I was immediately intrigued by the topic. Economists have devoted a great deal of attention to market allocation of resources and government allocation of resources, but have had less to say about philanthropic organizations. The foundations examined in this book are perhaps the most interesting of philanthropic organizations because they have the smallest amount of accountability to anyone. Businesses are accountable to customers and stockholders, and cannot survive without producing products people want. Government is accountable at the ballot box, and even typical charitable organizations rely on a continuing flow of donations for their operation, creating some accountability to donors. But nonprofit foundations, once established, fund their activities from endowment income, making them answerable to nobody, except to the extent that they must satisfy the general requirements of tax law to retain their nonprofit status. The issues are quite interesting, and this book is the product of my research.

The irony that this study, done for the Independent Institute, might be subject to many of the criticisms that the book makes about foundation-sponsored research has not escaped me. Surely they had good reasons for asking me (rather than someone else) to do this study, but if the study appears to be biased in any way, I can assure the reader that those are my biases and the study's conclusions are my conclusions. I did not work in a vacuum, however, and along the way I have received comments and advice from a number of readers. David Theroux offered helpful suggestions throughout the project, and while any listing is sure to leave someone out, I also want to thank Robert Higgs, Lora Holcombe, Alan Reynolds, John Smith, and Alex Tabarrok for their assistance. In addition, as any author can verify, writing a book is a time-consuming project, and I owe a debt of gratitude to my family for the understanding they have shown for allowing me the time to complete this book.

1

Introduction

In 1969 American nonprofit grant-making foundations were under attack. Foundations had been viewed with suspicion and distrust throughout the twentieth century, but that distrust had been growing during the 1960s, culminating in Congressional investigations and a tax reform act in 1969 that limited the allowable activities of foundations, subjected them to some minor taxation, required that they distribute a minimum amount of funds each year, and required more public accountability. Things could have been worse for foundations. Congress considered removing their tax-preferred status altogether, and also considered a proposal that foundations be required to have a limited life rather than be able to live in perpetuity, as they can now, but these more severe restrictions were not implemented. Still, the 1969 tax reform was the biggest public policy change ever undertaken with regard to America's nonprofit foundations. At the end of the twentieth century, several decades after the 1969 reforms, it seems reasonable to look back and consider those reforms. What were the problems that those reforms were intended to solve? Why were tax reforms used to try to solve them, rather than taking another approach? Have those tax reforms served their intended purposes? From a public policy standpoint, would additional reforms be desirable?

To understand the reason why reforms were demanded then, and why they might be desirable today, one must understand the role of nonprofit foundations within the context of the American economy. The largest and most influential foundations are the creation of prosperous Americans who have donated their wealth to serve the public interest.

1

The business empires of Rockefeller, Carnegie, and Ford, to name a few, generated tremendous personal wealth for their owners, and they placed the bulk of their wealth into foundations so that it could be used to further the public interest. The creators of those foundations have been dead for decades, but their foundations live on, now directed by foundation trustees. Foundations operate from income they earn on their endowments. They do no fundraising, but operate using the earnings from foundation assets. Not only are these assets sufficient to allow them to underwrite millions of dollars worth of projects every year, but most of the largest foundations earn enough every year that their endowments are actually increasing. They are bigger now than when they were first created. Foundations become wealthier and wealthier, and continue to undertake expenditures to further their visions of the public good.

The primary problem from a public policy standpoint is that foundation trustees have a tremendous amount of wealth at their disposal that they can spend as they see fit. While they are charged with acting in the public interest, they are accountable to nobody. Governments are run by elected officials. Business firms must satisfy their customers to remain viable. Even charities that operate from donations must satisfy their donors in order to keep the donations flowing. But foundations have an automatic source of income from endowment earnings, so they do not have to answer to anyone for their programs, and their income will continue regardless of the merits of the programs and projects they fund. Should foundations have to meet some higher level of accountability?

The issue has been raised throughout the twentieth century. When John D. Rockefeller, whose ruthless running of Standard Oil made him very unpopular as a public figure, established the Rockefeller Foundation in 1913, critics argued that it was just another way for this capitalist to try to extend his control beyond the American economy and into American social and political life as well. Rockefeller's attempt to create a foundation for the public interest was met with suspicion on the part of the general public, and hostility in Congress. In the 1960s the Ford Foundation, which was by far the largest foundation at that time, drew the bulk of the criticism for its attempts to influence public policy. The Ford Foundation supported many causes that were viewed as left-leaning, and even went so far as to become directly involved in some elections through voter registration drives. Undoubtedly foundations have the ability to exert a substantial influence over public policy debate, have often used this influence in the past, and continue to be active in public policy areas. The reforms enacted in 1969 were a response to this influence.

The reason why Congress used tax reform to try to control foundation activities is that so many characteristics of foundations are determined by tax policy. As nonprofit institutions, foundations must comply with certain provisions in order to retain their nonprofit status, and in 1969 Congress created additional requirements on foundations beyond those that other nonprofit organizations have to meet. The 1969 amendments to tax law dealt primarily with the rules foundations must follow in order to operate as nonprofit organizations, but the tax code is also relevant to the creation of foundations. Money used to endow foundations avoids the federal estate tax, and because such bequests are tax free, the tax code encourages people to create foundations. Thus, both income tax laws and inheritance tax laws are key elements in public policy toward foundations.

Several decades have passed since the 1969 reforms and it is now possible to look back and judge both the perceived problems and the effectiveness of the legislated solutions with a degree of objectivity. The perceived problems stem from the fact that a small group of foundation trustees are able to control a substantial amount of money that can have an impact on political and social policy without being accountable to anyone for their actions. The money is not theirs. It was earned by others who, for the most part, have long been dead. Now control of these fortunes has been given to a group of unelected and unrepresentative trustees. In general, when a vacancy appears on a board of trustees, the remaining trustees choose a replacement, creating a self-perpetuating dynasty that claims to act in the public interest. When foundation money is spent on public policy and political issues, foundation-funded ideas can compete with and sometimes overwhelm the ideas of individuals and groups who do not have such a ready source of funding. One of the main goals of the 1969 reforms was to limit the degree to which foundations could become directly involved in the political debate over public policy issues.

How successful were those reforms in retrospect? Were they too severe, or with hindsight should they have been stronger? Should foundations today be more accountable for their activities? Are there appropriate changes in public policy that might make them so? This study deals primarily with the public policy ideas that are financed with foundation grants, despite the fact that foundations fund many other activities. The link with tax laws is relatively direct, because donor money goes into foundations tax free, and foundations operate as nonprofit organizations that receive favorable tax treatment. Because of the tax break, those who finance the promotion of ideas through foundations do not pay full price. This suggests the question about the social value of ideas that foundations create. Can ideas that can be written off for tax purposes be as valuable as ideas produced by other means, or should the ideas themselves be written off as a product of the tax system rather than a product of unbiased intellectual endeavor?

In order to answer these questions, one must understand the historical context within which foundations developed in the twentieth century, the institutional environment within which they operate, and the activities that they finance. The unique environment within which foundations operate in the United States is largely a creation of tax law, and an examination of that environment reveals that there are indeed good reasons to be suspicious of the objectivity of the ideas that are developed as a result of foundation funding.

Foundations in the United States

Foundations have a long history in the United States. Ben Franklin bequeathed money to establish charitable foundations in Boston and Philadelphia, in addition to endowing the American Philosophical Society.[1] The Smithsonian Institution was created in 1846 through a $500,000 bequest, and the Peabody Education Fund was established as a foundation in 1867 to aid the postwar South.[2] While eighteenth- and nineteenth-century foundations played significant roles in American society, the modern American foundation is really a twentieth-century creation. Prior to the twentieth century, foundations were, for the most part, established to provide direct aid to the poor.[3] In the twentieth century, nonprofit foundations have grown substantially both in their financial importance and in the scope of their activities. Foundations are established to support college athletic teams, to fund hospitals and universities, to fund religious activities, the arts, and the development of ideas. This study will examine a subset of foundation activities by confining its scope to the intellectual implications of nonprofit grant-making foundations.[4] How do tax laws influence nonprofit foundations, and what types of ideas do foundations produce? How do the activities of foundations relate to the interests and intentions of their founders? Are there any policy changes that might be made to improve the performance of foundations?

The main reason that this study is limited to the intellectual implications of nonprofit grant-making foundations is that the issue raises interesting and important questions. To consider foundations in a broader context would dilute the primary message that the tax system affects the activities foundations fund and the ideological content of studies that are financed by foundation grants. Foundation funding affects the ideas that think tanks and academics develop about society, affects the way that we view our society, our political system, and our world, and as a result has a profound effect on public policy. There are other interesting issues regarding nonprofit foundations, such as whether they provide tax loopholes that allow the wealthy to pass wealth to their heirs and avoid inheritance taxation, whether money is spent for the benefit of foundation personnel rather than for any public purpose, whether nonprofit foundations unfairly compete with organizations that pay taxes, and so on. But to cover all of these issues would not only unnecessarily broaden the scope of this study, it would take the focus away from the influence of tax-exempt foundations over the development of ideas and public policies.

Foundations, through their financing of research, publications, conferences, and programs at educational institutions, exert a tremendous amount of influence over the way in which the world's social and political structure is viewed. John Maynard Keynes, in the closing passages of his famous treatise on economics, *The General Theory of Employment, Interest, and Money,* remarked,

> [T]he ideas of economists and political philosophers, both when they are right and when they are wrong, are more powerful than is commonly understood. Indeed the world is ruled by little else. Practical men, who believe themselves to be quite exempt from any intellectual influences, are usually the slaves of some defunct economist. Madmen in authority, who hear voices in the air, are distilling their frenzy from some academic scribbler of a few years back. I am sure that the power of vested interests is vastly exaggerated compared with the gradual encroachment of ideas.[5]

At the close of the twentieth century, many of these academic scribblers are writing studies funded by nonprofit foundations. Is the tax system affecting the nature and quality of the ideas they are producing?

If ideas are as influential as Keynes suggested, then any effect that nonprofit foundations have on the production of ideas will ultimately affect the way we perceive our society, the political decisions we make, and the very nature of the world we live in. Keynes was quite prophetic in his own case, and Keynesian theories have transformed not only academic ideas but the way in which economic policy has been conducted in the latter part of the twentieth century.[6] Ideas have consequences, so a study of the way in which the tax system, through nonprofit grant-making foundations, affects ideas attacks an interesting and important subject.

In 1969 Congress considered substantial changes in the way that nonprofit foundations were treated by tax law, including restricting their activities, taxing the income of foundations, and even limiting the allowable life of foundations. J. Irwin Miller, then chairman of the board of Cummins Engine Company and a supporter of the tax-exempt status of foundations stated,

> [W]hile foundations are the most peculiarly American manifestation of the philanthropic impulse, they do not operate as simply as traditional charity; taking the long view, and working with professional skill, they have grown more sophisticated and specialized in their approach to problems and therefore are less easy to understand. Further, they represent relatively large concentrations of wealth, and bigness in any form stirs suspicion in the American consciousness. Foundations have also concerned themselves with some of the problems that are deeply troubling our society, and almost anything one does in these fields is apt to stir passions. Finally, certain abuses in the field have become apparent, and questions have been raised about the judgment of foundations in certain activities.[7]

If foundations are not easy to understand, even according to their promoters, and if they are able to marshal large concentrations of wealth to try to deal with controversial and troubling issues, then an examination of how foundations influence the ideas and actions of American society is certainly worthwhile. Abuses of foundations, while not of primary interest in this study, often result from the same factors that lead to questions about foundations' promotion of ideas: lack of accountability. Once a foundation is endowed, its directors have an almost unlimited amount of freedom to use the foundation's resources as they see fit, without having to answer to benefactors or the general public.

Miller went on to state,

> At bottom, foundations operate under a public trust agreement. Through exemption statutes, American society encourages the application of private

wealth to public purpose. Society must be assured both that the privilege is not abused and that the responsibility to deliver a social dividend is met.[8]

What kind of a social dividend does society see from the ideas generated by nonprofit foundations? Does the tax-preferred status of foundations affect the types of ideas that they finance, promote, and disseminate? Can the tax laws be modified to increase the social dividend reaped from tax-exempt foundations? The lack of accountability of foundations, which has led to some of the questions of judgment referred to by Mr. Miller, also affects the type of research a foundation might sponsor and the types of ideas and programs it might fund and promote.[9] Perhaps the tax laws could be changed to create more accountability, and to create more of a social dividend from the work of foundations.

Characteristics of Foundations

What makes an organization a foundation? While there may be no definitive answer, the Internal Revenue Service distinguishes foundations from other philanthropic organizations based on the breadth of their donor bases. Foundations are supported by a relatively narrow base of donors while other charitable organizations have a broader base of donors. Foundation operations also tend to be financed from endowments rather than continued donor contributions. That is especially true of the large foundations which make most of the grants that finance the production of ideas. Furthermore, foundations tend to operate by giving grants to individuals or other organizations rather than operating programs of their own. F. Emerson Andrews, former president of the Foundation Center, has defined a foundation as "a nongovernmental, nonprofit organization having a principal fund of its own, managed by its own trustees or directors, and established to maintain or aid social, educational, charitable, religious, or other activities serving the common welfare."[10]

The purpose of this section is not to try to supply an authoritative definition of the term foundation, but rather to identify those characteristics of foundations that are of interest for this study. The definition supplied by Andrews does a good job of identifying those characteristics. The nonprofit aspect of foundations is important because nonprofit status confers tax benefits, and foundations must comply with the federal regulations involved in maintaining their nonprofit status. One idea that will be developed throughout this book is that the tax laws do have a substantial influence on the ideas generated by foundations. The characteristic that foundations have principal funds of their own is also a critical element in this analysis, because by having their own funds and being able to operate from the earnings of their endowments, they are freed from much of the oversight that polices the actions of other organizations in our society. Government faces the control of the democratic decision-making process, and businesses must respond to the pressures of the market, but with a steady income from an endowment, there is much less oversight of the activities of a foundation.

The managers or trustees noted in Andrews' s definition are also an important part of the equation, for ultimately they decide on the disposition of a foundation's resources. What will be accomplished by the foundation's expenditures? Andrews's definition suggests that some purpose furthering the common welfare will be accomplished. But that remains as a question at this point. Do nonprofit foundations really undertake expenditures that further the public interest? What incentives do trustees and foundation managers have to see that their activities further the public interest rather than just indulging in the whims of those trustees who allocate the money endowed by others?

The accounting firm of Arthur Andersen & Co. goes a bit further in describing a foundation:

> A private foundation is a charitable organization that generally has been established by an individual donor for the purpose of controlling, to the fullest extent possible, the use of his charitable dollars. The foundation's character generally reflects the objectives and purposes of its founder. Private foundations often are established to engage in what has been described as 'venture philanthropy,' or imaginative pursuit of less conventional charitable purposes than those normally undertaken by established public charitable organizations.[11]

This description suggests two reasons why foundations might warrant closer scrutiny than other charitable organizations. First, they are often established with the idea of providing more donor direction of funds than a typical charity, and second, the funds may be put to more imaginative or unconventional uses, which naturally will raise the question of the degree to which the public interest is served by the foundation.

Nonprofit foundations are primarily a twentieth-century American phenomenon. Along with industrialization came the amassing of substantial fortunes in the late nineteenth century and throughout the twentieth century, and many of those who amassed these fortunes wanted to use a substantial part of their wealth to enhance human welfare. They found that on their own, they were able to use only a small part of their total wealth for public interest activities, and the nonprofit foundation was designed as a vehicle through which these individuals could more effectively use their wealth to further human betterment. The names of Rockefeller and Carnegie, in addition to conjuring images of great nineteenth-century fortunes, are also associated with the modern foundations that operate on earnings from the endowments they left.

Foundation Facts

In 1998 there were over 44,000 grant-making foundations in the United States. These foundations issued approximately $20 billion in grants from an endowment base of some $329 billion.[12] About 78 percent of foundations are independent, with corporate foundations making up 14.3 percent of foundations and community foundations composing 6.5 percent. Grants to educational institutions account for about one quarter of total grant dollars, which is a far-greater amount than any other category of recipient. Health ranks second at 17 percent, and human services, which is a large category including awards for recreation and sports, youth service centers, emergency assistance, employment, and housing and shelter, among other areas, follows closely behind with about 15 percent. Arts, Culture and the Humanities, and Public/Society Benefit, which includes funding for civil rights programs, community development, and public policy research, are the only other double digit categories, at 13 percent and 12 percent respectively. Each of the categories of funding contains significant funding for ideas. Obviously many of the grants to educational institutions impact the creation of ideas but so also does some funding in the category of health. In 1997, for example, the Robert Wood Johnson Foundation gave $30 million of funding for anti-tobacco and anti-drug media campaigns. In 1997, funding in the Arts, Culture, and Humanities includes the Annenberg Foundation's $5 million grant to the Corporation for Public Broadcasting as well as funding from other foundations to museums and the performing arts (which also involve ideas even if abstract ones). Grants in the Public/Society Benefit area include $5 million from the Florence and John Schumann Foundation to establish a new national organization to advance public participation in campaign finance reform and $2.6 million from the Lannan Foundation to support the Independent Traditional Seminole Nation.[13]

Many foundations are small, but even when limiting the tally to foundations with more than $1 million in assets or more than $100,000 in annual giving, there are still more than 12,000 foundations, and that group is responsible for more than 90 percent of total foundation grants. In fact, the important foundations are concentrated quite highly, over half of the total grant dollars are awarded by the largest 1000 foundations.[3] That group of foundations excludes foundations established for a specific purpose or to fund a specific cause. The largest foundations are much larger than the typical foundation, so the activities of a few will be much more visible than the activities of foundations in general. The Ford Foundation's activities in the 1960s gained the attention of Congress, for example, when it was by far the largest foundation, and the questions Congress raised about the Ford Foundation's activities may have been primarily responsible for the major tax reform in 1969 that placed substantial restrictions on foundations. The Ford Foundation remained the largest foundation from its founding in 1951 until the late 1990s.[14]

Table 1.1 lists the 21 largest U.S. foundations by asset value. Although it will not come into official existence until Jan 1, 2000 the Bill and Melinda Gates Foundation will at that time be the largest US foundation with assets of at least $17 billion. Close behind is the Lilly Foundation with assets of $15 billion. The Gates foundation and the Lilly foundation have benefited enormously in recent years from the huge increases in the value of their stock holdings, but the same is true of many foundations. The Ford Foundation was for a very long-time the largest foundation, and its diversified portfolio of assets had a 1998 value of $9.5 billion. Foundation size declines rapidly from the top. The Gates Foundation is more than five times as large as the Andrew Mellon Foundation, the tenth largest. One of the oldest foundations, the Carnegie Corporation, had assets of $1.4 billion; it is number 28. The Conrad N. Hilton Foundation is the 75th largest foundation with assets just over $500 million. The Z. Smith Reynolds Foundation the 100th largest foundation, had 1998 assets of $443 million. While there are many foundations with substantial assets, one can see that a few of the largest foundations are in a position to dominate foundation activity.

The right-most column in Table 1.1 shows the year in which the foundation was established, and gives a good indication that the largest foundations have, with obvious exceptions, been around for decades. In many cases the dates in the table understate the age of a foundation because the foundation may have been set up as a trust long before it

TABLE 1.1
The 20 Largest Foundations by Assets, 1998

Rank	Foundation	Assets($Millions)	Year Established
1	Bill and Melinda Gates Foundation	17,000	2000*
2	Lily Endowment, Inc	15,780	1937
3	The Ford Foundation	9,654	1953**
4	David and Lucille Packard Foundation	9,527	1964
5	J. Paul Getty Trust	8,002	1953
6	Robert Wood Johnson Foundation	6,734	1972**
7	W.K. Kellogg Foundation	5,549	1930
8	Pew Charitable Trusts	4,734	1957****
9	John D. and Catherine T. MacArthur Found.	4,030	1970
10	Robert W. Woodruff Foundation	3,677	1937
11	Andrew W. Mellon Foundation	3,431	1969*****
12	Annenberg Foundation	3,349	1989
13	Rockefeller Foundation	3,094	1913
14	The Starr Foundation	2,541	1955
15	Charles Stewart Mott Foundation	2,346	1926
16	Duke Endowment	2,108	1924
17	Kresge Foundation	2,102	1924
18	McKnight Foundation	1,889	1953
19	Harry and Jeanette Weinberg Foundation	1,845	1959
20	William and Flora Hewlett Foundation	1,766	1966

*As of January 1, 2000 the William H. Gates Foundation and Gates Learning Foundation will merge to form the Bill and Melinda Gates Foundation. Gifts received in 1999 from Bill and Melinda Gates will give the foundation assets worth over 17 billion dollars. Since asset values for the other foundations are from late 1997 or 1998 the figures for the Gates foundation are not fully comparable but almost certainly the Gates Foundation will become the largest private US foundation.

**Incorporated in 1936; fully endowed in 1951 with the settlement of the Henry and Edsel Ford estates.

***Incorporated in 1936;became a national philanthropy in 1972.

****Created with the merger of five separate foundations.

*****Trust originally established in 1940. Merged with Old Dominion Foundation and renamed in 1969.

Source: "Top 100 U.S. Foundations by Asset Size" as of August 6, 1999 compiled by the Foundation Center and available on the center's web site at http://fdncenter.org/

was incorporated, or may have been the result of a combining of other foundations. A few special cases are noted in the table's footnotes. The newest foundation in the top 20 is the Bill and Melinda Gates Foundation followed by the Annenberg Foundation, the 11th largest, which was established in 1989 and the Robert Wood Johnson Foundation, which became a national philanthropy in 1972 even though it was created in 1936. The John D. and Catherine T. MacArthur Foundation was created in 1970, and the Andrew W. Mellon Foundation, which is listed in the table as being established in 1969, was created by merging two existing foundations.

The concentration of financial power changes only slightly if foundations are listed in order of the total amount of grants they make rather than by assets, as is shown in Table 1.2. The Bill and Melinda Gates Foundation again leads the list though by not as much as in asset size. The top three foundations in terms of giving each gave more than twice the total grants of the fourth largest giver the W.K. Kellogg Foundation. Kellogg in turn, is about twice as large as the tenth ranked Andrew Mellon Foundation. As would be expected, the largest foundations in terms of assets also turn out to be the largest in terms of total grants. One exception is the J. Paul Getty Trust, which is fifth largest in assets but not within the top twenty in grants. The J. Paul Getty Trust makes some grants, but primarily uses its income to operate foundation activities, the most notable of which is the Getty Museum. The Getty Trust is an anomaly, however, most large foundations make grants rather than operate their own programs.

Another interesting case of a Foundation no longer in the current top 20 grant-makers is the Lucille P. Markey Charitable Trust. The Markey Trust was one of the largest grant givers throughout most of the 1990's. Established in 1983, it made all of its grants for basic medical research, but was set up so that all of its assets would be distributed by 1997. This points directly to one of the key policy questions with regard to foundations. One of the problems that foundations can run into is that as they age, their activities are less and less tied to the intentions of the donor. Donors can set very broad agendas for their foundations, in which case much of what the foundation will do will be at the discretion of its trustees. When donors provide more specific direction, it may turn out that over time causes that donors believed were in the public interest can become less and less relevant in a changed world. One way around these problems is to endow a foundation with very specific intent, as with the case of the Lucille P. Markey Charitable Trust, but give it a limited life so that its expenditures will continue to be relevant. Chapter 6 deals specifically with the issue of donor intent. Meanwhile, it is worth considering whether foundations should have limited lives, along the lines of the Markey Trust.

TABLE 1.2
The 20 Largest Foundations by Total Giving, 1998

Rank Assets	Foundation	Grants($Millions)	Rank by
1	The Bill and Melinda Gates Foundation	500+	1*
2	Ford Foundation	439	3
3	Lilly Endowment Inc.	425	2
4	W.K. Kellogg Foundation	260	7
5	David and Lucille Packard Foundation	257	4
6	Robert Wood Johnson Foundation	241	6
7	Pew Charitable Trusts	161	8
8	John D. and Catherine T. MacArthur Found.	156	9
9	New York Community Trust	144	22
10	Andrew W. Mellon Foundation	142	11
11	The Danforth Foundation	105	**
12	The Annenberg Foundation	105	12
13	Open Society Institute	102	**
14	The Rockefeller Foundation	99	13
15	The Annie E. Casey Foundation	91	24
16	Robert W. Woodruff Foundation, Inc.	86	10
17	Robert R. McCormick Tribune Foundation	84	25
18	Charles Stewart Mott Foundation	84	15
19	The Duke Endowment	77	16
20	The Starr Foundation	74	14

* As of January 1, 2000 the William H. Gates Foundation and Gates Learning Foundation will merge to form the Bill and Melinda Gates Foundation. The figure on giving covers about 3/4 of 1999 and is the combined amount from the William H. Gates Foundation and Gates Learning Foundation. If all funding announced in 1999 is credited to that year the Gates Foundation may end up donating over 1 billion dollars in 1999.

**Not among the largest 100 foundations.

Source: "Top 100 US Foundations by Total Giving" as of August 9, 1999 compiled by the Foundation Center and available on the center's web site at http://fdncenter.org/

The modern era of foundations began early in the twentieth century with the creation of the Carnegie Corporation in 1911 and the Rockefeller Foundation in 1913. Both of those foundations remain large although they have been eclipsed somewhat in recent years by "new-economy" based foundations like those of Gates, Packard and Hewlett. The Ford Foundation remains one the largest foundation more than four decades after it was established and close behind is the Kellogg Foundation established twenty years before the Ford Foundation. Once created, foundations tend to last a long time and they exist relatively independently of both market forces and government oversight. Within broad general guidelines, their resources are spent in order to further what their trustees view as the public interest. Sometimes foundations themselves have been given narrower guidelines by their creators, but the norm among the largest foundations is that the original donors placed very little in the way of restrictions on what types of activities the foundations could fund. Is it in the public interest to allow this much independence over foundation expenditurs that might continue in perpetuity?

Certainly one could make a strong argument for allowing those resources to be spent as the donors wished, but over time there is an increasing separation between donor intent and foundation activity. This becomes more of a public policy issue because foundations are given favorable status under the tax laws, and it is reasonable to ask what foundations ought to be required to do in order to maintain their tax-preferred status. Tax laws had little to do with the creation of the earliest foundations, but as the twentieth century has progressed, tax laws have become increasingly relevant.

The Growth of American Foundations

The growth of nonprofit foundations in the twentieth century has at least two major causes. First, around the turn of the century a few individuals amassed substantial wealth, and wanted to direct some of it toward activities that would further the public interest.[15] Their individual motives may have varied. John D. Rockefeller was interested in deflecting public criticism by using his wealth to further the public interest. James B. Duke, who endowed Trinity College in North Carolina under the condition that its name be changed to Duke University, wanted to enshrine his family name.[16] Whatever their other motives, the fact that their founders could choose (within limits) the foundations' mission means that their founders intended for their money to further some purpose. What were the purposes? How well do the foundations' activities match the intents of their founders? This study will examine those questions primarily by looking at specific examples. The number of foundations and the diversity of their purposes is too large to pretend to do any type of exhaustive survey.

The second reason why nonprofit foundations have grown is that contributions to them are tax-deductible. This would have relatively little influence on founders in Rockefeller's generation, when income and inheritance taxes were relatively low, but has played an increasingly important role as tax rates have risen through the twentieth century, and especially after World War II. Federal estate taxes were established in 1916, and rose to as high as 25 percent (on estates over $10 million) during World War I.[17] The top rate was 20 percent in 1926, was increased to 45 percent in 1932, and was increased again to 70 percent (on estates over $50 million) in 1935. Beginning in 1942 the top rate was raised to 77 percent on estates over $10 million, where it remained for decades. The top rate is now 55 percent for estates over $3 million. These substantial estate taxes provide the incentive for wealthy individuals to establish tax-exempt foundations rather than leave the major fraction of their estates to the government. The Ford Foundation, which is discussed in greater detail in chapter 2, provides an excellent example of a major foundation established largely because of the impact that the tax system would have had on the Ford family fortune in the absence of the foundation.

In 1969 a survey of eighty-five people whose median annual philanthropic giving over the past five years was $375,000 asked what effect the removal of tax deductibility from charitable contributions would have on their giving. The median response was that they would reduce giving by 75 percent, and only 4 percent of those surveyed said they would continue their same level of giving.[18] It appears that income and estate tax laws can have a substantial influence over the amount of money flowing into foundations.

One might conjecture that the substantial tax cuts in the 1980s would have therefore led to a decline in foundation activity, but in fact the increase in wealth in the 1980's and the 1990s has lead to a surge in the number of new foundations. From 1980 to 1989, 3,082 foundations with assets in excess of $1 million were created, which is 31 percent of the larger foundations. Thousands more large foundations have been created in the 1990's. After the 1980s, the 1950s was the decade that saw the second-highest rate of foundation formation, with 1,858 foundations formed, or 19 percent of the total. The 1960s saw 17 percent of the total number of large foundations formed and only 10 percent of large foundations were formed in the 1970s. While some large and visible foundations like Carnegie and Rockefeller predate World War II, only 527 foundations, or 5 percent of the total with more than $1 million in assets, were formed prior to 1940.[5]

The 1980s, marked by substantial tax cuts for upper-income tax payers, also saw substantial income gains to upper-income taxpayers, and it appears that the positive effects of income gains outweighed the negative effects of tax cuts on the formation of foundations. Yet another factor might be that with income tax rate cuts, the relative tax advantages of charitable giving during one's lifetime is lower when compared to leaving a bequest, so some foundation giving in the 1980s may be the result of a deferral of charitable giving until death. The contrast is especially striking when the 1980s are compared with the 1970s. The economically troubled 1970s gave birth to only 10 percent of the total, compared to 31 percent in the 1980s. While the 1990s are not yet over, from 1990 to 1994, 687 large foundations were established, which is 7 percent of the total. Based on the first half of the decade, the rate of formation of foundations in the 1990s is running substantially ahead of the pace from the 1970s, but substantially behind the pace of the 1980s.

Tax laws also influence the amount of money flowing out, because foundations are required to make minimum disbursements from their endowments in order to retain their tax-preferred status. Furthermore, the activities foundations can engage in are limited by law. Violations can cost the foundations their tax-preferred status. Thus, foundations like the Carnegie and Rockefeller Foundations, established prior to confiscatory estate and income tax rates, are influenced today by the requirements they must meet to retain their tax-preferred status.

Long-Run Stability of the Largest Foundations

The last half of the twentieth century has seen an increasing number of foundations be created, but despite the large number of foundations created, there is considerable stability at the top. As Table 1.1 showed, the largest foundations in the 1990s have been around for a long time. To get a better idea of the degree of stability among the largest foundations, Table 1.3 lists the twenty largest foundations in 1969 — the year in which the major tax reform placed additional restrictions on foundation activity.

Only one of the top twenty foundations of 1969, the Bernice P. Bishop Estate, was no longer operating in 1998. That foundation ranked number 14, with assets less than ten percent the size of the Ford Foundation, which was the largest in 1969. Of the twenty largest foundations in 1969, all but Bishop and the Danforth Foundation (which is still large)

TABLE 1.3

The 20 Largest Foundations by Assets, 1969

Rank	Foundation	Assets($Millions)	Rank in 1998*
1	Ford Foundation	2,922	3
2	Rockefeller Foundation	890	13
3	Duke Endowment	629	16
4	Lilly Endowment	580	2
5	Pew Charitable Trusts	541	8
6	Charles Stewart Mott Foundation	413	15
7	W.K. Kellogg Foundation	409	7
8	Kresge Foundation	353	17
9	John A. Hartford Foundation	352	78
10	Carnegie Corporation	335	27
11	Alfred P. Sloan Foundation	329	35
12	Andrew W Mellon Foundation	272	11
13	James Irvine Foundation	250	38
14	Bernice P. Bishop Estate	234	**
15	Longwood Foundation	226	46
16	Rockefeller Brothers Fund	222	91
17	Houston Endowment	214	30
18	Moody Foundation	200	43
19	Danforth Foundation	173	***
20	Emily and Earnest Woodruff Foundation	167	10****

*Including the Bill and Melinda Gates Foundation

**No longer operating.

*** Not in top 100.

****Robert W. Woodruff Foundation, created from other foundations, had a 1998 rank of 10. Woodruff family wealth created primarily from Coca-Cola Company.

Sources: 1969 data from Joseph C. Goulden, *The Money Givers* (New York: Random House, 1971), pp. 321-322; 1998 data from "Top 100 US Foundations by Total Giving" as of August 9, 1999 compiled by the Foundation Center and available on the center's web site at http://fdncenter.org/

are in the top 100 in 1998. Ten of the top twenty foundations of 1969 are still in the top twenty in 1998. It is clear that although new foundations are being created, few die. Most of the large foundations continue to be large and indeed they grow in absolute dollar assets. Recent history suggests that some of the largest foundations at the end of the twenty-first century will be based on computer and internet fortunes made in the late twentieth century (e.g. Gates, Packard, Hewlett). Equally likely, however, is that many of the largest foundations of the twenty-first century will have been founded on early to mid-twentieth century fortunes (e.g. Ford, Rockefeller, Carnegie, Kellogg, Heinz). The fact that these foundations can continue to operate from the earnings of their endowments in perpetuity, and with little accountability, is one of the factors that gives people pause when considering public policy toward foundations.

When comparing Tables 1.1 and 1.3 one must be struck by how much larger the assets of the largest foundations have become in only a few decades. In most cases this growth in nominal assets is due to inflation. Consumer prices increased by a factor of 4.3 from 1969 to 1998, so the Ford Foundation's 1969 assets would have been $12,564 million expressed in 1998 prices. Adjusting for inflation, Ford Foundation 1998 assets were only 76 percent of what they were in 1969. The W.K. Kellogg Foundation, in contrast, grew even after adjusting for inflation. It's 1969 assets, expressed in 1998 prices, would have been $1,758 million and its actual assets were more than three times that amount. The Pew Charitable Trust, which ranked fifth in 1969 and eighth in 1998, had assets of $2,326 million in 1969 when measured in 1998 prices. It's 1998 assets were $4,734 million, so after adjusting for inflation, its assets more than doubled over about thirty years. This is all the more remarkable when we remember that the Pew Trusts have consistently been among the largest givers of funds over these same years. The Kresge Foundation fell in rank from 8th to 17th from 1969 to 1998, but after adjusting for inflation its assets increased by about 38 percent, from $1,517 in 1998 dollars million to $2,102 million. The Kresge Foundation is typical in that most large foundation showed an increase in real assets over the 1969 to 1998 period even if they fell in size due to the growth of new foundations.

A comparison over time shows that the largest foundations are getting larger, and that there is a great amount of stability in foundations. Some foundations are designed to have a limited life, like the Lucille P. Markey Charitable Trust, but most are designed to last in perpetuity, and foundation managers have been successful at increasing the wealth of individual foundations in addition to making grants. Because foundations operate from endowments, there is no market check on the value of the output financed by foundations, and there is very little government oversight either. Ultimately, democratic governments are subject to the mandates of voters, and private sector firms can survive only if they produce output that their consumers value more highly than the firm's cost of production. Foundations are accountable to nobody, and can survive and even grow forever. They are designed to operate in the public interest, so it is reasonable to consider whether they actually do, or even if they do, whether public policy toward foundations might be altered to get them to operate even more in the public interest.

One problem with allowing foundations to live in perpetuity is that the foundation's management can become more interested in perpetuating the foundation than in performing activities in the public interest. A report prepared by the DJB Foundation noted, "Our observation has been that the preservation of capital becomes the main concern of too many foundations, causing them to worry more about investments than about programs. Foundation trustees derive their prestige from foundation assets, but more significantly, foundation managers derive their incomes from foundation assets. When foundations are allowed to exist in perpetuity, perpetual life can become the long-run goal of the foundation's management, displacing concerns about the public interest. Is it really in the public interest to create foundations that can last forever? The general public should be interested in the question, but so should foundation managers and trustees, if they really want to operate to further the public interest.

Tax Laws and the Ideas Promoted by Foundations

The issues considered in this volume encompass only a small part of the total activities of foundations, but a potentially significant part. Foundations finance studies, conferences, and educational programs designed specifically to develop ideas. Do the scholarly activities promoted by foundations actually further the public interest? Foundations have been actively involved in domestic and foreign policy issues, which clearly promote ideas, and have been substantially involved in supporting educational institutions, which more generally promote ideas. Even when foundations support medical and agricultural programs, there is an element of the promotion of ideas, and often there may be a strong ideological component even to grants that go toward science, medicine, and agriculture. The issue is considered further in chapter 10, which looks at policy questions. There is a fuzzy division between the promotion of ideas and less ideological programs, but the promotion of ideas would have to account for at least 5 percent of foundation funding, including only the direct funding of studies, conferences, publications and the like, and perhaps 25 percent could easily be included under the heading of the promotion of ideas, if all educational grants are included. The percentage would be even higher if ideological overtones are read into other programs.

One need not make a clear division in order to see that this is an important area for inquiry. Regardless of how it is measured, the promotion of ideas is a substantial part of foundation funding, and the ideas promoted with foundation grants change the way that Americans, and indeed citizens of other nations, view their society. In short, ideas developed and promoted by foundation grants have a significant impact on the social and political system.

Public policy toward grant-making foundations is embodied primarily in the tax code. Foundations are nonprofit organizations, and in order to qualify for their nonprofit status they must meet certain conditions. Those conditions, detailed in chapter 4, require foundations to undertake a certain level of expenditures, dependent upon their assets and income, require certain forms of disclosure, and prevent foundations from engaging in certain types of activities. Activities that are prohibited fall into two general categories. First (and of less interest here), foundations are not allowed to expend resources for the direct benfit of those who have a relationship with the foundation. In other words, foundations are not supposed to be set up in order to allow people to obtain benefits tax-free that normally would be purchased from after-tax income. Second, foundations are restricted from engaging in some types of political and public activities. Such restrictions clearly influence the types of ideas that foundations can promote, and many were instituted in 1969 in response to perceived abuses of foundation activities. Are such restrictions warranted? Should more restrictions be placed on foundations? How effective are the restrictions currently in place?

Tax law also influences foundations because people can bequeath assets to foundations and avoid paying inheritance taxes on the assets. Thus some foundations are established as much to avoid inheritance taxes as to further any public purpose. But once established, the activities of foundations do have an impact on the public interest. There is a connection between the tax laws and the ideas foundations promote both because money goes into foundations to avoid taxation, and because the money that comes out of foundations must meet certain requirements in order for foundations to retain their tax-preferred status. The ability to use foundations as a mechanism to avoid taxation means more resources go into foundations than would otherwise be the case. Then, those resources are directed, at least in part, by the tax law requirements foundations must meet to retain their tax-preferred status.

Thus, there is a clear connection between the tax laws and the ideas promoted by nonprofit foundations. While there are some restrictions on foundation activities, foundations operate with relatively little accountability, spending money to promote their visions of the public interest within the constraints imposed by tax law. Foundations are directed by trustees whose vision of the public interest may be biased, because trustees are selected from a biased sample of the population. Is this a problem? The role of trustees is discussed in chapter 7. When looking at the ideas foundations promote, it is clear that over the course of the twentieth century foundation activities have been biased toward the liberal end of the contemporary liberal-conservative political continuum. This is documented in chapters 3,4, and 5. Why this bias hasoccurred, whether it will continue, and whether it is something to be concerned about, are all more difficult questions.

Chapter 5 notes that since about 1970 the nonprofit sector has turned somewhat toward the conservative side of the political spectrum, although liberal ideas still receive substantial promotion. This may be because those who establish foundations have made their fortunes in a market economy and tend to view the market mechanism favorably, whereas those who become foundation trustees after the donor dies tend not to be people who have made their own fortunes. Those from academia, and especially those with substantial backgrounds in the public sector, are more likely to be sympathetic to the ideas of government control over the economy. This would place the ideas of foundation trustees at odds with the donors who created the foundations, and would imply that as foundations evolve they move increasingly toward the liberal end of the conservative-liberal spectrum. These ideas are considered in chapters 3, 4, and 5, while chapters 10 and 11 consider the policy implications in more detail.

Public Policy Toward Foundations

One would want to consider carefully any public policy changes toward foundations. Pragmatically, one would want to ask whether changes would actually result in an improvement in the allocation of foundation resources. Often, policy changes have unintended consequences that do not become apparent until one sees how those who are affected respond to new policies. One would also want to consider policy issues more broadly to evaluate how foundations ought to be treated in the context of the American economy, which is built on the principles of limited government, private property, and free enterprise. Foundations are created when donors leave the money that they earned to the foundation, and a system that is built on the respect for private property rights ought to have good reasons for interfering with the way in which individuals want to allocate the resources they have earned. This would be especially true when, as in the case of foundations, those resources are earmarked for the promotion of the public good.

An obvious policy change in the tax treatment of foundations would be to subject money donated to foundations to inheritance or income taxes, rather than to allow the money to be passed tax free. But many causes are tax exempt, and this would seem to lead to the larger question of what activities one would want to allow people to contribute to tax free. Why should opera houses, symphony orchestras, and other activities that primarily entertain wealthy people be tax exempt? Furthermore, if donations made during an individual's lifetime were deductible as a charitable contribution but bequests to establish foundations were not, potential donors could easily rearrange their affairs to create their foundations before their deaths. Another way to place foundation endowments on an equal footing with other bequests would be to do away with the inheritance tax altogether. Naturally, one would want to consider the impact of inheritance taxation more broadly than just its effects on foundations, but possible modifications of the federal tax on bequests is considered in more detail in chapters 10 and 11.

If one is considering the taxation of bequests that go toward endowing foundations, one would want to consider not only how foundations would be affected, but also how resources would be reallocated between the public and private sectors. If bequests to foundations were taxed, less money would go to foundation programs and more would go to the government. Would the government spend the money more in the public interest than a foundation?

One advantage that foundations as a group have is that there are many of them. Each will see the public interest a little differently, and while some money may be spent unwisely, or even counter-productively, other foundations will innovate and further the public interest in ways that most people might not have imagined. With government expenditures (and especially federal government expenditures) there is little opportunity for experimentation. With only one federal government, there is only one Congress that collectively determines how resources should be allocated in the public interest. Rather than central planning for the public interest, a multitude of foundations can experiment with more options in a more decentralized way.

Public policy could curtail resources going into foundations by placing bequests into foundation endowments on an equal footing with other bequests, either by taxing them or by exempting all bequests from taxation. If bequests to foundations were taxed, then evaluating from a public interest standpoint whether additional taxation would be beneficial would require weighing the public benefits of foundation versus government expenditures. But once in foundations, government could further regulate how the money can be used. This is also done through taxation, indirectly, because the tax laws determine what qualifies foundations for their nonprofit status. Without the benefit of nonprofit status, a foundation could operate like a money-losing business, paying taxes and having as much legal latitude as any other business in its activities. Foundations are restricted only because they accept nonprofit status for tax purposes. Thus, public policy toward foundations means adjusting the tax laws to redefine the nature and activities of nonprofit foundations.

How do tax laws influence the activities of nonprofit foundations? How might the activities of foundations be different were it not for the requirements of the tax code? How might possible reforms of the tax code influence the activities of foundations? These are the issues that will be examined in this study of the influence of tax laws on the ideas generated by nonprofit foundations.

Notes

1. Joseph C. Goulden, *The Money Givers* (New York: Random House, 1971), p. 26.
2. Goulden, *The Money Givers*, pp. 27-28.
3. Amos G. Warner, *American Charities: A Study in Philanthropy and Economics* (New York: T.Y. Crowell, 1894).

4.   John G. Simon, "The Tax Treatment of Nonprofit Organizations: A Review of Federal and State Policies," chap. 5 in Walter W. Powell, ed., *The Nonprofit Sector* (New Haven, CT: Yale University Press, 1987), discusses the different types of foundations and other nonprofit organizations. Grant-making foundations are treated differently under tax law than operating foundations, which must use at least 85 percent of their revenues to ac conduct a charitable program (as opposed to making grants). Museums, symphony orchestras, and similar organizations are the types of activities that tend to be funded by operating foundations, and fall outside the scope of the current study.

5.   John Maynard Keynes, *The General Theory of Employment, Interest, and Money* (New York: Harcourt, Brace and Company, 1936).

6.   Many observers would argue that Keynesian ideas had a detrimental effect on the economy. See, for example, James M. Buchanan and Richard E. Wagner, *Democracy in Deficit: The Political Legacy of Lord Keynes* (New York: Academic Press, 1977).

7.   J. Irwin Miller, "The Role of Foundations in American Life," in *Foundations and the Tax Bill* (New York: The Foundation Center, 1969), pp. 5-6.

8.   Miller, "The Role of Foundations in American Life," p. 6.

9.   James T. Bennett and Thomas J. Dilorenzo, *Unhealthy Charities: Hazardous to Your Health and Wealth* (New York: Basic Books, 1994) discuss abuses of well-known charities such as the American Cancer Society, the American Heart Association, and the American Lung Association. Factors they discuss apply equally to foundations devoted to the dissemination of ideas.

10. Quoted from Thomas Parrish, "The Foundation: 'A Special American Institution,'" ch. 1 in The American Assembly, *The Future of Foundations* (Englewood Cliffs, NJ: Prentice-Hall, 1973), p. 10.

11. Arthur Andersen & Co., *Tax Economics of Charitable Giving,* 8th ed. (Chicago, 1983), p. 85.

12. These facts come from the Foundation Center's internet home page at http://fdncenter.org.

13. Foundation Center, *The Foundation Directory, 1994 Edition* (New York: The Foundation Center, 1994), p. v.

14. The Ford Foundation was actually incorporated in 1936, but it was not until the estates of Henry and Edsel Ford were settled in 1951 that the foundation undertook any major activities.

15. Goulden, *The Money Givers,* p. 28.

16. Warren Weaver, *U.S. Philanthropic Foundations: Their History, Structure, Management, and Record* (New York: Harper & Row, 1967), p. 72 notes that Duke claimed that the University was named for his father.

17. Information on the history of estate tax rates is in Carl S. Shoup, *Federal Estate and Gift Taxes* (Washington, DC: Brookings, 1966), chapter 1.

18. As reported by Goulden, *The Money Givers,* p. 25.

19. This information is from the Foundation Center internet home page.

20. Alan Rabinowitz, *Social Change Philanthropy in America* (New York: Quorum Books, 1990), pp. 60-61

2

The Origins and Development of Foundations

Foundations devoted to the development and dissemination of ideas have a long history. After Plato's death in 347 B.C., he bequeathed income from his estate for the perpetual support of his academy. Control of Plato's "foundation" passed through heirs who designated their successors, and Plato's academy survived until 529 A.D., when Roman Emperor Justinian terminated it for spreading pagan doctrines.[1] Benjamin Franklin left 1,000 pounds sterling to the cities of Boston and Philadelphia, with detailed instructions for the money's use. It was to be used for loans to young married couples, allowing principal and interest to grow, with the first expenditures of the accumulated funds to be made 100 years after the endowment. The Franklin Institute of Philadelphia and the Franklin Institute of Boston were financed by part of his endowment, and the remainder continues to grow.

Most foundations in the United States and elsewhere have been established for charitable or religious purposes. The establishment of the Smithsonian Institution was unusual in that regard because James Smithson's bequest to the United States government of $500,000 created an institution devoted to research and the dissemination of knowledge. Smithson's bequest was unusual not only because of its research orientation, but also because it left the United States government in charge of the money. Foundation endowments, both now and then, are not ordinarily managed by governments, and there was substantial debate in Congress at the time regarding whether Smithson's bequest should be accepted. While Smithson's bequest, received in 1846, was philanthropic in nature, the money was not used for charitable purposes.

The Smithsonian Institution was not the first noncharitable foundation to have been created, but it was a highly visible example of the way that foundations could be established for the creation and dissemination of knowledge.

Because of the unusual aspects of Smithson's bequest, the creation of the Smithsonian Institution was truly a significant innovation in the history of philanthropy. While the practice of bequeathing money to create a government-managed endowment remains unusual, it has become common in the twentieth century for governments to create their own foundations, especially for the purpose of funding public institutions of higher education. Every public university has its own foundation. Perhaps more innovative was the idea of leaving the money to produce benefits for the general public, rather than for benefits targeted at those members of a society who are least well-off. Smithson's bequest illustrates a clear distinction between charity and philanthropy—a distinction that has become more controversial because of the tax breaks given to philanthropic activity. Charitable activity is clearly aimed at the needy, whereas philanthropic activity is more broadly aimed at the general public.[2]

Undoubtedly the libraries that Andrew Carnegie built produced great social benefits, and benefits that were spread generally among the population. Can the same be said for philanthropy aimed at supporting art galleries or symphony orchestras that mainly cater to the well-to-do? In addition to philanthropic support, operas and symphonies are also typically supported by ticket sales, with the price of admission being considerably greater than the cost of a movie or a visit to a public park, which excludes the needy from direct benefits from this type of philanthropy. Yet the tax laws treat a donation to support the opera the same as a contribution to the homeless shelter.[3] One can justify such philanthropic activity on the grounds that it helps preserve the culture, although the culture being preserved is mainly that of the elite. Rap and country music seem to thrive without subsidization, but perhaps this is because they appeal to such pedestrian tastes.[4] The larger point is that philanthropy and charity are different, and Smithson's bequest thrust the difference into public attention and made it a matter of public debate.

Another innovation in the development of foundations occurred with the establishment of the Peabody Education Fund in 1867. The foundation's purpose was to provide assistance to the post-Civil War Southern states. Investment banker George Peabody, who endowed the foundation with a bequest of $2 million, left instructions that the foundation provide a public accounting of its expenditures and activities.[5] Unlike most foundations, Peabody was not committed to having his foundation last forever, and gave explicit instructions that it could be dissolved after thirty years. The foundation was closed in 1914, when its assets were transferred to the John F. Slater Fund, which was established in 1882 with goals consistent with Peabody's. Many who have chronicled the history of foundations in the United States cite the Peabody Education Fund as the model for modern American foundations. But if Peabody provided a model for nonprofit foundations, the influence of foundations took a substantial step forward when the newfound wealth of several American industrialists was channeled into foundations.

Prior to the twentieth century most foundations limited their activities to specific purposes. Early in the twentieth century, however, a number of foundations were established by very wealthy individuals for general purposes. The first of these was the Russell Sage Foundation, created in 1907, established for "the permanent improvement of social conditions."[6] Within a few years, the Carnegie Corporation of New York and the Rockefeller Foundation were established for the general purpose of improving the well-being of mankind.

Russell Sage had made his fortune as a financier, and had a reputation for being exceedingly frugal. The Russell Sage Foundation was established by his widow after his death. It is unlikely that the frugal Sage himself would have set up such a philanthropic foundation. The Carnegie and Rockefeller Foundations, in contrast, were established during the lives of Andrew Carnegie and John D. Rockefeller for philanthropic purposes. Several decades later, the Ford Foundation was created, again out of the fortunes of an American industrialist, which at the time of its creation was nearly as large as the Carnegie and Rockefeller Foundations combined. Have these foundations lived up to the expectations of their founders? Before that question can be answered, one must look into the circumstances surrounding their creation.

The Changing Concept of Foundation Activities

Foundations as they now exist are primarily a twentieth-century development. Prior to 1900 only eighteen foundations were established in the United States, and their missions were primarily charitable in the most straightforward sense of the word.[7] The earnings of foundations were used to provide assistance to needy and deserving individuals. Furthermore, most foundations were oriented toward providing financial support to specific institutions or groups of people. For example, the Baron de Hirsch Fund was established in 1891 to assist Jewish immigrants in the United States. This concept carries over to university and medical foundations today. But around the beginning of the twentieth century the orientation of foundations began changing, in large part because of the nature of the Carnegie and Rockefeller Foundations. Those foundations popularized two ideas related to the activities of foundations. First, they were oriented toward attacking the causes of problems rather than their effects. Second, they were established with very broad mandates.[8]

The most straightforward way in which to aid those in need is to provide for them those things that they need. The hungry need food, and the homeless need shelter. The sick need medical care. Another way in which to attack these problems is to try to deal with their causes rather than their effects. If people lack adequate food, a short-run solution is to provide food for them, but a longer-run view would fund agricultural research in order to create a greater supply of inexpensive food to allow them to feed themselves. Similarly, economic improvements can allow people to obtain their own housing rather than rely on the charity of others. And medical research can prevent the spread of disease. Foundation money used in this way can keep people healthy rather than trying to treat them once they become ill. Rather than providing charity to the unemployed, foundations can fund studies into the causes of unemployment that might lead to better jobs and higher incomes for everyone. Robert Treat Paine, president of the Associated Charities of Boston in 1893, anticipated the twentieth-century trend when he said, "Pauperism cannot be wisely considered alone, but the problem of how to uplift the general level of life must be studied as *one whole problem.*"[9]

Going beyond these specific examples that show how foundations can attack the causes rather than the effects of human suffering, education can be funded to more generally improve the well-being of mankind. Foundation support for education can both improve the condition of those receiving the education and provide the knowledge that will allow those educated individuals to better solve mankind's problems. Seen in this way, philanthropic contributions to educational institutions and to basic research finance a more permanent solution to the problems of those least well-off in a society. Giving money to the poor does not help them in the long run, whereas financing social, economic, and medical improvements provides lasting benefits.

One observer of philanthropic organizations has gone so far as to argue that charity is the enemy of philanthropy.[10] In this view, philanthropy is a strategic investment intended to improve the human environment. When emergencies arise that require charitable activity to help those in need, resources are diverted into the provision of immediate relief for those in need and away from philanthropic investments that enhance the social welfare over the long run. This idea embodies the twentieth-century view of the role that philanthropies try to fill.

While noble in principle, this is the first area in which one might want to question the social benefits of foundation programs. Providing food and shelter to the needy may not be the best way to help them in the long run, but at least the benefits are tangible and can be observed. Research and the development of ideas is much less tangible, and leaves open the question of whether a foundation's activities are really in the public interest. Oftentimes the results of medical research can be readily seen and appreciated, but not always. Thanks to grants from the Rockefeller Foundation, hookworm was eradicated in the Southern United States, but at the end of the twentieth century billions of dollars have been spent fighting cancer, with no cure in sight. Heart disease and lung disease are other popular targets of philanthropy are in a sense even more questionable, because many of those medical problems are brought on by the life-style choices of those who have the problems.

If there are questions about the efficacy of medical research, the questions must be much more serious with regard to research in the social sciences. The ideas financed by the grants of nonprofit foundations may not be in the public interest, and indeed may often work against the public interest. One of the major innovations in philanthropy made by the Rockefeller and Carnegie foundations was to develop the ideas to attack the causes of social problems, but this innovation raises one of the major questions to be examined in this study. Are those ideas funded by foundations really in the public interest?

The second major innovation of those early twentieth-century foundations was that they were established under a very general mandate so that the foundation's trustees and management could be flexible in deciding how to best spend the foundation's resources for the public good. Most previous foundations had been tied to a particular cause, like the Peabody and Smithsonian foundations, or even to particular institutions, such as the foundations that help support hospitals and universities. The Carnegie and Rockefeller foundations, in contrast, allowed the foundation trustees complete latitude in order to determine how they could best further the very general mandates of those foundations. This provides an opportunity to respond to society's most pressing needs as they emerge, and prevents future generations from being shackled by the inability of the donors to be able to see into the future. At the same time, it provides considerable discretion to the foundation's management. Because the foundation's operations are financed from the earnings from the donor's bequest, this also frees the foundation's trustees from almost all external oversight. They do not rely on any outside source for funding, so they are not accountable to anyone.

Thus, the potential benefits from a general mandate also bring with them potential problems. If a foundation is established to benefit a particular university, one could envision the university exercising oversight over the activities of the foundation, and even bringing suit against the foundation if it was mismanaging or misappropriating funds. In contrast, it is difficult to see who might have the incentive, or the standing, to sue the Rockefeller Foundation, arguing that its activities were not "promoting the well-being of mankind," following Rockefeller's mandate. Is the benefit of increased flexibility on the part of the foundation's management worth the cost in terms of reduced accountability? This is another question that will be dealt with in this study.

In many ways the Carnegie and Rockefeller foundations make a good point of departure for examining the ideas that are developed and disseminated with foundation funding. One reason is that they were the first major foundations that aimed more at eliminating the causes rather than the consequences of human problems. Another is that they were the first major foundations to be established under very general mandates. A third reason is that when they were established they were by far the largest foundations in terms of assets, and they continue at the end of the twentieth century as large and influential foundations.

Rockefeller the Philanthropist

John D. Rockefeller was born in 1839 in the small town of Richford, New York, about 125 miles from New York City. He was the son of a traveling salesman who hawked herbs, patent medicines, horses, salt, and furs, among other commodities. Rockefeller's father was away from home months at a time, requiring his mother to make ends meet on very limited means. When Rockefeller's father returned home, the family would be temporarily well-off, before Mr. Rockefeller left again on one of his trips. The family moved to Ohio where Rockefeller finished high school and studied basic business subjects at Folsum's Commercial Academy in Cleveland.[11]

Rockefeller's first lesson in business came before he finished high school, however. He had earned $50 raising turkeys and loaned the money to a farmer, for which he received $3.50 in interest. Rockefeller saw the advantage of having his money work for him. After school he worked for a few years for a shipping firm, but then went into business for himself. He got into the oil business in 1862, and by the end of the Civil War he was a wealthy man. Rockefeller established the Standard Oil Company in 1870, and by 1879 the company was worth $70 million. By the early 1900s Standard Oil controlled almost 90 percent of the nation's oil refinery capacity. By 1911 Standard Oil was worth $885 million, and Rockefeller owned about one-fifth of the company's stock.

This brief account of Rockefeller's rise to become the world's wealthiest man overlooks some important details. Because of his high visibility, his extreme wealth accumulated over a short period, and the often heavy-handed exercise of monopoly power by Standard Oil, Rockefeller was surely one of the most disliked individuals in America. He was accused of unfair competition that drove other oil companies out of business, of conspiring to keep railroads from shipping competitors' products, and even of bribing U.S. senators in order to purchase legislation favorable to Standard Oil.[12] In several states the attorneys-general argued that Rockefeller should be jailed for his crimes.[13] In 1906 the government accused Standard Oil of being in violation of the Sherman Act for monopolizing the industry, and in 1911 the Supreme Court decided against Standard Oil and ordered it broken up into smaller companies. By that time, Rockefeller's substantial fortune had already been made.

Rockefeller recognized that he was widely regarded as a villain by the general public, and cynics have argued that the reason why Rockefeller engaged in such substantial philanthropic activities was to try to present a better public image. Indeed, some philanthropies considered not accepting donations from Rockefeller because the donations would appear to be tainted money.[14] Nevertheless, it was not difficult for Rockefeller to find organizations that were willing to accept donations from him, and after an announcement of a donation by

Rockefeller to a church or university, he would receive thousands of requests for donations in his next month's mail.

Indeed, in fairness to Rockefeller, he had always been a charitable individual, and his generous assistance to philanthropic causes stand in contrast to his ruthlessness in running Standard Oil. In 1882 he was named vice president of the Theological Union of Chicago in recognition of his contributions to the organization, and he regularly gave to a number of charitable causes long before he was viewed as a villain for his business activities. Rockefeller was also instrumental in (re)creating the University of Chicago. Established in 1858, the university closed its doors in 1886 because it lacked funding. When a group of individuals expressed an interest in reviving the institution, Rockefeller donated $600,000 to its endowment in 1888. The University of Chicago reopened its doors in 1890, and Rockefeller continued to support it with cumulative gifts of more than $7 million.[15]

In 1892 Rockefeller hired Frederick Gates, a former Baptist minister, as an advisor to help him determine to whom he should donate money. In addition to his donations to existing organizations Rockefeller, with the assistance of Gates, established a number of foundations early in the twentieth century to undertake activities that they believed worthwhile. Gates believed that the most effective way for Rockefeller's fortune to have a favorable impact was to create groups of independent trustees with expertise in particular areas and endow them with sums of money for specific purposes. Thus, in 1901 a $200,000 endowment was given to the newly created Rockefeller Institute for Medical Research, $1,000,000 was given to establish a General Education Board to improve schools "without distinction of sex, race, or creed," and in 1909 $1,000,000 was given to establish the Rockefeller Sanitary Commission, which had as its mission the eradication of hookworm in Southern states.[16]

Despite the fact that Rockefeller was giving away substantial sums of money under Gates's direction, his fortune was growing more rapidly than he was able to give it away. Gates believed that Rockefeller needed to set up a more enduring way for distributing his fortune, or within a few generations it would be disbursed, possibly squandered, and possibly used for undesirable purposes. To that end, in 1905 Gates suggested to Rockefeller that he establish a great foundation that might promote education, the arts, culture, and ethics.[17] Gates envisioned a foundation that would be so large that just being a trustee of the foundation would make one a well-known public figure. The activities of such a large foundation would automatically be a matter of public concern, and because of the visibility of such a large undertaking, Gates believed that it would attract the most talented and intelligent people in the world. As Gates envisioned it, this foundation would be well beyond the scope of any foundation that had been established before, and would be a fitting tribute to Rockefeller's accomplishments. Thus, the idea behind the Rockefeller Foundation was born.

The Establishment of the Rockefeller Foundation

The Rockefeller Foundation was created in 1909 with Rockefeller's donation of 72,569 shares of Standard Oil Company of New Jersey. The foundation was created "to promote the well-being and to advance the civilization of the peoples of the United States and its territories and possessions and of foreign lands in the acquisition and dissemination of knowledge, in the prevention and relief of suffering, and in the promotion of any and all of the elements of human progress." [18] In 1910 Rockefeller asked Congress to incorporate his foundation, as it had done for many similar organizations in the past, but Congress refused.

Many critics felt that Rockefeller was trying to use his charitable donations to buy a more favorable public reputation that might help his business activities, and the timing was undoubtedly bad. Rockefeller asked Congress to charter his foundation at the same time that the Supreme Court was considering the case that broke up Standard Oil, and Congress was still debating the proposal when the Court decision was rendered. [19] In an effort to appease Congress, Rockefeller was willing to make many concessions, including having the trustees of the foundation be selected by a board consisting of the president of the United States, the chief justice of the Supreme Court, the president of the Senate, the speaker of the house, and the presidents of Harvard, Yale, Columbia, Johns Hopkins, and the University of Chicago. [20] Despite this and other concessions, many members of Congress felt that the stated mission of the foundation was to vague and too broad, and they distrusted Rockefeller. Theodore Roosevelt, president at the time, was proud of his reputation as a trust-buster. In an era of progressive reform, with Roosevelt as the leader, Rockefeller symbolized everything that the Roosevelt administration opposed.

Congress debated whether to charter the Rockefeller Foundation for years without coming to a resolution. Rockefeller's supporters argued that regardless of his public image, Congress should not stand in the way of his trying to do something good with his money. Furthermore, they argued, the foundation could operate without a Congressional charter, and by not chartering it Congress was giving up the opportunity to exercise some control over it. Finally, in 1913, Rockefeller approached the legislature of the State of New York about a charter, and the Rockefeller Foundation was rapidly incorporated in New York.

The Carnegie Corporation of New York

The Carnegie Corporation of New York, the general purpose foundation set up by Andrew Carnegie, was not established amid the degree of controversy that surrounded Rockefeller's foundation. Carnegie's foundation predated Rockefeller's by a few years, having been chartered in 1911 by the State of New York. Like Rockefeller, Carnegie, who made his fortune in steel, coal, and railroads, had a long history of charitable activity during his lifetime. In addition to a number of foundations, he established 2,500 libraries, and in 1889 published an influential essay titled "The Gospel of Wealth" in which he wrote about the "disgrace of dying rich"[21] and discussed how philanthropy could be undertaken on a large scale. Carnegie's activities were undoubtedly an influence on Rockefeller, his contemporary.

Born in Scotland in 1835, Carnegie was brought to the United States in 1846 by his parents who had trouble holding onto jobs in the face of the industrial revolution. Carnegie's father was a master weaver, but found it difficult to use his skills when steam-driven machinery replaced hand-weaving, and Carnegie held odd jobs throughout his childhood to help his family make ends meet. But Carnegie was shrewd and industrious, and the growth of his Carnegie Company made him one of America's wealthiest individuals. In his early thirties he already controlled a number of companies, and was already quite wealthy. Obviously able to spot opportunity, he met Henry Bessemer in 1872 and adopted Bessemer's methods to mass-produce steel, which enabled Carnegie to create his steel empire in Pittsburgh. The wealth he made in steel enabled him to challenge J.P. Morgan's banking empire, and at age sixty-five Carnegie pushed Morgan to buy him out. In 1901 he sold the company to J.P. Morgan for $492 million, which would be a lot of money today, and was an even more substantial sum at the beginning of the twentieth century. He spent the rest of his life giving away the fortune he had made.[22]

When Carnegie was only thirty-three years old, but already quite prosperous, he had written a note to himself promising to devote his wealth to benevolent activities. "Thirty three and an income of $50,000 per annum," Carnegie remarked in his note, and further went on to say that by the age of thirty-five he expected to have all he would need.[23] At that point, he would no longer need to increase his fortune, so would concentrate on how to distribute it to others. Carnegie's note was not written to obtain good publicity; indeed, it was not discovered until after his death, when he had already done what the note had promised. Throughout his life he considered not only how he could make money, but how he could dispose of it in a manner that would further the public good. His "Gospel of Wealth" published in 1889 shows that even before selling his company to give away the proceeds, he had thought deeply about the disposition of his wealth and developed a philosophy of giving.

According to the "Gospel of Wealth," Carnegie viewed the wealthy, including himself, as stewards of wealth that should be used for the greatest good for mankind. Equating the ability to earn wealth with the wisdom to dispose of it for the public interest, he argued that he was "called upon to administer in the manner which, in his judgment, is best calculated to produce the most beneficial results for the community." This means avoiding "indiscriminate charity" to "the slothful, the drunken, the untrustworthy," and using his wealth instead to "provide part of the means by which those who desire to improve may do so." [24] Following this philosophy, although Carnegie paid for the construction of thousands of libraries in his lifetime, he refused to provide money to buy books, or to provide for library maintenance. Carnegie felt that the libraries would be most useful, and most used, if the communities in which they were located felt a sense of proprietorship for them, and if the local communities were not willing to stock the libraries or care for them themselves, Carnegie felt that the library was likely to be neglected and that his money would not be well-spent.

Carnegie's own philanthropic activities reveal the philosophy preached in his "Gospel of Wealth." He believed that anyone with sufficient means should establish a university, and that the best service one could provide to a local community would be the creation of a library. As a youth, Carnegie himself had spent many hours in libraries familiarizing himself with the ideas of great writers that he otherwise would not have had the opportunity to read. The first library that Carnegie built, in 1881, was in Dunfermline, Scotland, where he was born in 1835. When his family had left the town in the 1850s they were poor, and were migrating to the land of opportunity. With great pleasure, Carnegie had his mother return triumphantly to Dunfermline in a coach to lay the cornerstone for the library in the town she had left, much poorer, three decades before. Other public works, such as hospitals, laboratories, parks, meeting and concert halls were also worthy causes that Carnegie wanted to support. As a person who appreciated organ music, he donated money for more than 7,600 organs for churches. Carnegie worked hard to distribute his wealth in ways that would further the public interest.

Andrew Carnegie was obviously a benevolent and public-spirited man, but at the same time he was a man who had unfailing confidence in his own abilities and believed that men of wealth should work to dispose of their own fortunes within their lifetimes. His view that dying wealthy was a disgrace traced partly to his belief that the wealthy had a moral obligation to direct the disposition of their wealth. Those who earned the money were in the best position to determine how it should be used, he believed, and he wanted to give away the bulk of his fortune before he died. He wanted to improve the well-being of mankind, but there is no indication that he believed that a more equal distribution of income or wealth would be desirable. His philanthropic activities were more aimed at producing public goods for communities, for the nation, and for causes that helped everyone than they were at targeting the needy directly.

Carnegie retired in 1901, selling his Carnegie Company to J.P. Morgan for $480 million. Between the time that the Carnegie Company was sold and 1910, Andrew Carnegie gave away huge sums of money, but he began with so much that he found it difficult to find enough worthy causes on which to spend it. Although his gospel of wealth preached that wealthy men should dispose of their fortunes within their lifetimes, it became apparent to him that despite his heroic efforts, he was going to be unable to do so. As a result, Carnegie established the Carnegie Corporation of New York in 1911, where he left the bulk of his fortune. It was quite clear that Carnegie intended to determine the disposition of his fortune himself, and that he felt that his money would do more good if he was in charge of directing it than if the responsibility were passed on to others. Nevertheless, his inability to find sufficient worthy causes to dispose of such a sizable fortune led to the establishment of his foundation. His foundation continues as a major influence through its philanthropic activities. By 1995 the Carnegie Corporation had assets of $1.1 billion, and made annual grants of approximately $55 million.[25]

The Establishment of the Ford Foundation

Circumstances behind the creation of the Ford Foundation were substantially different from those behind the Carnegie and Rockefeller foundations, and more related to tax law. When the Carnegie and Rockefeller foundations were established, the United States had not yet established an income tax, and if Rockefeller's employee Frederick Gates is to be believed, the primary motivation behind the establishment of his foundation was to use his wealth as effectively as possible for public purposes. Even if Rockefeller was trying to purchase a better public image with his philanthropic activities, the motivation was still primarily charitable. Henry Ford, in contrast, viewed charity as counterproductive. Recipients tended to become dependent on their benefactors, Ford believed. The profits of business are better spent reinvesting in the business, in Ford's view, in order to provide additional opportunities for individuals to earn a living. Furthermore, Ford viewed endowing a foundation as creating inappropriate incentives for those who would run the foundation. Endowments, Ford believed, might benefit the donor with a feeling of smug satisfaction, but would create inertia in the endowed organization, and would sap its imagination and initiative.[26]

Given Ford's hostility to foundations, how did the Ford Foundation come to be established? The tax laws at the time had everything to do with its establishment. Nearly all of the Ford Motor Company stock was owned by Henry Ford and his son Edsel, and Ford recognized that if they were to bequeath that fortune to Edsel's children, they would have had to have sold off a majority of Ford stock in order to pay the estate taxes. In addition to the huge tax payment that would have been due, it also would have meant that the Ford family would lose control over Henry Ford's company. Thus, in 1936 Ford created the Ford Foundation, which during the lives of Henry and Edsel was financed by small cash grants from Ford's family, mostly used to aid Michigan charities.[27]

The Ford Foundation lived in relative obscurity throughout the lives of Henry and Edsel. Edsel died in 1943 and Henry in 1947, leaving a substantial estate that was finally settled in 1950. They had left ten percent of the Ford Motor Company stock to members of the Ford family, and bequeathed the other 90 percent to the Ford Foundation, which was established in 1951.[28] Despite this generous endowment from Henry Ford, who was so uncharitable during his lifetime, the bequest to the foundation left much for Ford's family. The stock that was left to the foundation was nonvoting stock, leaving control of the company with the Ford family who held the voting stock. Furthermore, the bequest stipulated that the stock left to the family was to be tax free, leaving the foundation to pay more than $42 million in inheritance taxes for the Ford heirs.

The creation of the Ford Foundation in this way was legal, but raised enough questions that Congressional hearings were held on the subject in 1952. When Henry Ford II was asked whether the Ford Foundation was set up as a way to allow the Ford family to retain control of the Ford Motor Company, he responded that with the creation of the foundation in the 1930s Henry Ford felt that he had continuing obligations to a number of charities, and given the condition of the nation in the 1930s, he created the foundation as a way to ensure that these obligations would be satisfied after his death. This was an odd justification for the charitable activities of someone who, in life, publicly held charitable activity in such low regard. But when Ford stock was transferred to the foundation, estate tax rates were 77 percent. Undoubtedly Ford wanted to preserve family control of his company, and it may also be that Ford felt his foundation would use the money for better purposes than the government. If the family had inherited all of the Ford Motor Company stock, they would have owed federal estate taxes of about $321 million. In 1950, when the estate was settled, total federal budget receipts were $39 billion, so the Ford family estate taxes would have been equal to about eight percent of total federal receipts in that year.

After the Ford Foundation was established, its trustees chose a course of action substantially at odds with the ideas expressed by Henry Ford during his lifetime. The details are related in chapters 3 and 4. But the foundation trustees also had to be concerned with issues specifically related to the management of the endowment. The endowment came in the form of Ford Motor Company stock, and in the late 1940s the Ford Motor Company was struggling. By the early 1950s the company had turned around and was very profitable, providing the foundation with so much income that the trustees found it difficult to spend it. Suspicious observers of this new foundation, which was much larger than any of its predecessors, were concerned about the impact of the foundation's programs. Yet another concern for the trustees was the lack of diversification in the foundation's portfolio, and in 1955 the foundation began divesting itself of its Ford Motor Company stock.[29]

The divestiture was complicated by the fact that the foundation had only nonvoting stock, and the Ford family controlled all of the voting stock. A deal was struck that divided Ford Motor Company stock into three different classes. Class A stock was the nonvoting stock owned by the Ford Foundation. Class B stock was the voting stock originally held by the Ford family. A new class of common stock was created with voting rights, and whenever a share of Class A stock was sold by the foundation, it was converted into one of these new voting shares. Regardless of the number of shares outstanding, however, the new common stock would have 60 percent of the voting rights, and the other 40 percent of the voting rights would be retained by the Class B stockholders. In 1956 the Ford Foundation held 88 percent of the Ford Motor Company. After a major divestment in that year, followed by later sales, the foundation's share of the company's stock dropped to 16 percent by 1972. The creation of the Ford Foundation was as much a financial undertaking as it was philanthropic.

The Carnegie and Rockefeller foundations were established before federal income and estate taxation that made up the bulk of federal revenues when the Ford Foundation was established. While tax considerations had to be far down on the list of concerns for Carnegie and Rockefeller, they were the primary motivation for the establishment of the Ford Foundation, and this was the cause of considerable controversy when the foundation was established. The Ford Foundation has not remained free of controversy since then either. Operating as a nonprofit organization sheltered by favorable tax laws, some of the foundation's activities raised questions in Congress in the 1960s, only a few decades after the foundation was established. The Ford Foundation became actively involved in policy issues, social problems, and political activities. Despite restrictions placed on foundation activities in public policy areas as a result of tax reforms in 1969 the Ford Foundation continues to be actively involved in policy issues.[31] When relating the effect of tax laws to the promotion of ideas by foundations, the Ford Foundation has been a major part of the story of public policy toward nonprofit foundations.

The Kellogg Foundation

As the second-largest foundation in the United States in the early 1990s, the Kellogg Foundation deserves mention. In a book about foundation grants and their effect on the development of ideas, the Kellogg Foundation has largely kept out of visible programs to develop and promote ideas, sticking instead to more basic education, community, youth, agriculture, and health programs. The foundation was created by Will Kellogg, whose wealth came from selling Americans cornflakes.

Kellogg was born in 1860, and until middle age worked as a book-keeper at a health sanitarium Battle Creek, Michigan. Will's brother, Dr. John Harvey Kellogg, was the chief physician at the sanitarium, and became nationally famous as an author of health books. Dr. Kellogg would only accept patients to the sanitarium if they agreed not to smoke, drink, or eat meat. The reputation of the sanitarium caused people to flock to Battle Creek as a health mecca. Dr. Kellogg was constantly experimenting with new ways to package vegetarian food, and Will would assist his brother. They invented a number of novel foods, including peanut butter, which they declined to promote because they felt the public would not accept it, and in 1894, cornflakes. They sold food to former patients of the sanitarium, and because of the popularity of their cornflakes, Will sensed a commercial opportunity if they could market their cornflakes nationally.[32]

Will's brother opposed the commercial marketing of the cornflakes, feeling that it would undermine the reputation of the sanitarium, so Will acquired the majority interest in the cornflakes company and left the sanitarium to begin selling cornflakes. As the story is told, Will Kellogg was transformed from a quiet, unassuming, and slightly unhappy bookkeeper into a dynamo of mass marketing. He was a pioneer in the infant industry of advertising, coming up with many novel promotional ideas himself. He aggressively pushed door-to-door marketing. In one advertising campaign in New York City in 1911 he encouraged housewives to "wink at their local storekeeper to see what would happen." When they did, they got a free sample of Kellogg's Cornflakes, and in six weeks sales in New York City jumped from 200 cases a week to 200,000 cases a week.[33]

Kellogg was a political conservative who consistently voted Republican, and who believed Herbert Hoover was a hero. Kellogg was openly critical of Franklin Roosevelt and the New Deal, believing that the federal government was trampling on individual freedom and harming private enterprise. In 1925, when Kellogg was sixty-five years old, his attention turned from his business toward philanthropy. He was concerned about children, donated money for civic causes, helped the Boy Scouts, and established a day nursery. He disliked being called a philanthropist, insisting that he was giving money for worthy causes because he got "a kick out of it," rather than because he was trying to do good. His giving was a selfish act rather than a charitable one, he insisted. After engaging in five years of helping others, he established the Kellogg Foundation in 1930. Still, he was cautious, and made only annual gifts to the foundation until 1935, when he endowed the foundation with a substantial gift. He retained an interest in the foundation's activities until his death in 1951.

The Kellogg Foundation programs have focused on health, education, and agriculture since it was established, and still does not venture into more controversial areas of social science and public policy. Thus, the foundation stands in contrast to the Carnegie, Rockefeller, and Ford foundations that have moved more aggressively into the public policy arena. The issue of donor intent, discussed in chapter 6, would be less of an issue if all foundations chose their programs as the Kellogg Foundation has.

The MacArthur Foundation

The John D. and Catherine T. MacArthur Foundation was established in 1978 at the death of John D. MacArthur, who had made his fortune in insurance and real estate. The youngest of seven children, John D. MacArthur was a slow starter. He had a tough time in school, and quit in the eighth grade. He joined the Royal Canadian Air Force, but crashed three planes during his training. In 1935, in the midst of the Great Depression, he purchased Bankers Life and Casualty, a bankrupt Chicago insurance company, for $2,500, which looked like another dubious move on his part. But when other insurance companies failed during the Depression, he was able to capture their business. In the 1950s he channeled his profits into Florida real estate when the market began booming. MacArthur was a ruthless competitor, and often skirted on the edges of the law. He was frugal and had few friends. When he died in 1978 he had no funeral, at his request, because he felt that people only attended funerals as a sense of duty, and from accounts of MacArthur's life, in his own case he may have been right.[34]

Like other large foundations, the MacArthur Foundation has a very broad mission statement. It is "a private, independent grantmaking institution dedicated to helping groups and individuals to improve the human condition." [35] This mission statement provides relatively little specific guidance, and when the foundation began operating there was a tremendous amount of disagreement among the trustees. MacArthur appointed his wife, Catherine, and son Roderick, along with a handful of business associates as trustees. Catherine never attended a board meeting, believing that the family fortune should be turned over to established charities rather than run through a foundation. Rod MacArthur wanted the foundation to spearhead social change, and viewed the government as the most promising vehicle for social change, while the remainder of the board had a strong antigovernment bias, so initially there was a great deal of confusion as to the role the foundation would play. This confusion was compounded by the federal requirement that foundations must distribute their income in order to retain their tax-exempt status. Thus, initially there was little continuity as the foundation searched for its identity while being required to disburse tens of millions of dollars annually. [36]

Animosity between Rod MacArthur and the other trustees continued as Rod accused the trustees of raiding the foundation's assets for their own benefit and of general mismanagement. Those disagreements ended only after Rod MacArthur's death in 1984. Despite the foundation's inauspicious beginning, Rod MacArthur had some interesting ideas about how foundations might contribute to society. MacArthur noted:

> This is the only institution in our society that does not have constituencies that it has to keep looking to. All the others have to worry about pleasing a lot of people, so they're bound to tend toward conventional wisdom, respectability, and the lowest common denominator.... Foundations should be striving to do the kinds of things that the government cannot do. I repeat, *cannot do:* things that are not politically popular, things that are too risky, things that are just too far ahead of what the public will put up with.... A private foundation, where the board of directors is answerable only to itself, is in a completely different situation, and if it doesn't take advantage of that uniqueness, it's just blowing its opportunity, and perhaps even its moral obligation. [37]

Rod MacArthur's ideas are interesting in the context of this study, because one of the problems considered at some length is the lack of accountability of foundation trustees and management. MacArthur viewed this lack of accountability as a virtue of the foundation. Was he being overly idealistic, or is this lack of accountability over such tremendous wealth a good thing? MacArthur raises an important policy issue.

The MacArthur Foundation has matured, but still is a bit of a maverick and a newcomer among foundations. The foundation provides more than $100 million in grants annually, so its programs have a substantial impact. At the end of the twentieth century the total dollar value of grants from this relatively new foundation are about twice that of the Carnegie Corporation. The foundation gives grants for peace and international cooperation, environmental programs, population issues, health, and education. The foundation gains some visibility for its MacArthur Fellows Program, which provides unrestricted grants to "exceptionally creative individuals, regardless of field of endeavor." While relatively new, the activities funded by the MacArthur Foundation make this foundation fit into the same framework as the Carnegie and Rockefeller Foundations. They have broad mandates intended to promote the trustees' vision of the public good.

The Duke Endowment

James Buchanan (Buck) Duke was a native North Carolinian who made his fortune as owner of the American Tobacco Company, and later with the Duke Power Company. Like Rockefeller, he was relatively unpopular, especially in North Carolina where the locals viewed his domination in the tobacco industry as the cause of low tobacco prices that kept the prevailing wage and the standard of living lower than they should be for those in the industry. One of Duke's motivations in creating his endowment was to preserve his Duke Power Company, and he did so by bequeathing the foundation Duke Power Company stock. Duke's action to protect control of his corporation after his death undoubtedly provided inspiration to the Fords who had similar motivations when they established their foundation.

Buck Duke was a shrewd man who realized that it is difficult to control the world from beyond the grave, but designed his foundation in an attempt to do so. He believed that there were three major groups of people who had substantial influence over public opinions toward business, and who might be able to alter his plans after his death. Lawyers dominate government, preachers influence people's religious and moral attitudes, and physicians have a major influence over the public through their influence on people's health. Duke's plan was to design a foundation that would win the support of these three major groups. In contrast to other large foundations, Duke set up his foundation with explicit instructions on how its income should be distributed, and those instructions would help preserve Duke's intentions by appealing to those groups of people who he thought might be influential enough to alter them.

The largest portion of the earnings from Duke's foundation were to go to Duke University. Prior to the receipt of Duke's money, the university was Trinity College, a Methodist institution with a name that was symbolically valuable to the college trustees and to the college community. But the college would get Duke's money only under the condition that the name of the school be changed. One trustee facetiously questioned whether Duke's wishes could be satisfied by renaming the school "The Father, Son, and James B. Duke University," but in the end the college accepted the money and changed the institution's name. Duke University is entitled to 32 percent of the endowment's income. Duke reasoned that with this money, Duke University would have first-rate law and medical schools, and an outstanding theology school. Thus, the three groups of people to whom Duke wanted to appeal would all be grateful for the work done by the Duke Endowment.

Duke also instructed that 32 percent of the endowment's income be used to support hospitals in the Carolinas, and that 5 percent each from the endowment would go to Davidson College and Furman University. Johnson C. Smith University was to receive 4 percent of the endowment's income, 10 percent was to go to orphanages in the Carolinas, and 10 percent was to go to the construction and maintenance of Methodist churches in small North Carolina towns. Two percent was left for the support of retired preachers, their widows, and their orphan children.

Duke's logic in leaving a substantial share of income from his endowment to health care was that people needed to be healthy in order to work, and that people who were not working were a burden on society. One can see both similarities and differences when comparing the Duke Endowment with those left by Carnegie and Rockefeller. Duke, unlike his predecessors, left very specific instructions regarding the disposition of income from his foundation, and even now one can see some of the problems with such specific instructions. A healthier population leaves fewer orphans today, and there is an increasing trend toward foster care rather than orphanages. And with government becoming increasingly involved in financing the health care of those who are least well-off, one might well wonder whether Duke would be so charitably inclined to the health care industry today. This shows the wisdom in Carnegie's idea that it is difficult to anticipate now how money might best be spent for the public interest in the future.

The fact that it is difficult to anticipate future areas of expenditure for the public good does not necessarily imply that future trustees will wisely allocate a foundation's income either. Another alternative goes back to an earlier idea of Carnegie's: that a person's wealth should be allocated by the one who earns it, and within that person's lifetime. Carnegie was unable to do this, but perhaps he should have stipulated a rate of expenditure rapid enough that the foundation would have allocated all of its resources within a few decades.

Duke's endowment was different from Carnegie's and Rockefeller's in some respects, but it shares one striking similarity. It targets the foundation's expenditures primarily toward activities that can help prevent future problems and keep people from suffering rather than targeting money toward those who are currently feeling hardship. It attacks the causes of problems, not the effects.

Duke's endowment also shares the common feature with the Ford Foundation that both were designed to retain control of corporate stock in the donor's companies. Buck Duke endowed his foundation with a sizable amount of Southern Power System stock, which was Duke power and subsidiary companies, and instructed that the stock could not be sold except with the unanimous approval of the endowment's trustees. In 1962 the trustees of the Duke Endowment went to the North Carolina courts and asked that this restriction be lifted. When Duke's will was written in the 1920s the restriction made sense, they argued, because of stock market speculation and because there was no Securities and Exchange Commission to ensure the honest representation of investments. But in the 1960s, they argued, Duke's proviso was overly restrictive, and a more diversified portfolio would be in the best interest of the foundation. The courts turned down this request, arguing that Duke "had as much right to name the securities in which the funds should be invested as he had to name the beneficiaries," [39] so Duke's plans for his fortune did hold up decades after his death.

The Russell Sage Foundation

Perhaps the most colorful stories about those who earned the wealth to endow foundations are told about Russell Sage, whose fortune endowed the Russell Sage Foundation. Sage was a nineteenth-century financier, well-known for his miserly habits. He once sent a boy out to buy him a sandwich for lunch, and when the boy returned with a fifteen-cent sandwich instead of one of the five-cent sandwiches that were available, Sage deducted a dime from the boy's pay. Sage rode the streetcar to work and to meetings, and would haggle with street vendors over the prices they were asking for their goods. Once, when an enemy walked into his office with a bomb and threatened to blow him up, Sage grabbed a stockbroker and used him as a shield. The broker was injured in the blast, but because of Sage's refusal to offer any compensation the broker sued Sage. At one point a jury awarded the broker $40,000, but Sage appealed and eventually won the suit. The injured broker never collected anything, and Sage vowed that he would be willing to spend $100,000 to fight the suit rather than turn his money over to that undeserving broker.[40]

Sage remained miserly until his death in 1906, and his will left the bulk of his $64 million fortune to his widow, and not a cent to charity. His widow was much more charitable, and in 1907 established the Russell Sage Foundation "for the purpose of receiving and maintaining a fund, or funds, and applying the income thereof to the improvement of social and living conditions in the United States of America." To accomplish its mission, "it shall use any means to that end which from time to time shall seem expedient to its members or trustees, including research, publication, education, the establishment and maintenance of charitable or benevolent activities, agencies and institutions, and the aid of any such activities, agencies or institutions already established." [41]

The Russell Sage Foundation was largely oriented toward social work, and the collection of data on social problems. At the turn of the century, social work was called charity, and in large part because of the efforts of the Russell Sage Foundation to professionalize social work, it is now looked at as a vocation. Philosophically, the activities of the Russell Sage Foundation are in line with those of the Carnegie and Rockefeller foundations, in that they are geared toward eliminating the causes of human suffering rather than addressing the consequences. Now its activities are geared largely toward social science studies in economics, the causes of poverty, immigration issues, and other related social science topics.[42]

Other Foundations

Every foundation has a story behind it, and the stories often reveal much about the character of the foundation and the intent of the donor. A few more stories can lend some insight into the origin of this fascinating and underappreciated sector of the economy.[43]

S.S. Kresge earned a fortune creating the dime store chain that bore his name, but had a reputation, like, Sage, of being exceedingly frugal. Married in 1897, his wife divorced him in 1924 because he was so miserly. Kresge bragged about never spending more than thirty cents for lunch, and his friends said that he was a poor golfer because he spent his time on the links looking for lost balls. After his divorce in 1924, Kresge began giving away money, and by 1966 when he died had endowed the Kresge Foundation with more than $300 million.

Walter H. Annenberg inherited a substantial amount of wealth earned largely from his father's activities in gambling wire services, and while he was wealthy, to many old-line wealthy families Annenberg's fortune appeared tainted because of its origin. Annenberg established the Annenberg Foundation which gave money to universities, museums, and other organizations, and in exchange was placed on numerous boards of trustees and advisors, buying himself prestige. When he purchased a portrait of Ben Franklin for the White House during Jacqueline Kennedy's campaign to refurbish the White House, he was invited to a private dinner with President and Mrs. Kennedy. He was appointed ambassador to England by President Nixon, and spent $1 million of his foundation's money to renovate the U.S. embassy there. Simply having money does not convey prestige, but as Annenberg showed, someone with money can use it to buy prestige.

Yet another example is illustrated by the Charles A. Dana Foundation, established by Mr. Dana from his earnings out of his business that supplied parts to the auto industry. Thanks to the foundation, many will remember the Dana name, although whether they will know anything more about Mr. Dana is questionable. Thanks to foundation gifts, Stetson University in Florida has the Charles A. Dana Law Library, Indiana Technological College has the Dana Science Building, there is the Charles A. Dana Building of Science at the University of Bridgeport, the University of Toledo's Charles A. Dana Auditorium, the Charles A. Dana Fine Arts Center at Agnes Scott College in Georgia, the Dana Arts Center at Colgate University, the Yale-New Haven Medical Center's

Charles A. Dana Clinic and Hospital Diagnostic and Service Building... and many other Dana buildings and clinics that will preserve Mr. Dana's name. Mr. Dana's charitable impulses shown by the establishment of the foundation bearing his name must be admired, but at the same time it must be recognized that Mr. Dana did not wish to remain an anonymous donor.

Amherst H. Wilder, who was Minnesota's first millionaire, had one child, a daughter, and viewed every suitor of his daughter as someone with eyes mainly on the Wilder family fortune. Mr. Wilder was able to repel a number of men with interest in his daughter, but in 1897 she married a doctor named Appleby. Wilder would allow the marriage to take place only under the condition that all property of the couple remain under the control of his daughter. When the daughter died in 1903 Dr. Appleby sued to retain some of the property owned by him and his deceased wife, and did manage to win a settlement of an annual income of $10,000, but the bulk of Wilder's estate went to establish a foundation to aid the needy people of St. Paul, Minnesota. Foundations are established for many different reasons, and the Wilder Foundation was established because Mr. Wilder had no heir he viewed as suitable to inherit his wealth.

The Hormel Foundation is a Minnesota foundation established to retain control of the Hormel Company. The founders of the company were concerned that after their deaths the company would be swallowed up by industry giants, so gave controlling interest in the firm to the foundation. The foundation trustees are required to have their chief financial interests in the company, in an attempt to ensure that the company would not be taken over. Thus, like the Duke and Ford Foundations, the Hormel Foundation owes its origin at least partly to the desire of its departed owners to continue to control the company after their deaths.

Foundation History and Public Policy Toward Foundations

A reflection on the history of the development of foundations can help illuminate any discussion of public policy toward foundations. As the situation stands at the end of the twentieth century, public policy toward nonprofit foundations is almost entirely a matter of tax policy. Essentially the law says that in order to retain the tax-preferred status of a foundation, the foundation must meet certain conditions (which are discussed in chapter 4). In the abstract, this certainly appears reasonable. If organizations are going to enjoy a favored legal status, then they must contribute something toward the public interest in exchange for that favored status. Individuals are always free to give their money to causes they view as worthy, such as passing a dollar along to the guy with the sign that says, "Will Work for Food." If donors want to deduct the money as a charitable contribution for tax purposes, however, certain criteria must be met on the part of the recipient. This is the spirit in which it is reasonable for tax laws to place restrictions and requirements on the actions of nonprofit foundations. Foundations can always avoid the restrictions by giving up their tax-favored status; to retain favored status, they must demonstrate that the cost of their tax-favored status is offset by the public benefits that they produce.

Federal income and inheritance taxes are a twentieth-century innovation, as is the modern American foundation. While some precursors can be found earlier, only a handful of foundations were created prior to the twentieth century, and the structure and activities of those created in the twentieth century have served to define the nature of that segment of the economy. There are several reasons why foundations are a creation of the twentieth century, and the income tax is only a part of the story. Prior to the twentieth century, business operated on a smaller scale, so individuals were not able to accumulate massive fortunes such as those accumulated by Carnegie, Rockefeller, and those who came after. As Adam Smith noted in his remarkable treatise, *The Wealth of Nations,* published in 1776, the division of labor is limited by the extent of the market. The extent of the market increased dramatically with the growth of the railroads, and advances in transportation and communication throughout the twentieth century have continued to expand markets for all businesses. Firms that at one time could hope to sell only to local markets can now sell to the world, thanks to lower transportation costs.

Wealthy individuals—and wealthy families—had existed prior to the twentieth century, of course, but wealth-building was a slower process that took generations. Rockefeller, Carnegie, and Sage, who made the fortunes that financed some of the first large general grant-making foundations, began their lives in modest circumstances and produced their fortunes in their own lifetimes. Their foundations were established because they wanted to provide some public good with their wealth. (In Sage's case, of course, it was his widow who wanted to do the public good.) All three of these foundations were established prior to the advent of the income tax, so tax considerations can be ruled out as a primary motivation in their acts. And because there was no income tax, their foundations initially were treated like any other venture for tax purposes. One can hardly object to Rockefeller, Carnegie, and Sage turning control of their fortunes over to others so that the fortunes might serve some public purpose long after their deaths.

The rate at which foundations have been established has accelerated rapidly throughout the twentieth century. Before 1900 only eighteen foundations had been established in the United States, and that same number had been established in the years from 1900 to 1909 alone. From 1910 to 1919, seventy-six foundations were created, and in the 1920s, 173 were established. The 1930s saw 288 foundations established, the 1940s produced 1,638 foundations, and 2,839 foundations were created in the 1950s.[44] This impressive growth in the creation of foundations goes hand in hand with increases in federal income and estate tax rates. While the creation of the Carnegie and Rockefeller foundations was clearly not motivated by tax reasons, the creation of the Ford Foundation just as clearly was. Thus, while the tax code supplies only part of the story of the growth of foundations, it provides a crucial part of the story, especially for public policy purposes. Donors are able to tax-shelter their wealth after their deaths in perpetuity, giving control over to trustees who have little connection to the original source of the wealth, who have little reason to consider the intent of the donor, and most significantly, who are not accountable to anyone for the way in which the foundation is managed or its income is spent.

This lack of accountability gives foundation managers and trustees a huge amount of latitude in determining what types of activities foundations undertake. Should the activities of foundations have more government oversight, or more regulations on their activities, in exchange for their tax-exempt status? One way to frame this question is to compare the actual activities of foundations with the visions of the foundations' donors. This chapter has shown that many of the donors who established foundations had clear ideas of their own about how foundation resources should be used, but that the largest foundations were established with mandates that gave trustees much room to interpret how foundation resources could be used to further the public interest. Have foundations remained true to the intentions of their donors? The next chapter addresses this issue by examining the ideas that have been promoted by some of the most prominent foundations once the donors no longer had control of the foundation's resources.

Notes

1. This background comes from Joseph C. Goulden, *The Money Givers* (New York: Random House, 1971), pp. 25-26.
2. This distinction is analyzed in more detail by Barry D. Karl and Stanley N. Katz, "Foundations and Ruling Class Elites," *Daedalus* 116, No. 1 (Winter 1987), pp. 1-40.
3. Tax treatment of noncharitable activities is questioned by Henry Hansmann, "Economic Theories of Nonprofit Organization," chap. 2 in Walter W. Powell, ed., *The Nonprofit Sector* (New Haven, CT: Yale University Press, 1987).
4. See Tyler Cowen, *In Praise of Commercial Culture* (Cambridge, MA: Harvard University Press, 1998), for arguments supporting market-generated cultural activities (like rap and country music) as opposed to government-subsidized culture.
5. See Warren Weaver, *U.S. Philanthropic Foundations* (New York: Harper & Row, 1968), p. 24.
6. Michael O'Neill, *The Third America: The Emergence of the Nonprofit Sector in the United States* (San Francisco, CA: Jossey-Bass Publishers, 1989), p. 144.
7. Weaver, *U.S. Philanthropic Foundations,* p. 58.
8. Barry D. Karl and Stanley N. Katz, "The American Private Philanthropic Foundation and the Public Sphere: 1890-1930," *Minerva* 19, No. 2 (Summer 1981), pp. 236-270, discuss the evolution of foundations from narrow charitable purposes to broad philanthropic ones.
9. Quoted from Robert H. Bremner, *Philanthropy,* 2nd ed. (Chicago: University of Chicago Press, 1988), p. 99.
10. Robert L. Payton, *Philanthropy: Voluntary Action for the Public Good* (New York: Macmillan Publishing Company, 1988), p. 28.
11. See Weaver, *U.S. Philanthropic Foundations,* pp. 31-38, for a discussion of Rockefeller's background.
12. Some background can be found in Peter Asch, *Economic Theory and the Antitrust Dilemma* (New York: John Wiley & Sons, 1970), pp. 237-240.
13. Waldemar A. Nielsen, *The Big Foundations* (New York: Columbia University Press, 1972), p. 48.
14. Goulden, *The Money Givers,* p. 33, reports that after a series of magazine articles by muckraker Ida Tarbell, the American Board of Commissioners of Foreign Missions rejected a $100,000 donation from Rockefeller, but the Board later changed its mind and accepted the gift. Tarbell's book, *The History of the Standard Oil Company* (New York: Macmillan, 1904) brought a substantial amount of bad publicity to Rockefeller at a time when the general public was increasingly clamoring for government intervention to curb abuses of power by large corporations.
15. Sarah Knowles Bolton, *Famous Givers and Their Gifts* (Freeport, NY: Books For Libraries Press, 1971, reprint of 1896 ed.), pp. 374-376.
16. Goulden, *The Money Givers,* p. 30.

17. Nielsen, *The Big Foundations*, p. 50.
18. Goulden, *The Money Givers*, p. 32.
19. Nielsen, *The Big Foundations*, pp. 51-52..
20. Goulden, *The Money Givers*, p. 36.
21. O'Neill, *The Third America*, p. 144.
22. Nielsen, *The Big Foundations*, pp. 31-32.
23. Ellen Condliffe Lagemann, *The Politics of Knowledge: The Carnegie Corporation, Philanthropy, and Public Policy* (Middletown, CT: Wesleyan University Press, 1989), p. 13.
24. These quotations from Lagemann, *The Politics of Knowledge*, p. 15.
25. This information from the Carnegie Corporation's internet site, at http://www.carnegie.org.
26. Goulden, *The Money Givers*, p. 41.
27. Goulden, *The Money Givers*, pp. 42-44, discusses the establishment of the Ford Foundation.
28. See O'Neill, *The Third America*, pp. 146-147, for a discussion of the creation of the Ford Foundation.
29. Nielsen, *The Big Foundations*, pp. 85-87.
30. Nielsen, *The Big Foundations*, p. 87.
31. Ford Foundation, *The Common Good: Social Welfare and the American Future*. New York, 1989.
32. The story of the founding of the Kellogg Foundation is told in Nielsen, *The Big Foundations*, pp. 107-118.
33. Nielsen, *The Big Foundations*, p. 109.
34. Waldemar A. Nielsen, *The Golden Donors: A New Anatomy of the Great Foundations* (New York: Truman Talley Books, 1985), ch. 5.
35. This statement and other information on the foundation is from the MacArthur Foundation internet site.
36. Nielsen, *The Golden Donors*, pp. 103-105.
37. Nielsen, *The Golden Donors*, p. 110.
38. Goulden, *The Money Givers*, pp. 46-49 for a discussion of Duke.
39. Goulden, *The Money Givers*, p. 48.
40. Horace Coon, *Money to Burn: What the Great American Philanthropic Foundations Do With Their Money* (London: Longmans, Green and Co., 1938), pp. 73-74, and Joseph Goulden, *The Money Givers*, pp. 44-46.
41. Coon, *Money to Burn*, pp. 75-76.
42. Russell Sage Foundation, *Biennial Report: 1990-1991*. New York: Russell Sage Foundation, 1992.
43. Goulden, *The Money Givers*, chapter 2, for a more detailed discussion of the motivation behind the establishment of many foundations.
44. Weaver, *U.S. Philanthropic Foundations*, p. 58.

3

The Ideas They Promote

The concept that a nonprofit foundation would promote ideas was developed in the twentieth century, along with the development of the modern American foundation. Prior to the twentieth century, foundations were smaller, more focused in their programs, and more geared toward distributing benefits to the needy. The Carnegie and Rockefeller foundations were much larger than those that preceded them, and so perhaps by necessity had to be more broadly oriented. To provide the greatest possible benefit with that much money surely required that it be spread among a number of causes rather than focused on a few. At the same time, those foundations developed the idea of providing opportunities for everybody, rather than focusing on the needy, and of enhancing the ability of individuals to take care of themselves rather than providing direct benefits to those who could not. In their lifetimes, Carnegie built thousands of libraries and financed organs for churches, while Rockefeller supported hospitals and initiated public health projects to help cure widespread diseases. Both men supported institutions of higher education, not to provide direct benefits for the needy but to improve the condition of the world for everyone. Because of Carnegie and Rockefeller, the direction of foundation activity had turned. Their foundations were so big that almost by default the direction of foundation programs would have to move with Carnegie's and Rockefeller's programs.

The concept of human capital was strongly entrenched in the programs that Carnegie and Rockefeller wanted to support. The adage, "Give a man a fish and feed him for a day; teach a man to fish and feed him for a lifetime," describes this general idea well. Yet even this is too

53

narrow to describe the direction of foundation funding. The dawn of the twentieth century brought with it new ideas related to scientific management. In corporate America there was the idea that better application of management principles could improve the performance of American business, and these same principles were being applied to the public sector as well. The Harvard Business School was established in 1908, and the ideas that gave rise to more scientific business management might also be applied to the management of government.[1] Of course, individuals needed human capital in order to be productive, but they also needed a social environment in which their productivity could be fully utilized. The Carnegie Corporation in particular was responsive to these ideas, and lent its financial support to the development of more scientific ways to deal with social problems. Thus, foundations and social science became intertwined, and foundation activities began exerting a significant influence over ideas in American society.

The Pioneering Work of the Carnegie Corporation

The Carnegie Corporation was established in 1911 and Andrew Carnegie served as its president from its founding until his death in 1919. During those initial years the foundation's activities remained true to Carnegie's ideas that the foundation could play a role in helping people to develop their individual talents through the building of libraries, the financing of educational institutions, and other activities that could help make communities more productive places for the development of human abilities. The orientation of the foundation changed dramatically after Carnegie's death. The foundation's trustees, in line with the times, adopted a progressive agenda that pushed the foundation into areas of public policy. In 1923 Frederick Paul Keppel became president of the Carnegie Corporation, a position he held until 1942, and Keppel kept the foundation focused on social issues.[2]

One of the things Carnegie himself is surely remembered for is the large number of libraries that he financed. Carnegie believed that by making public libraries available, every individual in the community from the millionaire to the pauper could avail themselves of the great ideas contained in books. While most of Carnegie's libraries were well-received, even this philanthropic activity had its critics. In 1901 the *Detroit Journal* questioned how Carnegie came to believe that the residents of Detroit were in need of Carnegie's charity, and argued that if

Mr. Carnegie felt the urge to distribute his fortune, he should have done so by being more generous to those that had worked for him when he was amassing it. Socialist Eugene V. Debs thought that communities should refuse Carnegie's grants, arguing that there would be an abundance of libraries once capitalism was overthrown and the working class was no longer being robbed by the likes of Carnegie.[3]

The foundation's library program met with some controversy among the foundation trustees as well. James Bertram, who was Carnegie's long-time assistant and a trustee, wanted to pursue the library program as Carnegie intended it by providing library buildings, but leaving local communities with the responsibility of stocking them, maintaining them, and operating them. Carnegie felt that this would give the local community a sense of proprietorship, and that they would be more likely to make good use of the facility. Other trustees felt differently, and commissioned a report on the state of Carnegie's libraries, along with recommendations. The report suggested that the libraries would be of better use to communities if they were stocked using foundation funds, and if they were run by library professionals, again financed through the foundation, rather then left to the nonprofessional management of local community volunteers.

Carnegie himself had more of a laissez-faire philosophy on the operation of the libraries, whereas his handpicked trustees were more oriented toward the newer view of social science and public management. Why leave the operation of libraries to communities, when often they were staffed by untrained volunteers, when they could be more effectively run by professionals who could guide library patrons and enable them to make better use of the facilities? As the foundation's library program was being debated, World War I erupted and was commanding a substantial amount of the trustees' attention. Surely the promotion of world peace should take precedence over library funding, at least for the time being. The Carnegie Corporation "temporarily" discontinued its program of funding libraries in 1917, and the program was never resumed.[4] One of Carnegie's favorite personal causes was abandoned as the trustees of the foundation recast the foundation's direction.

Foundations Turn to Social Science

Philanthropies from the Carnegie Corporation to the Rockefeller Foundation, and those before and after, have always supported the creation and dissemination of ideas through their support of institutions of higher learning. The push in the early twentieth century to make the study of social phenomena more scientific was clearly a part of the vision shared by the trustees of the Carnegie Corporation, and after the death of Andrew Carnegie his foundation turned even more in that direction. Both the Carnegie and Rockefeller foundations had supported the work of scientific elites in the hard sciences through grants to the National Academy of Sciences (NAS), the National Research Council (NRC), and the American Association for the Advancement of Science (AAAS).[5] As social sciences became more scientific, there was precedent for the funding of this type of activity in the hard sciences, but no ready vehicle for channeling the funds. The NAS, NRC, and AAAS all predated their foundation funding, but there were no comparable organizations in the social sciences.

Interest in founding such an organization began earlier in the century. Theodore Vail, founder and president of AT&T, called a conference in 1912 in which he expressed an interest in establishing an institute of economics that might assist in quieting some of the social unrest of the time. Vail believed that the antibusiness mentality of the general public, and their distrust of large corporations, was primarily due to their being misinformed, and he envisioned the creation of an institute of economics that could provide reliable and credible information to the public so that the public could better understand the economic system that was bringing them unprecedented production and prosperity. Vail's conference was attended by John D. Rockefeller, Jr., who was interested in the idea and sought the advice of a number of academic economists.[6]

Among those who were consulted was Welsey Clair Mitchell, an economist at the University of California who moved to Columbia University in 1913. Also in 1913, Mitchell published his pioneering study, *Business Cycles and Their Causes*,[7] which made heavy use of economic data to try to understand why economies periodically fell into recessions. Mitchell saw the value of an institute of economics as well, but thought that it should be oriented toward doing basic research in economics. For Mitchell, that meant collecting data, dealing with issues surrounding the measurement of economic magnitudes, and undertaking studies based on that data. Recall that when this discussion was going on, the concept of gross national product had not been developed, there was no consumer price index or other systematic way to gauge price level changes, and no measurement of other economic data like production, income, employment, or unemployment.

Shortly after Rockefeller expressed an interest in supporting some type of economics institute, the Carnegie Corporation also became involved, and in meetings were held which involved representatives from the Carnegie and Rockefeller foundations as well as Mitchell and Edwin F. Gay, a Harvard economics professor. It soon became clear that the foundation trustees and the economics professors had different ideas about the activities that such an institute would undertake. The professors favored basic research, data gathering and analysis, and studies that would help to measure the economy's performance, whereas the foundation trustees favored programs that would quell social unrest and further cooperation among the various economic interests in the nation, ranging from labor and labor unions to corporate management. Despite these differences of opinion on the details, all parties believed that the creation of an economics institute would be desirable, and that foundation money could be productively used to establish one. Such a move would signal a major change in the direction of these relatively new philanthropies.

The Creation of the National Bureau of Economic Research

The push to establish an economics institute finally came to fruition with the creation of the National Bureau of Economic Research in 1920. In a speech he delivered in 1919, Irving Fisher, president of the American Economic Association, suggested that such an institute could help advance economics as a science, because funding was needed to pursue economic research. Meanwhile, during World War I Edwin Gay had served the federal government as director of the Central Bureau of Planning and Statistics, while Mitchell had served as its research director, giving them a clearer view of what they thought might be done with such an institute. Mitchell viewed the Bureau of Planning and Statistics as a potential vehicle for undertaking statistical research on the economy, and wanted the bureau to continue through peacetime so that better economic statistics might be gathered. Woodrow Wilson, despite his academic background, had little sympathy for the idea, and terminated the bureau.

Shortly after the Central Bureau of Planning and Statistics was closed down, the National Bureau of Economic Research was established with Gay as president and Mitchell as research director. Quite clearly, they had in mind continuing the work in economic statistics that they had begun while with the federal government, and applied to the Carnegie Corporation for a grant to continue their work. Despite some differences of opinion that existed between the Carnegie Corporation's trustees and the new NBER management team, the Carnegie Corporation provided a series of grants to the NBER which enabled it to undertake major programs to gather and utilize economic statistics.

Almost immediately the NBER developed a close relationship with the federal government and became an important organization in the determination of economic policy. The conduit was Herbert Hoover, who was secretary of commerce throughout the Harding and Coolidge administrations from 1921 to 1929, prior to assuming the presidency himself. Hoover, an engineer by training, was a true believer in social science and believed that scientific principles could be applied to better manage the operation of government, but also to enable the government to better oversee the operation of the economy.[8] A major problem that faced economic policymakers in the 1920s, in the view of both Hoover and Mitchell, was that the economic data was so poor that it was very difficult to evaluate the state of the economy, to measure improvements, and to test ideas that might be more useful in shaping economic policy. The role of the NBER was to improve the quality of economic statistics and to develop the application of these statistics so that they could be a guide to policy.

Seeing a clear role for the NBER, Hoover promoted the idea to foundations. He believed that foundation funding was preferable to government funding for a number of reasons. First, he believed that private funding would give the NBER the appearance of being an objective and nonpolitical organization, whereas government funding might immediately cast suspicion upon the NBER's work as a product of partisan politics. Furthermore, Hoover believed that the relatively low wage rates that would be dictated by the government for employees would prevent the NBER from attracting the most competent employees. The creation of a technically competent, unbiased, and widely respected economic research organization therefore required private funding, as Hoover saw it. Despite having Hoover as its pitch man, the trustees at both the Russell Sage Foundation and the Commonwealth Fund rejected the applica-

tions of the NBER, leaving the Carnegie Corporation as a major supporter.[9]

The NBER owes much of its early success to the support of the
Carnegie Corporation, and it is interesting to contrast the NBER with
the types of philanthropic activities that Andrew Carnegie pursued in
his lifetime.[10] The NBER is far removed from the construction of libraries or the financing of church organs, which help provide a social
infrastructure within which everyone can be better off. The NBER is, at
its foundation, an organization designed to develop and apply ideas,
and to influence the government's social policy. Its early relationship
with Herbert Hoover shows also that there was an early connection
between the NBER's activities and the government's activities. When
establishing his foundation, Carnegie did give it a very broad mandate,
and expressed the belief that a good board of trustees could better direct the foundation's money than very explicit instructions from Carnegie
regarding the disposition of his money. Nevertheless, Carnegie himself
was the first president of the Carnegie Corporation and by his actions
showed his more specific intent. Only a few years after his death, there
was a major change in direction as the Carnegie Corporation began
providing grants for the purpose of influencing social policy.

The Brookings Institution

The grants provided by the Carnegie Corporation to the NBER were
not an isolated aberration, but rather the start of a systematic turn toward
funding organizations that dealt directly with economic and social policy. In
1916 the Institute for Government Research was established to undertake
social science research that would promote better management of government resources. This clearly falls within the social science paradigm
that was developing in the early twentieth century. In 1922 Robert S.
Brookings presented a proposal to the Carnegie Corporation for the establishment of an Institute of Economics in Washington, D.C., that would be
affiliated with the Institute for Government Research. The Carnegie Corporation provided grants in excess of $1 million to found the Institute of Eco-
nomics. In 1927 the Institute for Government Research and the Institute
of Economics were merged along with the Robert Brookings Graduate School
of Economics and Government to form the Brookings Institution.[11] The
Brookings Institution today remains an institution devoted to the undertaking of public policy studies, financed by foundation grants.

The Institute of Economics, which evolved into the Brookings Institution, was sold to the trustees at the Carnegie Corporation as the type of organization that could foster social progress through economic research. By providing a better fundamental understanding of economic processes, and by demonstrating the interconnectedness of the economic activities of all individuals, they would then be in a position to see the importance of economic policy. Thus, from the perspective of the fundraisers approaching the foundation, the sales pitches from Brookings and the NBER were much the same. The founders, especially at the NBER, had in mind an organization that would undertake more basic research, whereas the trustees had in mind organizations that were more oriented toward public policy and the dissemination of information to the general public. Both organizations undertake basic research, but also undertake a substantial amount of policy-oriented research. And in both cases the targeted audience of the research is not the general public but rather academics and policymakers. Decades of foundation support shows that this must be acceptable to the trustees, although the nature of the activities that are funded are quite different from those that Rockefeller and Carnegie themselves chose to fund.

Other Activities Funded by the Carnegie Corporation

The Carnegie Corporation funded the social sciences more broadly than just funding economic organizations. In 1919 the foundation financed a study entitled *Justice and the Poor,* which concluded that the ability to pay for legal services had a major impact on the ability of people to receive fair treatment by the legal system, resulting in a legal system that discriminated against low-income individuals. Problems with the American legal system were perceived not only for poor people, but also for the wealthy. Attorneys for corporations often found themselves unable to understand the law in certain areas, and with the "trust-busting" that began in earnest under the administration of Theodore Roosevelt from 1901 to 1909, it was often unclear what the limits of antitrust law were, in particular.[12] In response to this uncertainty, the Carnegie Corporation financed a study in 1922 to make recommendations for clarifying the U.S. legal system, and that study recommended the creation of a law institute that might work to clarify the contents of American case law.

Following that recommendation, the American Law Institute was established in 1923 with a grant of more than $1 million from the Carnegie Corporation. The American Law Institute was designed to synthesize and restate the results of court cases so that it would be easier for legal practitioners to understand the law. Such restatements would be created through legal research, following the ideas of scientific social policy, and while the legal scholars pushing for such a synthesis of the law hoped to simplify matters, they also viewed the possibility of improving the law. These ideas came from the deans of Yale and Harvard Law Schools, among others, and following the model of the university in other areas of science, they viewed that law professors should be in a position to advance knowledge as well as to teach, and that legal research could lead to social improvements just as much as research in other areas of social science.[13]

The restatements of law produced by the American Law Institute were not uncontroversial. While they did not have the force of law, the institute hoped that they would be accepted as accurate representations of the law, giving the institute considerable power to determine which cases were relevant, and why they were relevant. The restatements were more than a summary; they hoped to interpret as well as summarize. Critics viewed that the American Law Institute "was not restating but rather remaking law." [14] For a brief period, several law professors from Columbia and Johns Hopkins law schools who opposed to the American Law Institute's projects established an Institute for the Study of Law to try to counter the influence of the American Law Institute. The opposing institute did not last long, however, and a key factor is that it did not have financial backing of the type that the Carnegie Corporation provided the American Law Institute.[15]

In the 1920s the Carnegie Corporation also established the American Association for Adult Education in order to try to influence the educational system,[16] supported the American Federation of the Arts, and contributed to arts programs in a number of universities.[17] The trustees had taken on as one of their missions the safeguarding of American culture through support for selected educational programs. The American Association for Adult Education was almost entirely supported by the Carnegie Corporation until it discontinued its funding in 1941. The Association struggled along for another decade before being taken over by the National Education Association.[18]

These activities fit within the same framework as the Carnegie Corporation's support of the NBER and the Brookings Institution. After Andrew Carnegie's death, the trustees swiftly changed the orientation of the foundation away from providing cultural and community amenities and toward undertaking programs designed to change the course of ideas about American society and American culture.

The Carnegie Corporation and Race Relations

One of the problems facing American society in the view of the Carnegie Corporation trustees in the 1930s was race relations. Hindsight certainly confirms this perception, but the perception was common even at the time. Blacks have never been fully integrated into American society, and studies early in the century were not aimed at integration per se, but rather at what might be done in order to improve the conditions of blacks in America. Two major views on the problem were prominent in the early part of the century, and those views might be identified with their strongest proponents. Following the Civil War and the emancipation of the slaves, most blacks in the South lived agrarian lives, and Booker T. Washington viewed that the best way to improve their condition was to educate them by giving them the skills that they needed to succeed and prosper in this environment. Blacks needed to learn basic income-earning skills, Washington believed. The opposing view, associated with W.E.B. Du Bois, was that for blacks ever to become a part of mainstream America, they needed the same type of education that was being given to successful whites. They needed to study Greek and Latin, they needed a more liberal education, and they needed to be trained to think and to lead.[19]

The trustees of the Carnegie Corporation believed that they could devote some of their resources toward trying to solve some of the problems facing black America, and in 1935 began a project designed to come up with some answers to problems of black education and of blacks in general. They wanted a study to address the problem, but they wanted the right person to do the study and began a search. At the outset they had decided that the study would best be done by someone who was not an American, and drew up a list of about twenty-five candidates. Eventually, they chose Gunnar Myrdal, a Swedish economist. The result of that project was Myrdal's book, *The American Dilemma: The Negro Problem and Modern Democracy,* which was published in 1944.[20]

Prior to his working on the project, Myrdal had a limited familiarity with the United States, but he came to the United States in 1938 and stayed through 1940, when he returned to Sweden. Although the project was far from complete at that point, Myrdal was concerned that because of the outbreak of World War II he might not be able to get back to Sweden if he did not return at that time. Still, Myrdal had a substantial amount of time to familiarize himself with the problem he was analyzing. He talked to black leaders, visited black universities, and familiarized himself with black culture to a degree that alarmed some of the Carnegie Corporation management. After formally scheduled events, when others in Myrdal's party would return to their hotel rooms and segregated America, Myrdal would seek out black restaurants, clubs, and black culture more generally, because he did not recognize the norms against it. Myrdal thought that his work would be better because of his direct observations, and because as a foreigner, he came to the problem without any preconceived notions.

Myrdal concluded that black culture in the United States was really not a separate culture from White culture, but was distorted by institutions that kept blacks separated from the mainstream. Myrdal saw black society as repressed by laws and social norms that kept them segregated and held them back. The American dilemma that Myrdal saw and noted in his title was that a democratic society rested on the notion of equality, while in practice blacks in America were legally and socially treated as unequal. Myrdal's book had a substantial influence. It was recognized as an excellent study in academic circles and influenced legal and political thinking. It was even referenced in the Supreme Court's landmark *Brown v. Board of Education* decision in 1954 that declared that segregation was unconstitutional. Myrdal's book is probably the most visible piece of work ever funded by the Carnegie Corporation, but it follows the same general trend of the programs discussed earlier. It moves away from providing tangible amenities such as church organs and libraries, and toward producing ideas which then shape the direction of American society.

The Rockefeller Foundation

The Rockefeller Foundation did not make as much of a dramatic turn toward the production of ideas as the Carnegie Corporation, but followed the same general direction. Whereas the Carnegie Corporation was instrumental in establishing the NBER and the American Law Institute, the Rockefellers stood outside the spotlight, although they were directly involved in the early discussions that led to the creation of the NBER and assisted other programs in the social sciences. In the 1920s the foundation supported the establishment of the Social Science Research Council and funded fellowships in the social sciences. The Rockefeller Foundation also made grants to a number of American and European universities in order to promote them as centers of social science research. In the early 1930s, as the Great Depression profoundly affected the way in which people viewed their society, the foundation's trustees began looking more intently at ways in which support for the social sciences might help solve the social problems of the day. In 1935 the foundation's Division of Social Science decided to allocate its funds in three major areas: economic stabilization, public administration, and international relations.[22]

Once the Rockefeller Foundation was established, Rockefeller himself distanced himself from it and did not try to control its activities, as Carnegie had done with his foundation. Thus, when Carnegie died, his foundation showed a marked change of course, which might not have happened in the case of the Rockefeller Foundation for two reasons. First, as already noted, Rockefeller left the control of his foundation to others. Second, Rockefeller lived until 1937, so even though Rockefeller did not directly control his foundation, he was able to watch its activities for several decades, perhaps providing an inducement for its trustees to behave more conservatively. Nevertheless, the evolution of the Rockefeller Foundation's activities even before John D. Rockefeller's death is apparent.

Yet another inhibiting factor that inhibited the Rockefeller Foundation initially was the closeness of Rockefeller's business activity to social science subjects. In 1914 the Rockefeller Foundation created a program to undertake research in industrial relations, but shortly after that initiative was begun, a bitter strike occurred at Rockefeller's Colorado Fuel and Iron Company. The strike eventually led to a violent battle between strikers and the state militia which became known as the Ludlow Massacre. Federal troops were called in to control the violence and the tragedy was featured in the news headlines for weeks. The idea that the Rockefeller Foundation, or any other organization remotely associated with Rockefeller, might be involved in policy issues was very unpopular among the general public.[23] Thus, there was some reason for the

Rockefeller Foundation to tread cautiously into social science issues and to maintain a relatively low profile.

Despite several reasons why the foundation might have been reluctant to diversify into policy-related areas, an examination of Rockefeller Foundation grants in 1936, a year before Rockefeller died, shows the movement toward the production of ideas. About 40 percent of the foundation's grants in that year went to health and medical science programs, which was very much in line with Rockefeller's own philanthropic ideas, but about 45 percent went toward social sciences and humanities programs.[24] The activities of the Rockefeller Foundation were less visible than those of the Carnegie Corporation in part because the Rockefeller Foundation provided much social science support through grants to universities, rather than aiding in the formation of new institutions through which its funds could be channeled, and also perhaps because the foundation continued to support health care initiatives of the kind that provided such spectacularly successful results in earlier decades.

There was considerable debate within the Rockefeller Foundation leadership in the 1920s regarding the foundation's activities in the area of social science and public policy. Some felt that following the Ludlow massacre the foundation was far too cautious about financing policy-oriented research, but the onset of the Great Depression and the rise of fascism in Europe led the foundation toward more policy-oriented projects.[25] While the Rockefeller Foundation had supported projects aimed at advancing basic scientific knowledge, the view in the 1930s was increasingly that projects would better serve the public interest if they were more applied in nature. The evolution of the Rockefeller Foundation might have been partly due to circumstances surrounding the Rockefeller name, which faded in importance over time, but also was partly due to the changing times, which made programs more directly aimed at policy issues appear to be a better investment.

The Ford Foundation

The next chapter recounts the politically oriented activities of the Ford Foundation during the 1960s in some detail, because the foundation's agenda had a significant impact on the public impression of foundations, and on the impression held by members of Congress. The Ford Foundation's activities, more than any other, pushed Congress to the 1969 tax reforms that had such a significant impact on the way in which foundations do their business. But the Ford Foundation engaged in a much wider range of activities than those questionable political activities that incited the wrath of Congress, and attempted to influence the course of ideas on many fronts.

When examining the impact of foundations on the development of ideas and public policy, the Ford Foundation stands as an interesting example because Henry Ford himself was not a charitable individual. He believed that the best thing he could do to help mankind with his money was to invest it in productive business in order to provide his employees with good jobs. As noted in chapter 2, Henry and Edsel Ford created their foundation mainly as a way to maintain family control over the Ford Motor Company and to avoid a massive inheritance tax bill for their heirs. Thus, it is interesting to see that a foundation created by an individual who believed chiefly in the virtue of hard work and private sector initiative become so involved in social issues just a few decades after its creation. The Ford Foundation's programs began in earnest in the early 1950s, and within fifteen years the foundation was embroiled in controversy.[26]

The foundation, from its beginning, had intended to pursue work in the areas that were to give it such high visibility. Having been established from the estates of Henry and Edsel Ford after their deaths, the donors had no direct influence over the disbursement of the foundation's funds. In a 1950 report outlining the foundation's priorities, the trustees of the Ford Foundation stated their intentions to work within five major areas. (1) They wanted to further the cause of world peace, which included strengthening the United Nations and other world organizations. (2) They wanted to deal with the problems of democracy, including the strengthening of civil rights and the elimination of restrictions on freedom of thought. It was primarily the activities in this area that caught the attention of government policymakers. Recall that the United States was on the eve of the McCarthy era in which individuals would be persecuted for being communist sympathizers. In addition, the foundation's civil rights activities in the 1960s brought the foundation considerable Congressional scrutiny. (3) Economic problems, including labor-management relations, were on the foundation's agenda. (4) Educational problems, including issues of equal opportunity, were another area in which the foundation intended to work. (5) They also wanted to undertake a scientific study of man, including factors that motivate individuals, that create values, and that cause maladjustments.[27] One can see from the start that the ideas of Henry Ford were not a significant part of the Ford Foundation's agenda at its beginning, and that the Ford Foundation is, in this regard, considerably different from the Carnegie and Rockefeller foundations.

Almost immediately the Ford Foundation found itself under fire for the programs it was supporting. As Senator Joseph McCarthy rose to prominence with his anticommunist attacks, the House of Representatives, led by Congressman Eugene Cox, began an investigation of communist penetration into the leadership of philanthropic foundations. In 1953 the foundation made a $15 million grant to the Fund for the Republic, whose mission it was to protect civil liberties. While in principle civil liberties sound worthy of protection, in a decade where civil rights of minorities were an issue, and where there was a substantial amount of anticommunist rhetoric coming from Congress, the activities of the Ford Foundation were controversial enough that some individuals avoided buying Ford Motor Company automobiles because of the bad publicity.[28]

Foundations and Foreign Policy

After World War II foreign policy became a larger interest of foundations, and especially the Carnegie, Rockefeller, and Ford foundations.[29] These foundations stand out because of their dominant positions among foundations, and because of their nature as general-interest foundations that make international grants. The Carnegie and Rockefeller foundations have had a dominant influence because they were among the first very large foundations early in the twentieth century. The Ford Foundation, while much newer, attained instant dominance because it was so much bigger than any other foundation when it was created. By the end of the 1960s the Ford Foundation had assets of $2.9 billion, which was more than three times the assets of the Rockefeller Foundation, a distant second with $890 million in assets.[30]

From the beginning these foundations had shown an interest in providing grants for assistance outside the United States. Andrew Carnegie himself provided overseas grants while he headed the Carnegie Corporation, and the Rockefeller Foundation's overseas public health programs were among its earliest big success stories. These philanthropists did not intend for the benefits from their foundations to remain inside the borders of the United States. As the focus of foundation giving shifted from providing benefits that might directly affect the standards of living of individuals (such as health care programs) toward public policy, social science, and educational issues, the foundations began exerting a substantial influence over the cultures, economies, and governments of areas in which they provided grants. Their influences did not come from supplying arms for revolutionaries or by supporting American government intervention, but rather came more subtly in the form of educational aid, conferences, and studies that directed the intellectual climate of nations and that influenced their leadership.

The story overseas is little different from what was occurring domestically. Foundations, by providing financial support for educational institutions and by financing studies on developing nations were able to have a substantial impact on the intellectual climate there. Foundation money led foreign universities, especially in poorer nations, to be designed following the American model and to employ American-trained scholars. Foreigners—primarily Africans, Latin Americans, and Asians—would receive foundation fellowships to study in the United States and would then return to staff foundation-supported foreign universities, perhaps undertaking foundation-funded research projects. Foundation-funded conferences and studies would support the same types of agendas that were being supported by their domestic projects.

Foundations found themselves in a good position to have their research accepted as credible and unbiased. Their work was privately funded, as opposed to being supported by the U.S. government which (rightly) has been regarded with suspicion overseas. The foundations did not do any work themselves, but rather funded leading experts in their fields. The results, then, were those of top scholars, rather than the foundations. But foundations chose the individuals and institutions to whom they would provide grants, and by so doing were able to direct the nature of the research and control the dissemination of ideas overseas to a considerable degree. Individuals whose work was financed by foundation grants were undoubtedly pursuing work they believed in, and were not trying to push some foundation policy in exchange for payment. Despite the intellectual honesty of the individuals involved, they were chosen because the ideas they were interested in promoting were consistent with the policies that foundations wanted to further.

Philip Coombs, who was assistant secretary of state for educational and cultural affairs under President Kennedy, argued that a successful foreign policy could not be run by military and economic assistance alone, but needed to be cognizant of a nation's culture as well.[31] But it is difficult for one government to successfully interfere with the cultural development of another, as well it should be. Thus, foundations can play a crucial role by providing educational and cultural grants. Coombs was no stranger to the world of foundations, having been employed by the Ford Foundation from 1952 until his appointment to the State Department in 1961.

Overseas Programs after World War II

American foundations pursued overseas programs prior to World War II. The Rockefeller Foundation began its massive public health project in China in 1913, and stopped the Chinese program in 1949 only after the communists had triumphed there. The Carnegie Corporation began funding education programs in Africa in 1925. But the focus of the programs changed after World War II in response to a changed world climate. With the onset of the Cold War and a fear of a domino effect that might cause successive nations to topple into communist domination, the interests of foundations were more closely aligned with the foreign policy interests of American government. In 1967 Irving Kristol argued that foreign policy had three major goals. It should try to enhance national security, minimize the possibility of armed conflict, and "encourage other nations, especially the smaller ones, to mold their own social, economic, and political institutions [in ways to ensure values] that are at least not repugnant to (if not actually congruent with) American values." [32] Because foundations are institutionally separate from government, their programs have been instrumental in the pursuit of this third goal of foreign policy that Kristol espoused.

Post-World War II foundation policy was influenced by the War-Peace Studies Project begun in 1919 and completed in 1945, financed by more than $600,000 in Rockefeller Foundation grants. The conclusion of that project was that increased overseas trade and investment would create higher incomes abroad, and would foster a less hostile world political climate.[33] A 1956 paper by University of Virginia Professor John K. King, financed by the Carnegie Corporation, argued that the United States needed to remain on good terms with lesser-developed nations in order to retain access to low-cost raw materials, a sentiment that echoed a statement made a few years previously by Ford

Foundation President Paul Hoffman.[34] In a similar vein, in 1957 Carnegie Corporation President Alan Pifer justified the foundation's involvement in Africa as an attempt to try to influence African nations as they became involved in the struggle for alignment with either the Western bloc or Soviet bloc nations.[35]

The 1956 *Annual Report* of the Rockefeller Foundation notes,

> The officers and trustees of the Rockefeller Foundation are deeply impressed with the thought that the prospects for peace and orderly economic growth throughout the world during the next quarter-century can be decisively affected by what happens in the independent nations of Africa, the Near East, and Asia. If they succeed in establishing constitutional systems with friendly and easy exchange with the rest of the world, increasingly productive economies to supply their needs at rising levels and to play an active role in world trade, and educational systems which can train their leadership in adequate numbers, then peace and stability will have gained tremendous support.[36]

This quotation makes it apparent that the Rockefeller Foundation, like other major foundations of the time, saw the spread of American ideology throughout the world as an important part of their overall program.

Foundations worked closely with the World Bank, the Agency for International Development (AID), and universities in developing nations in order to further their goals. Foundations believed that by training local leaders they could have an influence over the future course of developing nations, which led them to support foreign universities and to provide fellowships so that future foreign leaders could study in the United States. Foundation grants were heavily skewed toward support for social science and public administration programs in overseas universities, echoing their turn toward social science in the United States.[37] Universities in less developed nations could have benefited from programs in engineering, agriculture, or medicine, so the emphasis on social science says something about the ideological nature of foundation grants.

When World War II ended only a few universities in the United States had programs in international affairs or offered courses in non-Western studies, and the growth of those areas since World War II has been largely due to the financial support of foundations. The Ford Foundation spent $26 million between 1959 and 1963 on foreign language and area studies programs at major universities. The beneficiaries included Boston, California, Chicago, Columbia, Cornell, Harvard, Indiana,

Michigan, Northwestern, Pennsylvania, Princeton, Stanford, Washington, Wisconsin, and Yale.[38] These are prestigious universities that produce a substantial number of Ph.D.s, and that have a significant influence on the types of ideas that are produced at other educational institutions. Ph.D.s from these schools go on to serve on faculties at other universities, and have a major impact on government and corporate policy. Studies supported by foundations also have had a significant impact. W.W. Rostow's prominent study, *The Stages of Economic Growth: A Non-Communist Manifesto,* published in 1960, was written while Rostow was on a sabbatical funded by the Carnegie Corporation.[39] Foundation resources have influenced the direction that these academic programs have taken and, indeed, have affected the ideas that have been developed in American universities and that have been applied throughout the world.

The potential for foundations to influence foreign policy was not lost on the United States government. From 1952 until 1967 the Central Intelligence Agency channeled money through foundations, and established its own foundations, in order to further U.S. foreign policy.[40] Relationships were also set up with U.S. universities to cooperate on overseas programs. One can only blame foundations to the extent they were involved, and direct involvement by the largest U.S. foundations was minimal. However, the fact that the CIA used foundations as a tool of foreign policy illustrates how influential foundations could be.

Human Capital

Perhaps no idea more embodies the influence of foundations over the development of ideas than the concept of human capital. The concept was developed by University of Chicago economist and Nobel Laureate Theodore Schultz, and was succinctly presented in his presidential address before the American Economic Association in 1960.[41] Essentially the idea behind human capital is that people are factors of production, and that investment in their skills can increase the return to labor in the same way that an investment in physical capital can increase productivity. If investment in machinery and infrastructure make sense, so does investment in the productive capacity of people.

The acceptance of this idea has affected the influence of foundations on the production of ideas in two ways. First, it provides the rationale for foundations' focus on education and training rather than benefiting mankind by providing food, medical care, infrastructure, and so forth. The concept is embodied in the notion, "Give a man a fish, feed him for a day; teach a man to fish, feed him for life." But more than just rationalizing expenditures on people rather than things, the concept also rationalizes a shifting of emphasis of expenditures from engineering, sciences, agriculture, and medicine, to social sciences and public administration. By designing a society to be productive, and by establishing appropriate public policy, foundation expenditures can have a large permanent impact. But ideas on what makes desirable public policy differ among individuals. We have seen how the Cold War in the post-World War II years influenced the ideas of policymakers, foundation managers, and academics, but in the post-Cold War era it is apparent that there remain substantial practical and ideological differences among individuals. There is an inherent difference between creating good public policy and creating good health care.

Thus, by funding programs designed to develop human capital, foundations must get into the business of promoting ideas. With such a diverse group of ideas to choose from, foundation managers are always more likely to choose the ideas for which they have more sympathy. Indeed, the role of a foundation is not to provide an impartial hearing for every idea, but rather to promote the public good by promoting good ideas. Who decides which ideas are good? The people who run the foundations. When we see how foundations operate, and how their programs have evolved over the twentieth century, it is apparent that they are promoters of ideas, and the questions then move on to what types of ideas foundations promote.

Foundations and Public Policy Think Tanks

Early in the twentieth century, foundations began funding think tanks as a method of generating ideas that could produce public policy benefits. The creation of the National Bureau of Economic Research and the Brookings Institution provided early models that showed how foundations could influence ideas by funding organizations with specific public policy orientations. Since then a number of other think tanks have emerged that specialize in public policy research, and that are supported by foundations. The American Enterprise Institute in Washington, D.C., has received big grants from many foundations, including the Ford Foundation, Smith Richardson, and Pew. The Hoover Institution on War, Revolution, and Peace, housed at Stanford University, has received grants from the same foundations. Other influential think tanks that have received substantial foundation support are the Heritage Foundation, the Foundation for Economic Education, and the Council on Foreign Relations.[42]

Think tanks create a natural conduit between foundation money and the creation of ideas. As foundations have become more interested in social science and public policy, they have looked for ways to expend the money for programs that fit the trustees' vision of the public interest. Universities provide a natural outlet of this type, but think tanks may offer advantages over universities because the products of the two types of institutions are viewed differently. University researchers are charged with the production of knowledge, and as such tend to focus on more fundamental, abstract, and theoretical issues. The reward structure at a university is such that faculty research will be better-received by colleagues if it appears to be a fundamental advance in knowledge (rather than an application to specific circumstances) and if it appears in an academic journal rather than in an outlet that is more accessible and commands wider readership. Academics, in their attempts to advance knowledge in their fields, mostly write for each other. Think tanks, on the other hand, try to tackle policy issues, and try to produce concrete solutions to existing social problems. The work is not as abstract and theoretical, and because it tends to be more timely it may become obsolete more quickly. However, it is meant to have an impact on real-world affairs. If foundations want to see immediate results rather than long-term development of a field, then think tanks may provide a better outlet for foundation grants.[43]

Another characteristic of think tanks that may make them appeal to foundations is that they tend to have an ideological orientation. The Brookings Institution has long been viewed as having a loose association with the Democratic Party. Democrats use Brookings research to build their own policies, and Brookings personnel are often tapped to be advisors to Democratic politicians. Similarly, the Heritage Foundation is viewed as having an association with the Republican Party. Thus, there is an ideological slant that might influence foundation grants. That slant can work in two ways to send grants to think tanks. First, a foundation with ideological views might finance work in a think tank because the foundation management believes that the think tank's ideology will make its output consistent with the foundation's view of the public interest. One might accomplish the same thing with a grant to some specific university scholar with a known ideology, however. Second, a foundation might be inclined to support work in a foundation because it will not only be supporting a particular project, but also will be helping to create an environment in which that ideology can thrive.

Ideological viewpoints in universities tend to be more diverse, whereas think tanks tend to have more consistent ideologies. If one wants to promote not only a specific study but also an environment in which similar types of work can be done in the future, grants to think tanks may produce better results. Furthermore, think tanks can be held more accountable for the results of their work because they tend to have an organization-wide ideology, and because they rely on donations for their survival. Nobody in a university will be critical of research results on ideological grounds. Thus, while one can get an idea of the orientation of an academic's research, one cannot count on the researcher arriving at a conclusion aligned with a specific ideology. Think tanks may be more reliable in that regard. Also, because the think tank relies on foundations as a continuing source of revenue, the think tank will want to produce results that are in line with the granting foundation's expectations.

A personal example might illustrate how unreliable academics are. In 1981, when I was on the faculty at Auburn University, I received a grant from the State of Alabama, financed by a federal grant, to undertake a cost-benefit analysis of a federal program. I tried to honestly evaluate the data and use appropriate methods to undertake the study, and concluded that the program cost more than the value it returned. Lobbyists for the industry that received the federal benefits angrily met with state officials, and with me, about my study. I defended my work, but told them that I wanted to make sure that it contained no errors, and said that if they could show me where I went wrong, I would gladly go back and fix any problems. When I asked what in the study they thought should be changed, one lobbyist was very forthright. "The problem with the study," he said, "is the conclusion. You need to change your conclusion." I was unwilling to change my conclusion unless I could be shown that the work that led up to the conclusion was not correct. The result of our meeting was that the state officials declared my study to be "confidential," and told me that there could be legal penalties if I released the study or discussed its results.

Undoubtedly the lobbyists were hoping for a study by an unbiased university professor that they could use to further their lobbying efforts. But on a study like this an academic researcher will be more interested in looking at the problem in an objective way (even though academics—me included—do have ideological biases), and the university certainly has little interest in which way the conclusions of an academic study fall. A think tank, on the other hand, is more likely to be interested in furthering a particular agenda. This is not to say that think tanks or the individuals who work in them are deliberately biased. Rather, given the ideological persuasion of a think tank, it will tend to recruit people with similar views, so that undertaking honest evaluations of issues, their results will reflect their ideological vision of the public interest. Foundations are the same way. If they are charged with spending their resources to further the common good, that requires that they have a vision of the common good and that they try to further it. Thus, by supporting think tanks with similar ideologies, foundations and think tanks can work together for their common vision of the public interest. Are there biases in those visions? That issue will be taken up in more detail in chapter 5.

Foundation Influence Over Studies They Finance

The preceding example comes from a government grant rather than a foundation grant, but foundations also attempt to influence the results that come from the studies they finance. One researcher, working on a Ford Foundation Grant in 1979, recounts that he was working with individuals with the Ford Foundation "who had very particular expectations about the kinds of research they wanted done and the uses to which it would be put in influencing legislative, regulatory, and public opinion." The Ford Foundation program officer told him the study placed too much emphasis on theory and too little on quantitative measures, so would not be relevant enough for the formulation of public policy. In effect, the researcher said, "the Program had been presented an ultimatum: if you want our money, do it our way." [44]

Another example involves a grant from the East-West Foundation to the Aspin Institute for Humanistic Studies in 1979. In this case, the Aspin Institute refused continuing funding from the foundation because it said that the foundation was trying to impart an anti-Israeli bias to their study. The East-West Foundation was established by the Fluor Construction Company, which did a substantial amount of business with Saudi Arabia. Mary Anna Culleton Colwell, writing about this case, conjectures that the foundation was a conduit through which Saudi Arabian interests could transfer money through Fluor to the East-West Foundation for programs that would be pro-Saudi, but would give the appearance of objectivity.[45] Setting up a foundation like this to act as a conduit for funds may be relatively unusual, but all foundation trustees must have their own biases in terms of what types of projects they believe are in the public interest, and have the ability to push research funded by their foundations in those directions. Think tanks doing funded research must take into account the preferences of those with the research money if they hope to get grants.

Employment Opportunities for Politicians and Their Advisors

Think tanks might promote ideological visions of the public interest in another way. A number of public policy think tanks provide employment for politicians who are out of office, and more commonly, for their advisors who have had government posts in past administrations. When the political winds change, those advisors can move back into government positions. For example, the Brookings Institution have developed ideas and supplied personnel for Democratic administrations for decades. The Hoover Institution in Palo Alto, California, has played a similar role for Republicans, as has the American Enterprise Institute and the Heritage Foundation. Thus, think tanks are actively involved not only in the production of public policy ideas, but also in the maintenance of a supply of public policy experts who can offer advice, or directly move into government policy positions.

There is a close link between foundations and think tanks. Over half of the membership of the governing boards of both the Brookings Institution and the Hoover Institution serve as trustees with grant-making foundations, for example.[46] One can easily see the advantages to a think tank of having trustees who also are foundation trustees. Thus, rather than being independent organizations, there is a closely linked network of individuals who connect the foundations that supply the funds and the think tanks that spend them. Further, the link between think tanks and government creates a conduit whereby foundations influence government policy. This is not meant to imply that there is any conspiracy or that individuals are attempting to act against the public interest. Rather, all individuals, when doing the jobs they are hired to do, end up creating a connection between the ideology of trustees and government policy.

Foundation trustees are supposed to spend the foundation's money to further the public interest, which means not supporting all points of view indiscriminately, but rather supporting those projects that appear to have the best promise of furthering the public interest. Often, this can be done by funding projects through think tanks that have public policy experts, and that can be relied upon to undertake work following the think tank's ideology. Think tanks, in order to raise funds, have the incentive to seek board members with connections to foundations. Think tanks also have the incentive to maintain connections with those in government. The foundation connection to government policy is less direct than if foundation trustees had the power to make public policy, but this loose connection also obscures the influence of foundations on public policy. The potential for biases arising in the process will be examined further in chapter 5.

Losing Ground: Social Policy During the Reagan Years

As this chapter has indicated, there has been a close connection among the grant-making foundations, the recipients of grants that undertake policy studies, and the federal officials who actually make the policies. In some cases particular projects that have been undertaken with the aid of foundation grants can be cited as major influences over public policy. One such study is *Losing Ground,* a book on social policy published in 1984 by Charles Murray.[47] When Ronald Reagan was elected president in 1980, he came into the White House with a strong philosophy of limited government. He championed national defense, arguing that we needed to increase defense spending in order to counter the Soviet Union, which Reagan referred to as an "evil empire." But in most other areas Reagan argued for reductions in federal government expenditures and programs. He wanted to cut taxes, reduce the role of the federal government and give states more freedom and responsibility, he wanted to reduce federal regulation, and he wanted to reduce welfare expenditures.

The changes that Reagan wanted to implement in the area of welfare and entitlement programs were radical departures from the trends of the past two decades, and a clear stab at the substantial expansion in social programs that were envisioned by President Kennedy and implemented as Lyndon Johnson's Great Society. The programs saw their largest funding increases during the Republican administrations of Nixon and Ford, and continued growing under Reagan's immediate predecessor, Jimmy Carter. Reagan's commitment to reining in welfare programs was supported by those who viewed the programs as a drain on the nation's economic productivity, was criticized as hard-hearted by those who championed the causes of the poor, but was viewed by many as unrealistic and idealistic philosophizing by a president who was committed to principle regardless of the pragmatic harm that it might bring.

Murray's book, *Losing Ground,* changed the whole nature of the debate when it was published in 1984, and has had a continued influence since then. Murray argued that, far from helping the plight of the Americans who were least well-off, federal social programs have actually made them worse off. Collectively, programs like Aid to Families with Dependent Children, food stamps, housing subsidies, and Medicaid offered meager benefits to poor people, but only if they met certain conditions. They had to have low incomes, little accumulated wealth, in some cases they had to have children to qualify, and single mothers might lose their benefits if they were married. The incentives behind the programs were all wrong, Murray argued, keeping people in a trap of welfare dependency, because if they did get jobs, or if single mothers did get married, they would run the risk of losing their benefits. Thus, federal policy had the effect of giving those at the lowest end of the income distribution an incentive to be unemployed, it gave single women an incentive to have illegitimate children, and it took away any incentive for those who were on welfare to get jobs, to get married, or to take care of themselves.

Murray built his case with persuasive arguments and a substantial amount of statistical evidence to support his case. From the time when reliable poverty statistics first became available shortly after World War II until the late 1960s, when the Great Society programs took off, the percentage of Americans in poverty consistently declined, and without much government assistance. When welfare programs grew, the poverty rate ceased declining, and it is at about the same level at the end of the 1990s as it was at the end of the 1960s. Murray's critics have argued that he has made selective use of the statistics and presented only one side of the argument, and by focusing solely on social programs has ignored other significant changes that have occurred at the same time. The purpose of this analysis is not to side either with or against Murray on the controversy, but rather to make the uncontroversial point that

Murray's analysis changed the course of the debate over welfare policy in the United States.

Murray's book is closely linked to foundation support. He had been interested in this line of inquiry and had written a monograph on the subject, but as he relates in the preface to *Losing Ground,* Joan Kennedy Taylor at the Manhattan Institute took an interest in the project and encouraged Murray to write the book with the Institute's support. Murray notes, "William Hammett, president of the Manhattan Institute, took a chance and decided to use the foundation's resources to underwrite the effort. Without them, the book would not have been written." [48] One need not agree with Murray's work to agree that it had a profound influence over the direction of social policy through the 1980s and 1990s, and if we take Murray at his word, the book was written only because of foundation support.

Subsequently, Murray took the position of Bradley Fellow at the American Enterprise Institute, which is a part of that network of organizations that is funded by nonprofit foundations. While there, he co-authored *The Bell Curve* with Harvard professor Richard Herrnstein, which was published in 1994, and also has had a profound impact on the debate over social policy.[49] *The Bell Curve* agues that social policies aimed at creating more equality among ethnic groups through the use of quotas and preferential set-asides for underrepresented groups cannot work as they are intended, and will have negative effects both for the groups the programs are intended to benefit and for the society as a whole. The book's argument is built on a substantial amount of statistical evidence, buttressed by careful argument, as was *Losing Ground.* Like *Losing Ground,* it was also subject to a substantial amount of criticism and accusations that the authors selectively and misleadingly used their evidence.

For present purposes there is no reason to side either with or against Murray on these studies. All sides would agree that both books have had a substantial impact on the policy debate, and it is apparent that without foundation support they would not have been written. Murray states this plainly in the preface to *Losing Ground,* and because of the acclaim that he received for that book, he was able to take a position as a fellow at the American Enterprise Institute where he worked on *The Bell Curve.* Both books dealt with important issues related to public policy, and both influenced the direction of public policy, showing the close connection between foundation support and the ideas that shape public policy.

Conclusion

This chapter has covered a lot of ground, and in so doing has illustrated that foundations, as a group, do not promote any particular ideas, but rather promote ideas on many different subjects, and across the ideological spectrum. Foundation support produced Gunnar Myrdal's *An American Dilemma* and Charles Murray's *Losing Ground.* Foundations make grants to the conservative American Enterprise Institute and the liberal Brookings Institution. Regardless of any ideological slant, however, it is apparent that over the twentieth century foundations have become increasingly interested in promoting ideas rather than undertaking other types of projects that might more tangibly benefit mankind. Early in the twentieth century men like Carnegie and Rockefeller believed that they could further the common good by providing public amenities that everyone could enjoy and that would draw the society together, as reflected in Carnegie's many gifts of libraries and church organs, or that would directly improve the well-being of individuals, as exemplified by Rockefeller's initiatives in public health. Programs that financed agriculture and public infrastructure would fall into the same category. While programs like this are still supported by foundations, the twentieth century has seen an increased flow of resources toward the social sciences and public policy areas.

Several underlying causes might be conjectured for this shift. First, the lot of humankind has improved considerably over the century, so that problems of famine and disease are no longer so common. Second, governments have increasingly moved into many of the areas which relied on private support in the past. Libraries, hospitals, public health programs, and redistribution to the poor are all areas that at the beginning of the century were supported largely by private and foundation efforts, but at the end of the twentieth century have fallen clearly within the bounds of the public sector. With government taking over, there is less room for foundation activity. Third, the twentieth century has seen an increasing set of social problems that might suggest a movement toward social science research. The largest of these has been war, with the two World Wars followed by the Cold War which, perhaps, was kept from erupting into the Third World War in part because of foundation initiatives. Underlying the Cold War were the ideological divisions between capitalism and socialism, dictatorship and democracy. Social problems in the United States, ranging from poverty to race relations to industrial relations, can be added to the list. The point is that there may have been some reason to believe that the public interest would be served by shifting resources into more policy-oriented areas.

Public interest arguments aside, one must also consider the self-interests of those who run foundations. They are undoubtedly public-spirited, but they have been left in charge of large sums of money which they did not earn, and which they are charged with spending to further the public interest. What constitutes the public interest? That is what foundation managers and trustees must decide. When foundations spend their money on the development of public policy ideas, the ideological inclinations of foundation trustees and managers must exert a substantial influence over the ideas they promote. With very limited accountability, and with no real market for their ideas, there is little in the way of a check on the power of foundation trustees to promote the ideas they believe in. In the 1960s the federal government took notice of this lack of accountability, especially in light of some politically-related activities in which foundations began to pursue. The result, described in the next chapter, was a major change in the tax laws affecting foundations.

Notes

1. See Stephen Skowronek, *Building a New American State: The Expansion of National Administrative Capabilities, 1877-1920* (New York: Cambridge University Press, 1982). These principles of scientific public management are glowingly reported in Charles A. Beard and William Beard, *The American Leviathan: The Republic in the Machine Age* (New York: Macmillan, 1930).
2. Ellen Condliffe Lagemann, *The Politics of Knowledge: The Carnegie Corporation, Philanthropy, and Public Policy* (Middletown, CT: Wesleyan University Press, 1989) provides an excellent overview of the Carnegie Corporation's programs.
3. Lagemann, *The Politics of Knowledge,* pp. 23-24.
4. Lagemann, *The Politics of Knowledge,* p. 26.
5. Lagemann, *The Politics of Knowledge,* ch. 2, discusses the foundation funding of these organizations in detail.
6. Lagemann, *The Politics of Knowledge,* p. 53.
7. Wesley Clair Mitchell, *Business Cycles and Their Causes* (Berkeley: University of California Press, 1913).
8. On the relationship between the NBER and the federal government, and more generally on the economic planning of the 1920s, see Guy Alchon, *The Invisible Hand of Planning: Capitalism, Social Science, and the State in the 1920s* (Princeton, NJ: Princeton University Press, 1985).

9. Lagemann, *The Politics of Knowledge,* ch. 3, discusses in more detail the relationship between the Carnegie Corporation and the NBER.
10. Carnegie Corporation support for the NBER notwithstanding, Judith Sealander, *Private Wealth and Public Life: Foundation Philanthropy and the Reshaping of American Social Policy from the Progressive Era to the New Deal* (Baltimore, MD: Johns Hopkins University Press, 1997), argues that the influence of the Carnegie philanthropies over public policy tends to be overstated by most analysts.
11. Lagemann, *The Politics of Knowledge,* pp. 65-66.
12. See Thomas K. McCraw, *The Prophets of Regulation* (Cambridge, MA: Belknap Press, 1984), pp. 145-146.
13. Lagemann, *The Politics of Knowledge,* pp. 73-74.
14. Lagemann, *The Politics of Knowledge,* p. 85.
15. Lagemann, *The Politics of Knowledge,* p. 85.
16. Lagemann, *The Politics of Knowledge,* p. 106.
17. Lagemann, *The Politics of Knowledge,* pp. 109-111.
18. Lagemann, *The Politics of Knowledge,* p. 121.
19. Lagemann, *The Politics of Knowledge,* p. 126.
20. Gunnar Myrdal, with Richard Sterner and Arnold Rose, *An American Dilemma: The Negro Problem and American Democracy,* 2 vols. (New York: Harper & Brothers, 1944).
21. Lagemann, *The Politics of Knowledge,* p. 53.
22. Edward H. Berman, *The Influence of the Carnegie, Ford, and Rockefeller Foundations on American Foreign Policy: The Ideology of Philanthropy* (Albany: State University of New York Press, 1983), p. 106.
23. Waldemar A. Nielsen, *The Big Foundations* (New York: Columbia University Press, 1972), pp. 53-54.
24. Horace Coon, *Money to Burn: What the Great American Philanthropic Foundations Do with Their Money* (London: Longmans, Green and Co., 1938), p. 40.
25. Nielsen, *The Big Foundations,* pp. 60-61.
26. Joseph C. Goulden, *The Money Givers* (New York: Random House, 1971), pp. 42-46, discusses the Ford Foundation's origins.
27. These areas are outlined in Nielsen, *The Big Foundations,* pp. 80-81.
28. Nielsen, *The Big Foundations,* pp. 83-84.
29. Berman, *The Influence of the Carnegie, Ford, and Rockefeller Foundations on American Foreign Policy.*
30. The Carnegie Corporation was the tenth largest foundation with assets of $335 million. These figures are for 1969, and are taken from Goulden, *The Money Givers,* pp. 321-322.
31. Philip Coombs, *The Fourth Dimension of Foreign Policy* (New York: Harper & Row, 1964).
32. Quoted from Berman, *The Influence of the Carnegie, Ford, and Rockefeller Foundations on American Foreign Policy,* p. 42. Berman quoted from an article of Kristol's published in *Foreign Affairs.*

33. Berman, *The Influence of the Carnegie, Ford, and Rockefeller Foundations on American Foreign Policy,* pp. 41-46.

34. Berman, *The Influence of the Carnegie, Ford, and Rockefeller Foundations on American Foreign Policy,* p. 47.

35. Berman, *The Influence of the Carnegie, Ford, and Rockefeller Foundations on American Foreign Policy,* p. 57.

36. Berman, *The Influence of the Carnegie, Ford, and Rockefeller Foundations on American Foreign Policy,* p. 58.

37. Berman, *The Influence of the Carnegie, Ford, and Rockefeller Foundations on American Foreign Policy,* pp. 79-98.

38. Berman, *The Influence of the Carnegie, Ford, and Rockefeller Foundations on American Foreign Policy,* p. 102.

39. W.W. Rostow, *The Stages of Economic Growth: A Non-Communist Manifesto* (Cambridge: Cambridge University Press, 1960).

40. Ben Whitaker, *The Foundations: An Anatomy of Philanthropy and Society* (London: Eyre Methuen, 1974), pp. 157-166.

41. Theodore W. Schultz, "Investment in Human Capital," *American Economic Review* 51, No. 1 (March 1961), pp. 1-17.

42. Mary Anna Culleton Colwell, *Private Foundations and Public Policy: The Political Role of Philanthropy* (New York: Garland Publishing, Inc., 1993), p. 127.

43. Richard H. Fink, "From Ideas to Action: The Roles of Universities, Think Tanks, and Activist Groups," *Philanthropy* 10, No. 1 (Winter 1996), pp. 10-11, 34-35.

44. Peter Dobkin Hall, "Dilemmas of Criticism," *Philanthropy Monthly* 23 (June 1990), pp. 23-27.

45. Colwell, *Private Foundations and Public Policy,* pp. 66-67.

46. Colwell, *Private Foundations and Public Policy,* p. 89.

47. Charles Murray, *Losing Ground: American Social Policy, 1950-1980* (New York: Basic Books, 1984).

48. Murray, *Losing Ground,* p. x.

49. Richard J. Herrnstein and Charles Murray, *The Bell Curve: Intelligence and Class Structure in American Life* (New York: The Free Press, 1994).

4

Tax Laws and Their Influence on Foundations

The previous chapters have shown that America's nonprofit foundations are heavily involved in the production and dissemination of ideas on public policy issues, and underwrite ideas in ways that are often not obviously related to the missions that their donors intended for their foundations to undertake. The trustees and managers of foundations can do this because they have virtually no oversight in their activities, and are accountable to nobody for their actions. But foundations are subject to outside influences, sometimes as subtle as public opinion, and sometimes as obvious as the tax laws they must comply with as tax-preferred organizations. The influence goes two ways. Foundations must shape their activities to conform to the tax laws, but tax laws are also subject to change if legislators become dissatisfied with foundation activities. This chapter examines that two-way influence. Tax laws affect nonprofit foundations in two ways. First, they influence the donations that are made into foundations. Second, they influence the activities of foundations that must comply with the tax laws in order to maintain their tax-preferred status.

The earliest major nonprofit foundations, such as the Rockefeller and Carnegie foundations, were established before federal income and estate taxes were instituted, and contributions going into them were little affected by the tax laws. That has changed substantially over the years, however, and it is likely that the Ford Foundation would not have been established were it not for the federal tax laws. Indeed, a survey of eighty-five large donors to philanthropic foundations done in 1969 indicated that if there was no tax advantage to leaving money to foundations, those donors would have reduced their giving by 75 percent.[1] Another study done a year earlier suggests that without tax advantages donations from large donors would have fallen by 42.5 percent, not quite as large an estimate, but still significant.[2] A more recent review of econometric studies suggests that large donors are very sensitive to tax law changes.[3] Large donors are very important to philanthropies because approximately 90 percent of the donations in any fundraising campaign come from one percent of the donors.[4]

In the 1980s tax rates fell substantially, and fell the most for those who were in the higher tax brackets and thus were most likely to make philanthropic contributions. Contributions to philanthropies did not decline in the 1980s as one might have expected, however, and substantially more foundations were created in the 1980s than in the previous decade.[5] This calls into question the connection between donations to establish foundations and the tax deductibility of donations. Other factors may have been at work, because one of the strongest determinants of philanthropic activity is the level of the donor's income, and rising incomes in the 1980s could have offset the falling tax benefits from contributions. An analysis of data from the 1980s suggests that the timing of charitable contributions is very sensitive to changes in the tax structure, but the long-run level of giving is more responsive to changes in income. Tax laws probably have less effect on lifetime giving than on how donations are timed over one's lifetime.[6]

Ironically, this suggests a relationship between philanthropic activities and tax rates exactly the opposite of the conventional wisdom. Lower tax rates increase the productivity of the economy, and lower rates in upper-income brackets lead to greater income among those with the highest propensity toward philanthropic activity. Higher marginal tax rates provide a greater incentive to give when contributions are deductible, but they also produce lower income among the largest givers. The evidence suggests that income levels are more important determinants of philanthropic activity than tax benefits, so lower tax rates, rather than higher tax rates, would encourage more charitable contributions. But for present purposes this may be a minor point. Laws regarding the tax deductibility of charitable contributions could be amended without making other major changes to the tax code. Furthermore, one would be reluctant to recommend tax law changes that might slow the formation of foundations if those changes worked by lowering the productivity of the economy.

The relationship between tax law and donations to establish the largest nonprofit foundations cannot be conclusively determined by looking at the data because the creation of large foundations is such a rare event. Surely the Carnegie and Rockefeller foundations were not established for tax purposes, but just as surely the Ford Foundation would not exist (in its present form, anyway) without the tax laws to prompt its creation. Overall, however, it appears that while donors claim that tax deductibility is a major factor, the overall level of charitable activity is not affected very much by the level of tax benefit received. At least in part, this may be because while many individuals may respond to changes in tax laws, the overall level of giving will not be affected as much because most total giving results from large contributions from a few donors.[7] When one considers that most foundation grants come from a handful of foundations endowed by only a few donors, however, one must consider seriously the possible effects of tax law changes on the few people who have the resources to endow very large foundations. Undoubtedly some major contributions would be affected, and contributions might be channeled away from foundations and into other charitable activities, like the Salvation Army or the Red Cross, if the tax laws were modified.

When one is considering the very large nonprofit foundations that operate entirely from endowment income, no fundraising is undertaken and all of the assets of these foundations come from the initial endowments made by the donors. Still, the motivations that underlie contributions to nonprofit organizations that solicit contributions are likely to be similar to the motivations of those who endow their own foundations. Quite clearly, the tax system has the potential to exert a significant influence on the resources that flow into the nonprofit sector of the economy, although predictions that if tax deductibility of contributions were eliminated the sector would lose most of its funding are likely to be overstated. The influence of the tax code on the operations of foundations is probably more substantial, however, both directly and indirectly, than on the amount of resources going into foundations.

The direct effect of tax laws on nonprofit foundations arises because foundations must comply with the laws that provide them with nonprofit status. The indirect effects come because the tax laws provide nonprofit foundations with an incentive to manage their resources in certain ways. This chapter looks directly at the tax laws in order to see what the laws are, and to try to understand why they are designed as they are. Tax laws affect the behavior of nonprofit foundations, but the behavior of foundations and their donors has also influenced the design of tax laws. Tax reforms enacted in 1969 brought with them major changes in the ways that foundations had to conduct their business — changes made as a reaction to the activities of foundations. Tax tinkering in other years has also affected the activities of foundations, but the 1969 tax reforms have had the biggest impact.

The interest of Congress and the general public in the tax laws that govern nonprofit organizations is understandable. Those organizations are given a privileged position in society by virtue of their tax-exempt status, and if the general public believes that they do not further the public interest enough to justify their privileged status, or if Congress believes that they are using their tax-exempt status for purposes at odds with those of the political leadership, their tax-exempt status will be put in jeopardy.[8] This has nothing to do with whether the organizations should enjoy a favored position under the tax laws. Rather, it is a statement about political realities. Organizations that antagonize Congress or that upset the general public will be targets of the political system.

Tax Expenditures for Public Purposes

Nonprofit foundations are not the only organizations that benefit from favorable tax treatment. A list drawn up by the Office of Management and Budget shows that there are forty-five categories of tax preferences that cost the Treasury more than $1 billion each in foregone revenues.[9] These tax preferences, intended to further some public purpose, are called tax expenditures because the federal government intends for these provisions of the tax code to provide an incentive for the beneficiaries of the preferences to do something in the public interest.

The term tax expenditures was coined by Stanley Surrey in 1973, in a book intended to direct public attention to the use of the tax system for purposes other than the collection of revenue.[10] The logic behind the concept of tax expenditures is that the government could collect taxes in order to undertake some activity in the public interest, or it could provide a tax break for individuals who do so on their own. The tax break lowers the government's tax revenues, but because individuals act on their own to further the public interest, the government does not need to spend that money directly. Thus, rather than spending money directly out of the Treasury for some public purpose, the government gives a tax break which lowers its tax revenues, giving the private sector an incentive to accomplish that same public purpose. Following this logic, tax expenditures make good fiscal sense if the tax revenues foregone to promote the public purpose are less than the direct expenditures the government would have needed to make to accomplish the same ends.

One can always raise a question about what constitutes a public purpose, and looking at the big picture, the direct revenue costs of nonprofit foundations are small when compared to other tax expenditures. According to the Office of Management and Budget list, the largest tax expenditure in the United States is the exclusion of contributions into qualified retirement plans, which reduced the Treasury's income tax revenues by $66 billion in 1995. Close behind is the deductibility of employer contributions for employee medical care insurance premiums, which cost the Treasury $61 billion in revenues. What public purposes are served by these tax expenditures? If people do not provide for their retirements, then when they reach old age and are unable to work, they will go on welfare and be a burden to the government. By encouraging them to save now for their retirements, the government reduces its future burden and reduces the number of indigent citizens. Similarly, by encouraging people to purchase health insurance themselves, the government keeps people from relying on government-financed health care.

The next largest tax expenditure is the deductibility of home mortgage interest on federal tax returns, which cost the Treasury $51 billion in 1995. While one might make an argument that a public purpose is served by this deduction, the argument is not as strong as for retirement plans and health insurance. Allowing the accelerated depreciation of buildings and equipment costs $26 billion a year. The deferral of capital gains on the sale of homes costs $17 billion. The deductibility of charitable contributions of all kinds cost the Treasury $23 billion in 1995. Of this, $19 billion goes for charitable activities other than education or health.

Occasionally the Treasury will forego a substantial amount of revenue in estate taxes when a wealthy individual creates a foundation rather than passing a large estate to heirs, but eliminating the possibility of creating a foundation from an estate will only push the donor to create the foundation before death, as was done by Rockefeller and Carnegie even without the incentives of the tax system. These figures show that in the big scheme of things, nonprofit foundations have a small impact on federal tax revenues when compared to other tax expenditures.

Interestingly enough, when Stanley Surrey coined the term "tax expenditures" in 1973 to point out how extensive they were, he was hoping to generate some opposition to them because they were costing the Treasury so much money. When out in the open, he hoped that people would see how the use of the tax system to further public purposes was compromising its ability to raise revenues, and that many of these tax preferences would be eliminated. Following this line of reasoning, the tax system should be used as an efficient generator of government revenues, and not as a broader tool of public policy that creates incentives for people to act in the public interest. While Surrey had hoped that his expose of tax expenditures would lead to a reduction in their use, in fact, the opposite happened. Many people liked the idea that the tax system could be used as a tool of social engineering, and the term was picked up by champions of the concept who wanted to encourage its further application.

Surely one must be sympathetic to the idea that those contributing to the Salvation Army or Care are doing so to help those less fortunate, and perhaps allowing their contributions to be tax deductible will encourage more charitable activity. Perhaps donations to colleges and universities could be looked at the same way, except that those who attend college tend to be from families with above-average incomes, and tax subsidies to the rich do not seem quite so charitable. Likewise, opera houses and art galleries are set up as nonprofit organizations that operate tax-free. Should people's consumption preferences be subsidized through tax preferences?

Nonprofit foundations established for education, scholarly research, and the development and promotion of ideas are worth questioning on the same basis. Nobody should object if someone wanted to devote some money to the development and dissemination of ideas, but when the individual does so through a tax-exempt organization, that creates a reason for the general public to scrutinize the activities of the organization to see if it promotes some public purpose. While the tax cost of these foundations is small compared to other tax expenditures, the cost still runs into the billions of dollars every year. The public has a legitimate interest in knowing whether the tax cost is worth the benefits generated, and the biggest questions have been raised when it has appeared that foundations have been acting in opposition to the public interest.

Donations

The largest foundations have been created by individuals or families. The foundations established by Rockefeller and Carnegie were created before income and bequests were taxed at the federal level, so tax laws had a minimal impact on the establishment of their foundations. The Ford Foundation, on the other hand, was established almost entirely with an eye toward avoiding estate taxes and maintaining family control of the Ford Motor Company, as chapter 2 noted. The Ford Foundation is not alone in this regard, as the Duke Endowment and the Hormel Foundation are two others described in chapter 2 that were designed in order to maintain control over corporations by endowing the foundations with corporate stock. Quite clearly, the effect of the tax code on the establishment of foundations in the twentieth century has not been trivial.

There are several reasons why one might be concerned about the influence of tax laws on endowments to foundations. Most obviously, if the donations are made tax free, then the government is losing the tax revenues, and there is good reason to ask whether the donations further a public purpose that is worth more than the tax revenues that are foregone. A second reason is that if the purpose of the endowment is to designate who will retain control of a corporation, the corporate sector of the economy may be affected, perhaps inefficiently. Private sector efficiency is enhanced because private firms can be bought and sold. The stock market assists because if firms are being run inefficiently, there is a ready market that creates an opportunity for people who believe they can more efficiently run a company to take it over and manage it themselves. If control of a corporation is vested in a nonprofit foundation that has little incentive to sell its shares or exercise any oversight, or if the foundation's shares are in some way inferior (as was the case when the Ford Foundation was given nonvoting shares), then this avenue of efficiency is closed off. Thus, the tax system with regard to nonprofit foundations might reduce the efficiency of the private sector of the economy.

Yet a third reason why one might be concerned about the influence of tax laws on the bequests into nonprofit foundations is that the money might be put to purposes that are not in the public interest. A foundation that finances studies that are politically destabilizing might be viewed as acting against the public interest, for example. In this case, not only might the cost to the tax system not be worth the benefits, and not only might private sector efficiency be compromised, the public interest might be best served if the foundation did nothing with its assets rather than use them in a counterproductive way. How might one judge whether the public interest is being served? This is a complex question, but one can see from the discussion of the ideas promoted by nonprofit foundations in chapter 3 that some foundation activities may not be in the public interest, and additional examples appear later in this chapter. Even without a detailed analysis, it should be obvious that with the discretion that the trustees and managers of foundations have, foundations could use their money in ways that oppose the public interest.

Many expenditures in the economy might be viewed as opposite of the public interest, of course. From time to time activities like music (rock and roll, rap) and religion (Satanism) have been viewed as antithetical to the public interest, but surely a free society must give great latitude to people to spend their money as they choose. The real question with regard to nonprofit foundations is whether the way in which the money is spent is sufficiently in the public interest to warrant privileged tax treatment. If the money would not have been donated except for the favored tax treatment, and if the activities financed by the expenditures are not sufficiently in the public interest to compensate for the loss to the Treasury of the tax revenue, then one need not have strenuous objections to the activities of foundations in order to argue that their favorable tax treatment should be altered or eliminated.

The Activities of Foundations

Nonprofit foundations engage in activities for public purposes, but the concept of public purpose is vague, and not everybody will necessarily agree on when public purposes are being served. Major questions about the activities of foundations were being raised in the 1960s, partly because foundations were being established at a more rapid rate. More than two thousand new foundations were created in 1968 alone, some for rather esoteric purposes. A foundation could be created to paint one's portrait, making a contribution to art. Foundations were established to recruit football players and to support mistresses. One creative individual established a foundation and donated his house to it, then continued to live in the house and to charge his living expenses to the foundation.[11] The activities of foundations fell under increased public scrutiny for several reasons in the 1960s. They were used as methods for avoiding taxes, and at times foundations supported what seemed to be offbeat causes. One foundation, for example, was established to provide hippie-oriented urban service, a very "sixties" kind of cause. But as much as anything, foundation activity came under scrutiny when it appeared to be politically oriented.

Many organizations engage in political activities. Labor unions, businesses, and veterans' organizations are examples. The political activities of these other organizations are accepted as an integral part of the political process, although in each case there are regulations that define the acceptable bounds of political activity. In some cases political activities of these other organizations are even tax exempt. But there are significant differences between these organizations and nonprofit foundations which led to Congressional scrutiny of the political activities of foundations. In the case of other organizations, whether businesses, unions, or other interest groups, they have well-defined political interests, and are trying to enter the political marketplace in order to gain governmental recognition of those interests. In the case of nonprofit foundations, they have no readily identifiable economic interests, except perhaps the retention of their tax-preferred status. Thus, when they engage in political activities, they do so at the discretion of a small number of foundation trustees and executives, and often are in a position to place substantial resources into the political arena for causes they wish to support.

The problem with political activities of foundations, then, stems directly from their lack of accountability in the direction of large sums of money. There is no reason to believe that those who allocate the resources of foundations will undertake expenditures in the public interest. Indeed, under one interpretation of democratic ideals, it would be almost impossible for them to do so, because foundation leaders would be put in the position of being able to use other people's money to further their own political agenda without consideration of donor intent or of the public interest. At least when political action committees or corporations spend money for political purposes, there is a close connection between the origin of the money and the interests it is trying to further. If one questions whether the expenditures of corporations and wealthy individuals have an undue influence over the political process, there is even more reason to question expenditures by foundation executives of other people's money for political activities the executives want to further.

Foundations became increasingly involved in political activities in the 1960s, and with substantial resources behind them began to be viewed as a "third sector" of the economy, along with business and government. While some approved of the social change that foundation money brought about, others questioned the wisdom of having foundations be so actively involved in the political process. When questions arose about the political activities of foundations in the 1960s, the Ford Foundation felt the most scrutiny. The Ford Foundation's political activities were more visible than those of other foundations at least partly because of its huge size, but also partly because of some specific activities it undertook.

The Ford Foundation in the 1960s

An examination of some of the activities of the Ford Foundation in the 1960s shows why the foundation focused attention on the political activities of foundations. The Ford Foundation had a reputation for supporting a wide range of extremist groups, and often groups who advocated violent activities as a means for furthering social change. The foundation supported Mexican American Youth Organization (MAYO), as one example, which was dedicated to furthering the welfare of Hispanics by supporting socialism. The president of MAYO, Jose Angel Gutierrez, gave speeches criticizing "gringos," and advocating eliminating their influence by killing them if necessary. Gutierrez also was employed by the Mexican American Legal Defense Fund, which received millions of dollars in funding from the Ford Foundation. Members of MAYO frequently went to Cuba, and disseminated pro-Castro propaganda to Mexican Americans.[12]

This is but one example of the Ford Foundation's support for extremist groups. Jeffrey Hart noted that the Ford Foundation supported those "who spouted the most extreme rhetoric, who presented the most exotic appearance, who were, in fact, fountains of anti-white racism. All this validated them as minority spokesmen, in the eyes of white liberals."[13] The Ford Foundation also supported the National Student Association (NSA), which in fact was not an association of students at all but an interest group that confronted faculty and students in an attempt to change campus policies. Through the NSA, the Ford Foundation financed the campus rebellion that was a visible part of 1960s social activism.

The Ford Foundation also financially supported programs to integrate housing in American suburbs. While one might be sympathetic with attempts to end forced segregation, the Ford Foundation went further to try to force integration. One might expect such programs to be politically controversial, in the same manner as forced bussing of school children.

In 1969 the Ford Foundation helped finance several experiments at school decentralization in New York City. While such decentralization might be beneficial, and it is worth considering at least, the Ford projects stirred considerable political antagonism. Teachers accused the foundation of attempting to destroy their union and of trying to lower school standards that had been built up over the years. The foundation was accused of trying to buy off school board members in order to further their designs by giving board members grants. Whatever the intentions of the Ford Foundation, Daniel P. Moynihan argued that the actual results of the foundation's activities was to organize poor communities to become more radical, to create resentment among lower-income groups, and to increase the amount of racial antagonism. The foundation's programs promised great changes, and when improvements failed to materialize the programs ended up creating feelings of powerlessness and bitterness among those who the grants were nominally supposed to help. In the end, the foundation-financed education experiments produced nothing in the way of educational improvements, but led instead to social activism and political unrest.

Many of the Ford Foundation's activities were even more overtly political in nature. In 1967 the foundation worked with the Congress of Racial Equality (CORE) to undertake a voter registration drive in the predominantly black areas of Cleveland, Ohio, when Carl Stokes, a black candidate for mayor, was running against white candidate Seth Taft. Following the registration drive, Stokes was elected. The foundation claimed that the registration drive was aimed at increasing "democratic participation," ignoring the fact that the drive targeted blacks in its efforts, and ignoring the fact that a particular black candidate was running for mayor. Critics rightly questioned why the Ford Foundation did not attempt similar registration drives in areas populated with Italian or Irish minorities, or why it focused on Cleveland rather than other cities. Despite the Ford Foundation's disingenuous denial, it was apparent to everyone that the foundation was using its resources to further the political fortunes of Carl Stokes. Their voter registration program, coupled with other programs, some of which have already been described, led critics of the foundation to see it as an organization that was using its money and power to support the Democratic political party, as well as to support social unrest, racial tensions, and socialist economic systems.

The foundation granted $5 million to the Center for Community Change, which was governed by a group of highly visible and politically active members of the Democratic Party. Supporters of Bobby Kennedy's presidential campaign, and later, of George McGovern's campaign, were featured prominently in the center's leadership. Frank Mankiewicz, who served as Bobby Kennedy's press secretary, received money not only through the Center for Community Change, but also separately received a grant to study Peace Corps operations in Latin America, before going on to work on McGovern's 1972 run for the presidency. In all, eight former aides of Bobby Kennedy received Ford Foundation money in 1969, in what appeared to be little more than severance pay to individuals whose political orientation was similar to that of the Ford Foundation's leadership.

While one might want to ask whether such expenditures are desirable, that is somewhat beside the point for present purposes. These activities that the Ford Foundation was undertaking appeared to have a clear political slant, and one can rightly question whether an organization with such an overtly political agenda, heavily endowed and accountable to nobody, freed from having to abide by the wishes of the original donors of the money, should be so heavily favored by the U.S. tax code. Furthermore, as described in chapter 2, the Ford Foundation was originally established as a method for avoiding estate taxes and retaining family control of the Ford Motor Company anyway. The tax law was instrumental in the establishment of the foundation, and then was instrumental in sheltering its political activities. As much as anything, it was the Ford Foundation's activities that caused Congress to question the tax laws as they applied to foundations in 1969, and to make major changes in the tax laws as they affected nonprofit foundations.

The 1969 Tax Reforms

Congress perceived a number of problems with nonprofit foundations, including their use of funds for political activities, the use of foundations as a tax shelter, the use of foundations to allow individuals or families to maintain control of corporations, and the general lack of accountability of a foundation's management. The tax code changes made in 1969 were mainly regulatory in nature, and restricted in many ways the activities of foundations. They also imposed a tax on foundation income that, while not very large, was viewed as a dangerous precedent by those in foundations. The 1969 tax reforms were a watershed event in the history of nonprofit foundations. They have changed the way in which foundations have had to operate in many ways, and are more significant than any tax other changes before or since. The next several sections consider the effects of the 1969 tax reforms on foundation activities.[14]

The Tax on Foundation Income

Prior to 1969 nonprofit foundations were completely tax exempt, like other charitable organizations. The 1969 tax law changed that by imposing a tax of 4 percent on the net investment income of a foundation. The justification of Congress was that foundations should share in the cost of financing government, and specifically, should share in the cost of IRS enforcement of tax laws regarding foundations. In order to implement this tax, Congress had to develop a clear definition of a foundation in order to distinguish foundations from other charitable organizations, which remained tax exempt. The law was written in such a way as to exclude certain classes of charitable organizations from foundation status. Excluded organizations are defined by their source of income. Organizations that are supported by the general public or by a large number of donors are excluded from the tax definition of a foundation, and thus do not have to pay the foundation income tax on investment income. The reasoning is that these organizations with a broader base of continuing support are more accountable to public opinion and therefore require less government oversight.

The 4 percent tax on foundation income was perhaps the provision of the 1969 tax reform most heavily criticized by those who were closely involved in the running of foundations. The rationale of having foundations shoulder some of the burden of financing the federal government seemed irrelevant. The tax rate is much lower than that levied on businesses, so foundations still enjoy tax-favored status, but at the same time other charities pay no tax. If foundations are merely being asked to pay their own way, why are not other charitable organizations not also asked to do so? Furthermore, a 4 percent tax on investment income can hardly be viewed as a user charge, because there is little relationship between the investment income of a foundation and the cost of enforcing the tax laws for that foundation. And while other provisions of the 1969 act aid in making foundations more accountable, the tax has nothing to do with accountability.

By taxing the investment income of foundations, foundations are put at a relative disadvantage when compared to other charitable organizations. Because of tax laws, potential donors would be more inclined to contribute to tax-exempt charitable organizations rather than foundations. One result is that fewer foundations are established than would have been the case without the tax. Prior to 1969 a moderately wealthy individual could include in his estate the provision for a modest foundation operated with a few hours a year of an attorney's time to undertake charitable activities. After 1969 the tax laws would push such an individual to contribute to an existing charity so that the money could be distributed tax free. Of course, one of the problems that Congress saw was that it was too easy to set up foundations as tax dodges, and making foundations more costly to establish was clearly one of the goals Congress had in mind when passing the 1969 reforms.

Probably the most serious problem that those in the third sector had with the tax on foundation income was that it set a precedent for the taxation of foundation income. With this foot in the door future tax increases might be on the horizon. While this has not yet happened, the possibility remains. Meanwhile, foundations are clearly set apart as poor cousins to tax-exempt charitable organizations.

Payout of Foundation Income

The 1969 tax act requires foundations to spend their entire current income, excluding capital gains, for charitable purposes. If their return on investment is less than a certain minimum amount, set by statute initially at 6 percent, then it is required to pay out this minimum amount. The minimum amount can be adjusted by the secretary of the treasury to reflect changes in interest rates and investment returns. Most of those associated with foundations agree in principle with the idea that foundations should spend their income for charitable purposes. The disagreement is in the details of the provision, and most specifically with the minimum payout requirement.[15]

The minimum payout requirement was written in order to deal with cases in which foundations are heavily invested in land, which generates no current income, or in stocks that pay little or no dividends. The investments are likely to accrue significant capital gains over time, but because capital gains are not current income, a foundation could continue to pay out all of its (meager) current income, or even more, and still continue to grow in wealth. Because foundations are allowed their tax-favored status in exchange for furthering some public purpose, a foundation that continues to grow in assets while paying out little for public purposes might be thought of as betraying its public trust.

Those who manage foundations argued that the minimum payout requirement was excessive, and that it would lead toward the erosion of foundation assets, eventually destroying the foundation. In cases where the minimum payout exceeds the current income of a foundation, its assets would have to be sold in order to meet the requirement, although if it had sufficient capital gains it still might see a growth in its capital value. Foundations with current income in excess of the minimum would still have to pay out all of their income. In years of high inflation, or when the foundation portfolio suffered capital losses, this might be an excessive financial burden on the foundation. Some individuals affiliated with foundations thought that it would be more reasonable to require a minimum payout based on the net asset value of the foundation, leaving current income out the equation altogether. And because foundations tend to be conservative investors, they thought that the minimum required payout should be somewhat below a market average rate of return.

There was another motivation for requiring a minimum payout by foundations. Congress felt that this could lead to better portfolio management by foundations, and would tend to weaken the ties between foundations and specific corporate assets. If stock had to be sold to make the payout, then this would create turnover in the foundation's portfolio, and it would also give foundation managers an incentive to look more closely at the rate of return they were earning on their investments.

Everybody on both sides of this issue agrees in principle that foundations should make generous payouts to further public purposes. Those opposed to the minimum required payout object not to the principle, but to the implementation of the rule, which they claim has the potential to weaken foundations and erode their assets over time. A few decades of history since the 1969 tax reforms have shown that, in fact, most large foundations have increased the values of their endowments, even after adjusting for inflation. The concerns of foundations did not materialize on this issue.

Should Foundations Have a Limited Life?

At least some of the proponents of minimum payouts support the idea precisely because it has the potential to erode the asset value of foundations over time. An amendment was added to the 1969 tax act that would have ended the favorable tax treatment of a foundation after forty years. The reasoning behind this is that after the establishment of a foundation, it becomes increasingly separated from the intentions of the donor, and because it operates on income from its endowment, it is essentially free from public accountability. Because these foundations operate independently of any outside constraints, they should not be able to maintain their substantial presence in the society, subsidized by tax preferences. Thus, the argument can be made that foundations should have a limited life.

Indeed, it is difficult for today's donor to foresee the pressing problems that might exist a century from now. In the 1940s polio was a major medical problem in the United States. Now, vaccines against the disease have almost eradicated it. Might cancer be defeated a century from now? Could the same argument not be made for current social and political problems? A broad mandate for a foundation, like improving the well-being of mankind, might overcome this argument about the limited scope of a donor's intent, but opens up other problems because it gives so much discretion to the foundation's management. By giving foundations a limited life, they can be made more accountable, and can be tied more closely to the intent of the donor. The idea was considered in 1969, and will be revisited in chapter 10, which examines policy alternatives.

Risky or Speculative Ventures

The 1969 reforms prevent foundations from investing in risky and speculative ventures that might place the foundation's charitable purposes in jeopardy. One can hardly argue with the intent of this provision, if it is to maintain the foundation's assets in order to further its public purpose. However, given the requirement that the foundation make a minimum payout, a foundation might be put in the position of having to make more speculative investments than it might otherwise like, or else risk having its assets eroded by a combination of conservative investments and the minimum payout requirement.

This provision requires one other comment: what constitutes a risky venture can only be known with certainty in hindsight. People have lost a lot of money over the years in what they thought were safe investments. How can the federal government know whether ventures are risky or speculative, let alone require that foundations avoid them?

Self-Dealing

The 1969 tax act prohibits foundations from engaging in financial transactions, either directly or indirectly, with donors or related parties. The intent of this provision is evident and nonobjectionable. Those who are donors, trustees, officers, or employees, or who have other associations with a foundation should not financially benefit from that association. Otherwise, foundations can be established as a tax-free way to funnel income to those affiliated with a foundation. A foundation could, for example, hold a conference and pay for all of the attendees to stay at a hotel owned by a trustee, hire catering services from a large donor, and so forth. Because there is no market discipline forcing foundations to be careful shoppers, the tax-favored status of foundations could be taken advantage of to provide income to those associated with the foundation.

While one can hardly object to the intent of the prohibition against self-dealing, it could raise difficulties when the trustees and donors of foundations are prominent individuals in a community. Foundations in smaller communities are likely to find themselves more vulnerable to these problems than those in larger areas. When prominent local citizens are board members of foundations, it may be hard to rent office space, find conference accommodations, or advertise a foundation's activities without self-dealing. What happens when the local newspaper is owned by a board member, for example? The prohibition on self-dealing has the potential of imposing substantial burdens on some foundations, although one can see the rationale behind it. Foundations should not be conduits for the support of those affiliated with the foundations.

Objectivity

Foundations may make grants to charitable organizations or to other organizations and individuals. When they make grants to noncharitable organizations or individuals, they must do so using nondiscriminatory and objective criteria that are approved in advance by the Internal Revenue Service. The idea here is similar to the prohibition against self-dealing. The foundation should be working to further its public purpose in the most effective way possible, rather than favoring particular individuals or organizations that have a relationship with the foundation.

Responsibility

When grants are made to organizations or individuals who are not charitable organizations, foundations must establish procedures to monitor the expenditures to see that they are spent for the purpose for which they were made. They must obtain a complete financial report from the grant recipient, and make a detailed report to the IRS showing that the money was spent as it was intended. Some foundations have reported that this requirement generates more paperwork than any other requirement in the 1969 tax act. While it is reasonable to want to ensure that money channeled through a tax-favored organization is used for a public purpose, the reporting requirements are potentially burdensome, and after the passage of the act one foundation noted that while the requirements were not hard to meet, they increased the paperwork done by the foundation by about one third. As with all such requirements, one negative side-effect is that time spent on government reporting requirements is time taken away from the public purpose of the foundation.

Foundations do have an alternative to implementing procedures to meet the IRS reporting requirements. They can simply make all of their grants to charitable organizations, as defined by the IRS. Indeed, many foundations do exactly this. The end result may not have a major impact on the financing of ideas by foundations, because there is a large number of qualified universities and think tanks that apply for foundation grants to support their work. The burden of the reporting requirements then falls on the recipients, although the reporting requirements are a part of the routine that all such organizations must practice in order to operate. Still, this requirement is likely to mean that more foundation grants are made to organizations that are a part of an established network rather than those who are working independently.

Ironically, provisions such as this are more likely to have a negative impact on those charitable activities intended to help those less fortunate in a society than on the production of ideas funded by foundations.

If one wants to help provide furniture for the needy, for example, there may be a substantial burden involved in showing that the money was spent as it was intended. (There is, of course, the possibility of fraud that the IRS would like to guard against. They do not want foundations to purchase furniture for college students who are children of donors, for example.) However, when foundations make grants to individuals in exchange for the production of ideas, often a large part of the grant will be made for the time of the writer or researcher, and a clearly defined product in the form of a report or study will be produced. This provision may actually help to channel funds into the production of ideas by making it relatively easier to document expenditures on studies than on providing material benefits for the needy.

Despite the burdens imposed by many of these requirements, such as the responsibility requirement, the objectivity requirement, and the prohibition against self-dealing, at least some individuals associated with foundations believed that these were desirable parts of the 1969 tax act. J. Irwin Miller, testifying on behalf of foundations in Congressional hearings on the subject said, "In contrast to the proposed tax, the Bill's measures to curb and prevent fiscal abuses are necessary to the public interest and vital to the preservation of private philanthropy." [16] Congress implemented the 1969 reforms because of abuses that they perceived by foundations that acted in irresponsible ways, with little accountability. Foundations saw the same problems themselves, as this quotation shows, and some of those associated with foundations felt that more government oversight would actually be beneficial to foundations, because the costs imposed in terms of complying with the new rules would be more than compensated for by the enhanced reputations that foundations might enjoy.

Limited Holdings of Stock

In order to limit the use of foundations as a method of maintaining control of a family-owned business, the 1969 act limits the amount of stock that can be held by a foundation plus related parties to 20 percent of the stock of a business. The Ford Foundation immediately comes to mind as one that was intended, at least in part, to aid the family in controlling the business. There are other reasons why this provision might be beneficial, besides just preventing the foundation from helping a family maintain control of a business.

When foundations hold a large share of a corporation's stock, the corporation may have less of an incentive to pay dividends to its stockholders. Stockholders see that a substantial payout goes to the foundation, so the use of retained earnings to finance the operation of the business might be more heavily favored by the corporation. This would have the effect of lowering the foundation's income, and also would have the effect of insulating the corporation to a degree from the pressures of the marketplace. In the interest of having a more competitive market, such restrictions may be warranted. If a large share of a foundation's assets are tied up in one company, the foundation's managers have an incentive to become involved in monitoring the performance of the company, which might distract them from the public purpose behind the foundation. Thus, it seems reasonable for foundations to diversify their assets, and for foundations not to have a substantial ownership interest in any one corporation.

Such a rule clearly prevents foundations from holding donated shares in closely held corporations, some of which might be large, profitable, and potentially good investments. For example, in 1996 Bill Gates owned approximately 25 percent of the stock of Microsoft Corporation. Because a foundation and related parties together cannot own more than 20 percent of the stock of a company, foundations would automatically be excluded from retaining any significant amount of Microsoft stock that Mr. Gates might wish to donate.[17] There are many profitable companies besides Microsoft, of course, and as Microsoft pays no dividend on its stock, it provides no income in that manner, so there is no particular reason why this exclusion would necessarily harm foundations. Nevertheless, the example shows the degree to which this requirement limits the range of investments available to foundations.

A study done in 1968, prior to this provision taking effect, showed that 41 percent of all foundation contributions, and 70 percent of contributions to foundations with assets greater than $100 million, were made in stock for which the donor and those related to the donor had in interest greater than 20 percent.[18] This makes some sense, and the Microsoft example provides a case to illustrate why. People who have amassed substantial wealth to contribute to foundations are likely to have done so by building a successful business of their own. Thus, the bulk of their assets are likely to be tied up in the ownership of the business. With this provision, foundations receiving such donations are placed in a position of having to figure out a way to divest themselves of a part of their portfolio that has proven itself a good investment in the past in order to avoid running afoul of this limited ownership provision. The result may be that foundation managers spend more time dealing with portfolio matters, not less, and because they must worry about following the rules devote less attention to the public purpose of their foundation.

Political Influences

The 1969 tax reform act limits the degree to which a foundation can influence the political process in a number of ways. First, it prohibits foundations from making expenditures to influence any specific election. That includes voter registration drives of the type undertaken by the Ford Foundation. Second, it prohibits foundations from making any payments to government officials except for reimbursing their domestic travel expenses. Both elected and appointed government officials are covered in this prohibition. Third, it prohibits foundations from attempting to influence legislation, either by trying to affect public opinion or by trying to influence government officials who participate in the formulation of legislation. The act does grant exceptions in cases where foundations make available the results of their own "nonpartisan" research or analysis, or when a governmental body requests information, or when the legislation would affect the foundation's tax or legal status.

This provision of the 1969 tax act has potentially the most far-reaching impact on the ideas generated by foundations. Examples given earlier of Ford Foundation activities suggest what activities Congress might have been interested in curtailing, but any foundation dealing in public policy issues must be especially concerned with the way in which this provision might be enforced. The prohibition against influencing legislation, for example, might be extended to prevent the types of public policy studies that many foundations on all sides of the political spectrum have funded, because public policy almost always works its way through the legislature. There are really two separate but closely related questions here: What constitutes legislation, and what constitutes attempts to influence it?

Studies advocating the passage of a particular bill would surely qualify, but for decades the IRS has been reasonable in its interpretation of influencing legislation. Public policy studies on issues are permissible, even when a study's conclusion takes a particular point of view, if the study makes a careful and reasoned analysis of the issue. However, there have been occasional suggestions that an administration was inclined to take a closer look at the activities of certain foundations—foundations that tended to advocate anti-administration positions—to see if they might not be in violation of this prohibition against attempting to influence legislation. Thus, the fact that this provision has been relatively benign to date does not guarantee that it will stay that way.

J. Irwin Miller, cited above as broadly supportive of additional regulations to control abuses by foundations, argued against this limitation when the 1969 tax act was being debated. Miller argued that this restriction "would fence off private foundations from activity in areas of public policy" and that "barriers that the new proposals would erect could well impair, not improve, the judgment and effectiveness of private foundations." [19] Miller's concerns arose because the act's limitations are "necessarily imprecise," and because penalties could be imposed on foundation managers and trustees for violations. "This could drive trustees and foundation officials into such an excess of caution that even innocent and benign activities that touch on public policy in such fields as education and conservation would be deprived of foundation support." [20] One could argue that Miller's fears have not been realized, but that does not mean that in the future threats to foundation activities might not be made. Indeed, there have been rumblings that some administrations might start scrutinizing the activities of foundations that oppose the incumbent administration more closely, and perhaps attempt to remove their tax-favored status.

In the same hearings a similar statement was made by Merrimon Cuninggim, then president of the Danforth Foundation, who questioned, "What, then is left for foundations to do? To play safe, they would feel that they must eschew working in any field of the social sciences, perhaps also the humanities, and even the natural sciences, at least in their applicability to human problems. Conservation of our natural resources? Air and water pollution? Beautification of our highways? Such innocent-sounding activities would be too dangerous, for they would sooner or later touch on legislation." [21] While it is true that foundations have continued to work in the areas that Mr. Cuninggim argued were risky, foundations are continually concerned about the boundaries beyond which they might be penalized.

It is interesting to note that the prohibition is limited to influencing legislation, and that attempting to influence policy through administrative proceedings or through legal action are not covered in the law. One might wonder why the law would allow foundations to pursue projects that would advocate litigation and administrative rule-making to affect public policy on specific issues, yet exclude legislation. Nevertheless, while efforts to influence the passage of specific bills is prohibited, the law has been interpreted in a way general enough to allow foundations to continue to finance and promote work on specific public policy issues. Indeed, some observers believe that this is an appropriate and socially desirable way for foundations to use their resources.[22]

Foundations Versus Charities

Many organizations with foundation in their names are in fact set up as public charities. The primary difference is that charities raise funds from a broad base of donors, whereas foundations are endowed by a more limited group.[23] The generally accepted delineation is that a charity receives more than one-third of its annual support from members and from the general public, and less than one third of its support from investment income and unrelated business income.[24] Thus, philanthropic organizations that do not qualify as charities are by default foundations. The advantage of being a charity rather than a foundation is that the tax laws are much less burdensome. After the 1969 tax act many foundations discovered that they already qualified for status as a public charity, or could if they made minor changes in their methods of operation. In addition, many smaller foundations simply terminated their operations by donating all of their assets to qualified charities.

Should foundations face more scrutiny than charities? Clearly they should because of the lack of accountability of foundations that was discussed in chapter 2. Despite the advantages of operating as a charity, there remains a substantial number of nonprofit foundations that operate to generate ideas and to alter the way that Americans think about a broad number of issues.

The Significance of the 1969 Tax Reform

Many federal tax reforms have occurred since the 1969 tax act, yet there have been no reforms before or since that have had as significant an effect on the tax status of foundations. Prior to 1969 foundations were treated as other nonprofit charities; after 1969 foundations found themselves in a separate category, facing greater accountability and having lost a small part of their tax-favored status. While there were major changes as a result of the 1969 act, many of the tax aspects that are important to foundations did not change in 1969 and still remain unchanged. This is especially true when the relationship of tax laws to the production of ideas is considered.

Many of the 1969 tax reforms dealt with preventing foundations from becoming a conduit through which those associated with foundations could receive tax-free benefits. Reporting requirements have tightened a bit since 1969, with all tax-exempt organizations being required to report when some payment in kind has been made in exchange for a contribution. Thus, when a foundation gives its donors a free trip to a banquet, or a free coffee mug, these must be reported as taxable income to the recipient. The ability to use foundations to control the management of corporations was reduced, and foundations were required to pay out a minimum amount in grants.

With regard to ideas, the prohibition on political activities looms as the largest impact of the 1969 tax reform. Also, reporting requirements and requirements that grant recipients be objectively selected might have a minimal influence on the intellectual products of foundations. In particular, there is a bias on the part of some foundations to give grants to charitable organizations rather than individuals. Still, the major issues of lack of accountability and a weak correspondence between foundation expenditures and donor intent remains.

With the benefit of several decades of hindsight, it is apparent that the 1969 reform left considerable latitude for foundations to finance policy-oriented studies, and did little to create accountability for foundations. The ability to stop wholesale abuses was enhanced, and Merrimon Cuninggim, writing in 1972 after being with the Danforth Foundation for more than ten years, argued that the reform was beneficial to foundations because by closing some of the loopholes to abuse, it made foundations appear more credible to the general public.[25]

Tax Laws and Foundation Policy

The major issues with regard to tax policy for foundations revolve around what conditions foundations should meet in exchange for their tax-exempt status. Such questions are relevant for any tax-exempt organization, but there are specific questions that apply to nonprofit foundations because of the fact that they lack the accountability of other charitable organizations.

Should donations and bequests be allowed to pass into foundations untaxed? While one can see that some foundations would be established regardless of the potential tax benefits, one can also see that others, such as the Ford Foundation, would have been unlikely to have been created without this substantial tax benefit. While people should be allowed to do what they want with their money, the question becomes one of public policy when some ways of disposing of one's assets receive preferred tax treatment. That question has remained the same before and after the 1969 tax reform.

Once a foundation is established, should it be allowed to keep its tax-preferred status in perpetuity? That question was raised in 1969, but ultimately no action was taken on it, and foundations are allowed to live forever. Two possible methods of altering the status quo would be to have the tax-preferred status of foundations expire after a certain number of years, or to increase the payout requirement that must be met in order to retain tax-exempt status.

After these two major questions come a host of minor ones, such as whether reporting requirements should be changed, whether restrictions on foundation activities should be altered, and whether more direct accountability of foundations should be designed in some way. The tax reforms in 1969 had a major influence on the way that foundations are treated under tax law, but the major issues are little different now than they were prior to that reform.

Having reviewed the interaction between tax law and the ideas promoted by foundations, it is apparent that there is a close connection between the two, and that the major tax changes in 1969 were largely in response to the left-leaning ideas supported by the Ford Foundation and others. The possibility of ideological biases in the ideas supported by foundations has been suggested before and is interesting to contemplate, because the antimarket ideas supported by some foundations seem so clearly at odds with the market mechanism that originally generated the resources of foundations.

Notes

1.   Joseph C. Goulden, *The Money Givers* (New York: Random House, 1971), p. 25.

2. T. Willard Hunter, *The Tax Climate for Philanthropy* (Washington, DC: American College Public Relations Association, 1968), p. 117.
3. Charles T. Clotfelter, *Federal Tax Policy and Charitable Giving* (Chicago: University of Chicago Press, 1985).
4. Hunter, *The Tax Climate for Philanthropy,* p. 114.
5. Rebecca Schaefer, "So, What Gives? How Tax Policies Affect Charitable Donations," *Issue Analysis* No. 19 (December 20, 1995), Washington, DC: Citizens for a Sound Economy Foundation.
6. William C. Randolph, "Dynamic Income, Progressive Taxes, and the Timing of Charitable Contributions," *Journal of Political Economy* 103, No. 4 (August 1995), pp. 709-738.
7. Teresa Odendahl, *Charity Begins at Home: Generosity and Self-Interest Among the Philanthropic Elite* (New York: Basic Books, 1990), p. 62.
8. While this discussion on tax laws and government oversight of foundations focuses on federal law, states also exercise some oversight, as discussed by Marion R. Fremont-Smith, *Foundations and Government: State and Federal Law and Supervision* (New York: Russell Sage Foundation, 1965). The focus on federal law is warranted, first, because federal law is more binding, and second, because taxpayers wanting to establish foundations will have the resources to be able to locate their foundations in the states of their choosing, making any one state's provisions largely irrelevant.
9. U.S. Department of Commerce, *Statistical Abstract of the United States, 1995,* 115th ed. (Washington, DC: 1995), p. 339.
10. Stanley S. Surrey, *Pathways to Reform: The Concept of Tax Expenditures* (Cambridge, MA: Harvard University Press, 1973).
11. Jeffrey Hart, "Foundations and Social Activism: A Critical View," in The American Assembly, *The Future of Foundations* (Englewood Cliffs, NJ: Prentice-Hall, 1973), p. 46.
12. Jeffrey Hart, "Foundations and Social Activism: A Critical View," pp. 49-53, describes the Ford Foundation activities recounted in this section.
13. Hart, "Foundations and Social Activism: A Critical View," p. 52.
14. John R. Labovitz, "The 1969 Tax Reforms Reconsidered," in The American Assembly, *The Future of Foundations* (Englewood Cliffs, NJ: Prentice-Hall, 1973), chapter 4, discusses and analyzes the effects of the 1969 tax reforms on foundations in detail.
15. This payout provision has been modified in minor ways over the years, but the principle behind the payout provision remains. See Bruce R. Hopkins, *Charitable Giving and Tax-Exempt Organizations* (New York: John Wiley & Sons, 1982), pp. 32-35, for a discussion of some modifications contained in the 1981 tax reform.
16. J. Irwin Miller, "The Role of Foundations in American Life," in *Foundations and the Tax Bill* (New York: Foundation Center, 1969), p. 7.
17. There is an exception that allows foundations to own not more than 2 percent of any company's stock, regardless of donor interest. See Arthur

Andersen & Co., *Tax Economics of Charitable Giving,* 8th ed. (Chicago, 1983), p. 87.

18. Labovitz, "1969 Tax Reforms Reconsidered," p. 115.
19. Miller, "The Role of Foundations in American Life," p. 8.
20. Miller, "The Role of Foundations in American Life," p. 8.
21. Merrimon Cuninggim, "Effect of Program Limitations, in *Foundations and the Tax Bill* (New York: Foundation Center, 1969), p. 77.2
22. See J. Craig Jenkins, "Nonprofit Organizations and Policy Advocacy," chap. 17 in Walter W. Powell, ed., *The Nonprofit Sector* (New Haven, CT: Yale University Press, 1987).
23. Note that this distinction between foundations and charities is made for tax purposes. As noted in chapter 2, another distinction might be made between charity and philanthropy, with charity being activities targeted at the needy and philanthropy being activities to promote the well-being of the general population. Barry D. Karl and Stanley N. Katz, "The American Private Philanthropic Foundation and the Public Sphere: 1890-1930," *Minerva* 19, No. 2 (Summer 1981), pp. 236-270, discuss this distinction.
24. See Arthur Andersen & Co., *Tax Economics of Charitable Giving*, p. 85-86.
25. Merrimon Cuninggim, *Private Money and Public Service: The Role of Foundations in American Society* (New York: McGraw-Hill, 1972), p. 195.

5

Trends and Biases in Foundation Funding

The previous chapter's discussion of the Ford Foundation's activities in the 1960s leaves little doubt that foundations have used their resources to promote their ideological biases in the past. Chapters 3 and 4 have documented many areas in which foundations have promoted government programs and left-leaning political causes, and have been involved in politically related activities in foreign countries. These examples are telling, yet by themselves do not tell the whole story of the trends and biases in foundation funding. This chapter attempts a more systematic examination of the topic.

Any attempt to try to draw a single bottom-line conclusion about trends and biases in the types of studies that nonprofit foundations fund would surely lead to an over-simplification. There are thousands of foundations with varied activities, and any analysis could be undertaken in a variety of ways. Should all foundations be treated alike? Should they be weighed by the dollar amount of their grants? Should trends in the formation of new foundations be charted, or would one get a more accurate picture by looking at trends in the grants made by a few of the largest foundations? There is no right answer to these questions, because any look at a trend or bias is an attempt to reduce all of these dimensions of foundations over time into a single dimension. What specific things one looks at to try to identify trends depends partly upon what one is looking for, and partly upon what data is available. It is easier to categorize the activities of more visible foundations, whereas smaller foundations that make a few grants for research projects will be more difficult. Even if one reads all of the studies produced by foundation grants, there still may be differences among individuals regarding their subjective evaluations of biases in them.

To see the problems involved in examining trends and biases, consider the measurement of economic data such as consumer prices or national income. Continuing controversies plague such measurements as economists debate how changes in product quality should be factored into price indexes, how to pick the appropriate mix of goods whose prices will be aggregated into a single index, and what weight should be given to each. Problems of the same nature are involved in looking at trends in foundation funding, but the problems are more severe because the data are less readily available, and because groups of researchers have not considered the measurement problems (such as what foundations should be included and how their work should be evaluated) in order to work out any problems.

Thus, this chapter begins with the disclaimer that it does not present the last word on trends and biases in foundation funding, and that there may be legitimate reasons to disagree with this analysis. Nevertheless, the issue is important for public policy purposes. If there is a legitimate public interest in the activities of foundations, there must be some attempt made to categorize what foundations do in order to see if it is in the public interest. This chapter is offered as an initial attempt to consider biases and trends in foundation funding to provide some background for discussing the issues of donor intent, the role of trustees and directors, and ultimately the policy alternatives that are considered in chapter 10.

There are (at least) two ways in which the trends and biases in foundation's might be analyzed. The first is fundamentally empirical, and looks at the types of activities that foundations have funded over the years. The second is fundamentally theoretical, and considers whether there are institutional reasons that would lead foundations to be biased in the activities they fund. This chapter builds on both approaches to draw its conclusions. Looking at the issue within the framework of the twentieth-century conservative-liberal ideological spectrum, an examination of the evidence shows a clear liberal bias in the ideas promoted by foundations. This bias began early in the twentieth century, and perhaps was at its peak in the 1960s. There is some evidence that the trend may be slowing, or even reversing, because younger foundations tend to be more conservative in their ideology. Is this a function of their age, implying that they will become more liberal over time, or is it a reflection of contemporary social changes in ideology? Arguments can be made both ways. Meanwhile, the older foundations have retained their liberal orientations. The next several sections review the evolution of foundations through the twentieth century to illustrate the origins and nature of the ideologies of foundations.

Foundations Find Direction: 1910-1930

The Carnegie and Rockefeller foundations, established early in the century, provided models for foundations that followed, and because of their substantial size, overwhelmed earlier foundations once they were created. Whereas foundations before Carnegie and Rockefeller were limited in scope and charitable in nature, the Carnegie and Rockefeller foundations changed the direction of foundation activity. Carnegie and Rockefeller themselves broke with earlier foundations by funding activities that were targeted toward improving the general well-being of a population rather than targeting specific causes or those in need of assistance. Carnegie's library program and Rockefeller's health programs typify this innovation in foundation financing. But after Carnegie and Rockefeller turned control of their wealth over to their foundations, the trustees moved increasingly toward public policy-related projects, and evolved from the financing of programs that might provide material benefits toward those that could enhance human capital, provide social benefits, and improve the operation of government.[1]

The turn toward social science must be viewed at least partly as in keeping with the overall philosophy of the times. Concepts of scientific management were coming into vogue, both in the private sector and in government.[2] The creation of the National Bureau of Economic Research was a cooperative effort that, while foundation funded, was supported by those in government, including Herbert Hoover, who served as secretary of commerce from 1921 until he was elected president in 1928. Hoover, an engineer by training, was a firm believer in scientific management of the public sector, and pushed research in social science and public administration as a way of enhancing the nation's ability to engineer a better society.[3] Foundations, as they moved more into the promotion of ideas, and as they increased their emphasis on social science, were following the trends of the day. They were, of course, helping to chart the course through their activities, but they were doing so in a manner consistent with government policy, with private sector initiatives, and with public opinion.[4]

In those formative years from 1910 to 1930 one can see the trend toward the production of ideas, and can understand it as a part of the times. One can also understand how foundation leaders would be interested in using the power vested in them to change the course of society in ways they might view desirable. Through the power of foundation grants and activities, foundation trustees saw that they could influence public opinion, change the course of government, and alter the direction of social change. Thus, one might rightfully question the degree of autonomous power granted through the endowments of foundations. Government leaders in the United States were democratically elected to influence the course of the nation, and by looking overseas, Americans could understand the danger of political power without representation. The private power of corporations, while held in low regard early in the century, was ultimately the result of voluntary market exchange. The power of foundations was a remnant of that market power, now given to trustees with virtually no accountability.

Trustees did use their power to influence ideas and public policy, as the previous two chapters have shown. Trustees were chosen from an American elite, educated at good schools, and accustomed to the better aspects of twentieth-century American life. If they had biases in their ideas and ideologies, it would be only natural that those biases would be those shared by the American elite, and following the revolution of Progressivism, which placed government more at the center of American economic life, one should be surprised if foundation leaders did not share these biases. But one must question whether this is a liberal bias, or merely an acceptance of the trends of the time.

Foundations Face World Problems: 1930-1950

When the Great Depression came on in the 1930s, followed by World War II in the 1940s, foundations had already begun to chart a course that would enable them to address the problems of the times. The change in direction came decades earlier, and it was only natural that foundation funding would now turn toward the social, economic, and political problems that beset the United States and the world. Increased acceptance of the tenets of Progressivism early in the twentieth century led Americans to believe that the government should come to the aid of its citizens to protect their economic well-being, in addition to protecting their rights. With the onset of the Great Depression, popular opinion was that government programs were necessary to stabilize the inherently shaky capitalist system. Mainstream economics turned toward the Keynesian ideas that gave government a prominent role to play in promoting full employment and economic growth, and argued that without government interference, the economy could be doomed to perpetually high unemployment and underproduction.[6]

The philosophy of the New Deal displaced ideals of laissez-faire capitalism, and at the same time a world still recovering from World War I could anticipate, with the rise of Nazism in Germany, additional hostilities on the horizon. Economic recovery and the promotion of world peace were goals that everyone could favor, even if there were differences among individuals regarding the most appropriate methods of achieving those goals. For foundations with general charters that were charged with improving the well-being of mankind, policy issues were natural areas of involvement. One might argue that foundations had a liberal bias, but at the same time one must recognize that the intellectual climate of the time also was moving toward the idea that government control in many areas was necessary for peace and prosperity. Again one must question whether there was a liberal bias in foundation policy, or whether the appearance of bias occurred because foundations are prone to follow the trends—and especially the trends in academia—of the time.

Foundations Set a Liberal Agenda: 1950-1970

In the decades following World War II foundations spearheaded a liberal agenda in the United States. Again one must consider the historical context, and when considering foundation policy, one must consider the creation of the Ford Foundation at the beginning this time period, which was by far the largest foundation in existence. Because of its size, the Ford Foundation's activities were more visible than those of other foundations, and the Ford Foundation could play a leadership role. The nature of that role was described in the previous two chapters. The overtly political nature of some of the Ford Foundation's activities are especially relevant. The Ford Foundation was not alone in its support of liberal causes, however, and the Carnegie and the Rockefeller foundations also were active in continuing their liberal agenda following World War II.

By the 1960s foundations found their reputations suffering because of their activism. Foundations were attempting to steer the course of public education, they were trying to impose their vision of race relations on the nation, they were actively involved in political campaigns, and they were influencing the course of foreign nations through their grants. Because their activities were financed from their endowments, foundations were accountable to nobody. Unlike elected officials, who had to win the approval of the masses, foundation trustees were chosen from an elite group, but were able to use their wealth to influence the course of public policy. The political result was the Tax Reform Act of 1969 that limited the powers and activities of foundations while imposing additional requirements on them. Once the equal of other charitable nonprofit organizations, nonprofit foundations were placed in a separate and less preferred position.

The liberal agenda of the Ford Foundation, undoubtedly the most visible of the liberal foundations, was detailed in chapter 4, as a prelude to describing the 1969 tax reform. But while the Ford Foundation was much larger than other foundations, its activities were not that different from an ideological perspective, as the record of ideas promoted by foundations, described in Chapter 3, shows.

Foundations and Public Policy: 1970-1990

The reforms initiated in 1969 had some influence over the most overtly political behavior of foundations. However, the worst fears of those in the third sector did not materialize. While foundations are not allowed to engage directly in political activity or attempt to influence pending legislation, they can offer their opinions if asked by public officials, and they can fund public policy studies aimed at more general policy areas, if not at specific legislation. In the main, foundations promote ideas in largely the same way after the 1969 reform as they did before.

One innovation that occurred early in the twentieth century was the funding of think tanks to create ideas. Following the creation of the National Bureau of Economic Research and the Brookings Institution with foundation money, additional think tanks have been created either explicitly with foundation assistance, or with the idea of applying to foundations for financial support. The Brookings Institution, founded in 1927, has promoted ideas consistent with the ideology of the Democratic Party, and beginning in the 1970s the American Enterprise Institute has been viewed as serving a similar role for Republicans. The

American Enterprise Institute was founded in 1943, although it was then called the American Enterprise Association, and assumed its current name in 1962. By funding the activities of think tanks, foundations have found a way to keep themselves at arm's length from policy issues, yet have a direct influence by funding public policy work that is consistent with their ideologies.

If the most visible ideas funded by foundations prior to 1970 tended to have a liberal bias, that has been countered somewhat by the emergence of a number of new think tanks that have been established after 1970. Two of the more influential have been the Institute for Contemporary Studies, founded in 1972, and the Heritage Foundation, established in 1973. The Institute for Contemporary Studies, based in San Francisco, was established by a group of individuals who had worked for Ronald Reagan when he was governor of California. The institute was established specifically to provide a free-market perspective on public policy issues, and the first book it issued was an attack on a project funded by the Ford Foundation calling for more government intervention in energy markets. Following Reagan's election to the presidency, the Institute for Contemporary Studies enjoyed increased visibility and influence, but the conservative Heritage Foundation, based in Washington, D.C., was even more influential. Its books and policy papers have had a substantial impact on the public policy debate in Washington.[8]

A number of other think tanks have been established both at the national level and at the state level. The National Center for Policy Analysis, based in Dallas, is a free-market think tank that has been influential in the health care debate, among other issues, in the 1990s. Meanwhile there is a national policy network of state-based think tanks that deal primarily with policy issues of state, local, and regional interest. These conservative policy organizations receive substantial foundation funding, but also rely on corporate and individual donations, so while they may offset some of the liberal policy initiatives funded by the larger and more established foundations, they rely more on marketing their ideas. Foundations, because of their endowments, are more insulated from market forces.

The turn toward conservative ideas might be viewed as a response to the times. The nation has become more conservative at the end of the twentieth century than it was when foundations began funding policy-oriented work. However, the think tanks that promote conservative public policies are not foundations, and the more established foundations have not changed their ideological courses appreciably, as can be noted by looking at their activities in more detail.

The Carnegie Corporation

Ellen Condliffe Lagemann, in her 1989 study of the Carnegie Corporation, describes the foundation's programs as "steadfast liberalism." [9] Lagemann's study was undertaken with the assistance of the Carnegie Corporation, and she looked into the corporation's archives in considerable detail when doing her research. Lagemann is sympathetic with the liberal agenda of the Carnegie Corporation, so the steadfast liberalism she describes is an ideology she finds praiseworthy. The point here is neither to praise nor condemn the Carnegie Corporation for its activities, but rather to document any trends and biases in the foundation's funding activities. Lagemann's reference to steadfast liberalism is credible, both because of the comprehensiveness of her study and because she is someone who is largely supportive of the foundation's activities over the years.

Andrew Carnegie himself was a generous philanthropist, but certainly not a liberal in the twentieth-century American sense of the word. Carnegie's personal gift, and those of the Carnegie Corporation when he was its president enabled the recipients to enjoy an enhanced appreciation of culture, to make themselves more productive, and to identify themselves more with their communities. Commitments to health care, donations of church organs, and of course his construction of thousands of libraries provided communities with opportunities they might not otherwise have had, but at the same time Carnegie wanted the communities themselves to participate in the activities he funded. Carnegie donated organs to churches, but he did not build the churches that housed the organs. He donated library buildings, but under the condition that the communities that received them agree to stock them and maintain them.

The activities of the Carnegie Corporation changed dramatically with the death of Carnegie in 1919. Whereas Carnegie himself wanted local communities to be responsible for their libraries, some of his trustees believed that professional management, and libraries stocked with foundation grants, would produce greater benefits. The disputes among trustees resulted in a termination of the library program. Meanwhile, the

1920s saw a turn away from the funding of tangible objects and toward the funding of ideas. The National Bureau of Economic Research was founded in 1920 with Carnegie Corporation funds. The American Law Institute was founded in 1923, again with Carnegie Corporation funds. In 1922 Robert Brookings used Carnegie Corporation funds to establish an Institute of Economics in Washington, D.C., which merged with other related organizations to form the Brookings Institution in 1927. The Carnegie Corporation has remained an important source of funding for the Brookings Institution, which is closely associated with American liberalism.

The movement toward the funding of ideas began at the Carnegie Corporation in the 1920s, immediately after Andrew Carnegie's death, and shows how substantially a donor's intentions can be altered after the donor is gone. Carnegie chose those trustees himself, yet his handpicked trustees dramatically changed the direction of the foundation's activities once Carnegie was no longer in charge. The ideas that the Carnegie Corporation funded earlier in the 1920s tended toward basic social science research, although the trustees always had in mind the application of ideas for social change. As time marched on, the projects the Carnegie Corporation funded were less and less related to basic research and more and more were related to fundamental policy issues. The commitment to steadfast liberalism described by Lagemann has manifested itself in two ways. First, the issues that the Carnegie Corporation was interested in funding tended to be liberal causes, and second, the individuals whose work the Carnegie Corporation supported were scholars with backgrounds that were easily recognized as liberal.

The Russell Sage Foundation

The Russell Sage Foundation, established in 1907, is credited with creating the profession of social work.[10] Prior to the foundation's activities, most aid to less fortunate individuals was charitable, and was done by volunteers. By promoting schools of social work and by professionalizing those who delivered benefits to the needy, the Russell Sage Foundation laid the cornerstone for the modern, organized income transfer activities of government. The foundation remains true to its initial mission, as one can see by looking at its publications. The foundation's 1990-1991 biennial report states, "Since World War II, Russell Sage has devoted its efforts to strengthening the social sciences

as a means of achieving more informed and rational social policy. To
that end, the Foundation supports external research projects that advance its programmatic objectives, invites visiting scholars to pursue
their writing and research in residence at the Foundation, and publishes
under its own imprint the books resulting from the research it supports."
An examination of the work published by the Russell Sage Foundation
can help provide an idea of the foundation's ideological orientation.

*The Decline in Marriage Among African Americans: Causes, Con-
sequences, and Policy Implications,* edited by M. Belinda Tucker and
Claudia Mitchell-Kernan, published by the Russell Sage Foundation in
1995, documents the decline in marriage rates among African Americans and looks for both causes and solutions. The book focuses on providing better economic and health care support for single parent families, providing better public education, and improving the economic
opportunities for African American men. From an ideological standpoint, this book can be contrasted with Charles Murray's book, *Losing
Ground,* which, as described in chapter 3, blamed many of the problems of those at the bottom end of the income distribution on the federal government's welfare programs. Murray would argue that these
programs should be cut back. Tucker and Mitchell-Kernan, in their
Russell Sage Foundation study, argue that they need to be expanded to
provide better support. Murray's book provided some of the intellectual foundation for the conservative ideas associated with the Reagan
administration. The contrast between these two works shows the continuing support for liberal ideas by the Russell Sage Foundation.

Other work published by the Russell Sage Foundation shows a similar orientation. *Closed Doors, Opportunities Lost: The Continuing Costs
of Housing Discrimination,* by John Yinger, was also published by the
Russell Sage Foundation in 1995, and argues that housing discrimination is rampant despite the passage of the federal Fair Housing Act in
the 1960s. Similarly, *Local Justice in America,* edited by John Elster
and published by the Russell Sage Foundation in 1995, argues that discrimination remains in many areas. Elster's volume looks at four areas:
immigration, college admissions, employee layoffs, and kidney trans-
plants, to document this discrimination. The book is clearly intended to
have an impact on debates over social policy. Liberal causes remain at
the core of the ideas promoted by the Russell Sage Foundation.

The Russell Sage Foundation not only finances studies and publishes
books, but also actively disseminates their publications in order to try

to have an impact on the world of ideas. The foundation mails advertisements for its materials to college professors to try to get them to use the books in classes. The mailings advertise, "SPECIAL OFFER FOR COLLEGE PROFESSORS" and "Complimentary Exam Copies of Books for Classroom Use." [11] As is customary for examination copies of potential textbooks, professors can order Russell Sage books at no cost by filling in a postage-paid postcard, and professors can obtain and read the books whether or not they adopt them for their classes. Thus, the Russell Sage Foundation is involved in the ideas it promotes from beginning to end. It funds studies, publishes results, and disseminates its publications by targeting college professors, who are the most likely group of individuals for spreading those ideas to an even larger audience.

Ford, Rockefeller, and Other Foundations

The Ford Foundation remained the largest nonprofit foundation in the early 1990s, and the grants that it makes continue in the liberal tradition that brought it so much attention in the 1960s. Its support in the 1990s, while retaining the philosophy that brought it attention in the 1960s, has not been for activities that are as controversial as they once were. In 1992 it provided millions of dollars for minority fellowships, and had a $3 million program to encourage minorities to enter careers in public service. It granted $2 million to the Joint Center for Political and Economic Studies for general support on projects designed to analyze the effects of public policies on blacks in the United States. Two million was also granted to the Watts Labor Community Action Committee. (Watts is a predominantly black area in Los Angeles.) More than $2 million was given to the Social Science Research Council for graduate student fellowships. The Ford Foundation also provided millions of dollars in support for AIDS programs.

The Rockefeller Foundation also continues to support liberal causes. In 1992 it made a $2 million grant to the College Board to aid minority students in middle schools, and gave $1 million to the Lawyers Committee for Civil Rights Under Law. [13] The foundation's 1994 annual report states its commitment to programs that can help design welfare reform. [14] The foundation budgeted $9.4 million in 1994 for equal opportunity programs, $5.6 million to school reform, and $13.4 million to population sciences. The foundation's 1994 budget also included $12.2

million for global environmental programs, $11.7 million for international health programs, and $17 million for agriculture. Someone looking for a liberal bias in Rockefeller Foundation programs is likely to find it, but at the same time most of the foundation's resources are going toward activities that would be considered more philanthropic than political or ideological.

The W.K. Kellogg Foundation, in 1992 the second-largest behind Ford, has less of a social science orientation. In 1992 the foundation gave $12 million to Gallaudet University to educate deaf students, and supported many neighborhood and health programs. The Pew Charitable Trusts, the third-largest foundation in 1992, supports education, health, and environmental programs. The John D. and Catherine T. MacArthur Foundation, the fourth-largest foundation in 1992 supports health programs, cultural and community development in the Chicago area, programs for international peace, and environmental programs. Perhaps the most visible program of the MacArthur Foundation is the MacArthur Fellows Program, which provides grants to highly talented individuals in any field of endeavor.[15]

The Foundation Center's *Foundation Directory* lists more than 5,000 independent grant-making foundations, each one different from the others, so one cannot really generalize about the programs funded by foundations. The review of a few of the largest shows how different foundations are in their activities, and also shows that when looking at the big picture, the promotion of ideas through the funding of social sciences and public policy grants is not the major activity of most foundations. It is worth emphasizing that when considering the ideas promoted by foundation grants, one is considering but a small part of what most nonprofit foundations do. This study is looking at the results of a small fraction of foundation activity, but still an activity that has a substantial impact on the development of ideas and the conduct of public policy. Even if the topic covers a small part of total foundation activities, it still covers an important activity of foundations. For that reason, it is worthwhile to look at biases in foundation grants and the relationship to ideas that foundations promote.

Institutions and Bias in Foundation Programs

The sources of potential bias in foundation funding lie in the lack of accountability that characterizes foundations. Because they operate from endowment income, they do not need to respond to the preferences of their donors, and because they do not sell their output, they are not accountable for the value of their output. Foundation trustees nominally serve the public, but they are not elected officials and are not accountable to the public. Rather, trustees are appointed according to the wishes of the initial donors, and in many cases by the donors themselves, and often boards of trustees are self-perpetuating. When a vacancy occurs, the remaining board members appoint a new member.

Foundation trustees are by no means a representative cross-section of the general public. Trustees would be expected to be educated and informed, and would be expected to have relevant experience so that they would be in a position to make wise use of foundation resources. Trustees would already have to have risen to positions of power and influence in order to be considered candidates for a position. This means that potential candidates for foundation trusteeships would be drawn from a relatively small group of elite individuals within a society. In short, foundation trustees will tend to be upper-class people with upper-class values.[16] In addition, because people who serve in such positions tend to know others of their status, and because trustees would undoubtedly prefer to admit into their group someone they already know and feel they can work with, there tends to be a network of people who are members of boards of trustees. Foundations share some of the same trustees, and share trustees with those organizations that receive foundation grants.[17]

In short, for institutional reasons, foundations tend to be run by an elite group of individuals who have very little accountability for their actions. Undoubtedly they are motivated to use foundation money for the social good, but their visions of the social good may be at odds with those of the original donors, and of the public at large.

Ideological Influences on Donors and Trustees

Foundation trustees are likely to be educated and successful, but they are not even an unbiased cross-section of educated and successful individuals. Consider the donors who created the wealth that found its way into foundation endowments. Those individuals tend to be hard-working entrepreneurs who in their working years have been able to devote little time to giving thought and energy to philanthropy. Making a fortune tends to be a full-time job. Trustees are more likely to be those with inherited wealth and those who have risen to power within the ranks of government or academia. One major difference between the ideological influences of donors and trustees results from the way in which they have come to success and power.

Even going back to Andrew Carnegie and John D. Rockefeller, men who did devote some of their personal energies to philanthropy, one can see that their values differed considerably from the traditional view of charitable activity. Carnegie's and Rockefeller's own philanthropic activities revolved around creating a better environment within which every person has a greater opportunity for success and fulfillment, rather than giving assistance directly to the needy. Rockefeller's health initiatives were intended to allow people to succeed on their own merits, unimpeded by health problems, and Carnegie's prominent library donations required of beneficiaries that they take the initiative to stock, maintain, and operate the libraries that he built. Those men wanted to create an environment within which people could help themselves, rather than directly providing assistance to the most needy.

If Andrew Carnegie and John D. Rockefeller provide examples of donors who valued hard work and private initiative, Russell Sage and Henry Ford provide even better examples. Sage's reputation as a great miser has already been described, and his foundation was created by his widow despite his own stingy views. Henry Ford believed that he could best serve the interests of the general population not by philanthropic activity, but rather by reinvesting his profits in order to provide good jobs and a decent income for his employees. While the stories of these high-profile donors are interesting, the attitudes and circumstances surrounding these wealthy donors must be typical, for wealth is made by working hard, taking advantage of opportunities when they arise, and not squandering the resources that one has available. Those who have made their fortunes in the market economy understand how markets work and see that to succeed, they had to provide people with products that they wanted on terms that the buyers believed were reasonable. They tend to believe in the virtues of the system within which they were able to prosper, and tend to believe that others, given the opportunity, can make comfortable livings within that system.

Those born into wealth do not share the experience of amassing it, and rather than beginning with hard work and little opportunity, start their lives with substantial advantages. While it is true that the children of those who made fortunes often faced demanding parents with high expectations, those children were also secure in the fact that they would inherit wealth, and they were expected to work hard, go to good schools, and perform well enough to uphold the family name. Their main concerns will be different in many ways from those of most people who know that they alone will be responsible for providing themselves with a comfortable standard of living.

Individuals who rise in academia and in government will also have ideas different from entrepreneurs. Entrepreneurs must be practical in order to survive, whereas in academia those with new and interesting ideas are rewarded, even when those ideas tend to be impractical or utopian. Furthermore, there is a tendency for academics to be inclined to think that societies can be designed to work better, and there tends to be a bias toward believing that centralized planning can help create a more desirable society. This tendency comes in part because if a society is more centrally controlled, those in academics tend to be the ones who will do the controlling. And if academics have such biases, they are likely to be even stronger among the elites in government, because those in government will be the ones to gain even more power. People choose careers in government because they believe in the efficacy of governmental institutions. Thus, entrepreneurs will tend to believe more in a laissez faire system with decentralized private markets, whereas academics and government officials will be biased toward the advantages of increased government oversight.

Biases of Academicians

Everybody has their own views of what would create a more desirable society and enhance the well-being of mankind. People's biases will be at least partly a function of their vocations, for two reasons. First, there will be self-selection. People choose their occupations partly for the life-style that it might provide them, but partly because they have a desire to practice in those occupations. Doctors want to help people live healthy lives (in addition to making money), and construction workers get satisfaction from creating new buildings (in addition to making money). Those in higher education believe that there is a social benefit to creating a more educated society. A second reason for bias as a function of vocation is that once in a vocation people more directly link their own self-interests with the public interest. Social scientists in academia develop an understanding about the way that a society works and grows, and having theories to explain what makes better societies, come to believe that they are in a position to improve conditions, if only they are given the opportunity. From a social scientist's viewpoint, who would know more about how to design an effective society than a social scientist?

At the beginning of the twentieth century, for example, academic economists had relatively little influence on public policy, although their influence was growing as they advocated antitrust laws and new forms of taxation. The establishment of the National Bureau of Economic Research, described in chapter 3, was done in order to provide better data so that government could more effectively implement public policy to improve the performance of the economy. Following World War II the President's Council of Economic Advisors was created to further give economic advice. Indeed, academic economists and other social scientists provide a pool of intellectual resources that the government routinely taps to find policy makers. If academics can create ideas showing how intelligent people can more effectively control the development of the economy, or of other parts of the society for the public good, academics are likely to be the people who are placed in charge of those activities. Even those who remain in academiaget more power and prestige because they develop the policy ideas that chart the course of society.

When these academics, largely sheltered from the realities of the market system by a tenure system, and in many cases working at state universities as government employees, advocate more government control of the economy, of businesses, and of private property rights, they are advocating taking power away from those who make their living in the private sector and transferring it to those in the government and nonprofit sectors. Some of the loss of power of those in the private sector is transferred to academics. Thus, from the perspective of self-interest, there is a natural bias in academics to favor more government control. This is bolstered by the fact that with most college faculty employed at state universities, their pay comes from the government. Furthermore, it is natural for individuals to value their own contributions to society highly, leading to the attitude that more power should be transferred from those who are engaged in more mundane commerce toward those who are in more lofty pursuit of ideas.

While those who have made their own wealth may have had modest educations themselves, their children are likely to have had the advantages of going to the best schools, and being indoctrinated with the ideas of academia. They are less likely to see what goes into creating wealth, because they have been born into it, and will be more likely to understand that if wealth were spread around, more people could enjoy the benefits of wealth that they enjoy. Thus, those with inherited wealth are more likely to share the ideological biases of academics than of the entrepreneurs that made the wealth they inherited. But many entrepreneurs, perhaps because of their lack of extensive formal education, are unlikely to be in a good position to eloquently articulate the ideas they may hold. As Barry Karl and Stanley Katz note, "American philanthropists, unlike monarchs and Popes, know they are an intellectually dependent class." [18] They often feel a responsibility to use their resources for the benefit of others, and often like the idea of funding educational programs because they are helping those who are motivated to help themselves. Yet academics, like the heirs of entrepreneurs, tend to have less appreciation for wealth-creating activities than for wealth-redistributing activities. [19]

If there are biases in academics, there are even more biases in government. The same self-selection argument applies. Those who go into government work are more likely to believe in the efficacy of government. People who choose careers in government will tend to be those who think that government can make a positive difference, and once employed in the public sector, government employees would like to think that they are doing meaningful work that contributes toward making a better society. The self-interest argument made above for academics also applies to government employees. Power transferred from the private sector to the public sector is power transferred to those who work in the public sector. Thus, many of the individuals who make up the pool of applicants for foundation trusteeships—those with inherited wealth, academicians, and public sector leaders—will tend to have biases in favor of government control rather than laissez-faire capitalism. If they tend to be more biased toward government intervention than the general public, they will be even more biased toward government intervention than those who made the fortunes that created the foundations, and who tend to view government intervention as an impediment.

Biases and Trends

By looking at the actual funding activities of foundations, one can see that there have been biases, and that foundations have leaned toward the liberal end of the liberal-conservative political spectrum. By looking at the institutional environment within which foundations exist, one can understand in theory why such biases would exist. This liberal bias has been criticized by conservatives, but also has been observed and been approvingly reported on by liberals.[20] Conservatives argue that the liberal bias of foundations tends to undermine the capitalist system that produced the wealth that endowed those foundations, whereas liberals look on foundation activities as partially offsetting the harsher realities of a market system. The point here is not to pass judgment, but rather to note the bias.

While the liberal bias in foundation programs is apparent, current trends in foundation programs are less easy to detect. Throughout the twentieth century there has been a trend toward the funding of more liberal programs for several reasons. First, foundations have turned more toward the funding of social science and public policy programs, rather than more value-free programs in health, agriculture, and basic education. Second, the crises of the century, ranging from economic depression in the 1930s, to a world war in the 1940s, to a prolonged cold war from the 1950s through the 1980s, have pushed foundation trustees to use foundation resources to try to solve some of these problems. Additional problems of poverty and race relations have drawn additional funding. Third, the increasingly liberal turn of academics in the twentieth century has influenced foundations. Foundation programs have not been immune to the intellectual trends of the century, which would be expected because of the close relationship between foundations and institutions of higher education. The record is clear that the trend over the twentieth century has been for foundation funding to move more toward the liberal end of the liberal-conservative political continuum.

What is less clear is whether that trend will continue into the twenty-first century. Perhaps the movement toward liberalism has already stopped. Beginning in the 1970s there has been an increasing number of organizations created that promote a more conservative viewpoint. The most visible of these organizations are think tanks rather than foundations. Think tanks operate from ongoing sources of funds rather than endowments, but much of the funding for think tanks comes from foundation grants. Furthermore, these new conservative think tanks are funded by new conservative foundations. The Pew Memorial Trust, founded in 1948 and the fifth largest foundation in the early 1990s, funds conservative causes such as the Freedom Foundation, Americans for the Competitive Enterprise System, and the Christian Anti-Communism Crusade.[21] Other foundations that lean toward conservative causes are the Brown Foundation, founded in 1951 and the Smith Richardson Foundation, founded in 1935. More recent foundations, such as the Adolph Coors Foundation, established in 1975, and the Scaife Foundation, established in 1959, have a much more conservative orientation than the older foundations that have been discussed through most of this volume. Thus, there may be an ideological change underway in the orientation of foundations.

One must be cautious when trying to extrapolate the types of programs that will be funded by newer foundations because they will be more under the influence of their original donors. Perhaps over time, as their boards of trustees evolve, they will become more liberal in their biases, for the reasons given earlier in the chapter. There is another reason to think that foundation biases may not continue to be so liberal in the future, however. There is a shift in the dominant ideology at the end of the twentieth century toward more laissez faire ideas, and if foundation trustees are influenced by the trends of academic opinion, and even by popular opinion, foundation programs might lose some of their liberal orientation.

At the beginning of the twentieth century, ideas of socialism were prominent throughout the world, while at the end of the twentieth century the collapse of the economies that tried socialist experiments has made government planning appear less attractive. Karl Marx's *Capital* was an influential treatise at the turn of the century.[22] John Maynard Keynes's book, *The General Theory of Employment, Interest, and Money,* published in 1936, was also very influential and kept alive the Progressive Era idea that increased government control over the economy could yield better economic performance. The idea was continued in works such as Abba Lerner's 1944 book, *The Economics of Control.*[23] As the twentieth century progressed, ideas on the merits of central planning began to give way to a new set of ideas promoting the virtues of the old system of laissez-faire capitalism. Friedrich Hayek's book, *The Road to Serfdom,* published in the same year as Lerner's *The Economics of Control,* argued that central planning would inevitably lead to a lower standard of living, and actively promoted the virtues of laissez faire.[24] Milton Friedman's 1962 book, *Capitalism and Freedom,* and his 1980 book, *Free to Choose,* co-authored with his wife Rose, also have had a substantial impact on the ideas of the late twentieth century.[25]

One might be premature in saying that the intellectual winds have shifted, but it appears that in the later twentieth century the ideas of Hayek and Friedman have begun to displace those of Marx and Keynes. If so, the trend throughout most of the twentieth century toward increasingly liberal programs supported by foundations might stop, or even reverse itself in the twenty-first century. One can detect the clear bias throughout most of the century toward a liberal agenda, and one can detect a clear trend throughout most of the century toward foundation funding for liberal programs. Yet developments in the last half of the twentieth century, and especially since 1970, make it appear that the programs funded by foundations are not becoming more liberal, and indeed may be becoming more conservative.

Notes

1. See Barry D. Karl and Stanley N. Katz, "The American Private Philanthropic Foundation and the Public Sphere: 1890-1930," *Minerva* 19, No. 2 (Summer 1981), pp. 236-270, for a discussion of this evolution.
2. Stephen Skowronek, *Building a New American State: The Expansion of National Administrative Capabilities, 1877-1920* (New York: Cambridge University Press, 1982).
3. Guy Alchon, *The Invisible Hand of Planning: Capitalism, Social Science, and the State in the 1920s* (Princeton, NJ: Princeton University Press, 1985).
4. See Charles A. Beard and William Beard, *The American Leviathan: The Republic in the Machine Age.* New York: Macmillan, 1930) for a discussion of the newfound capabilities of a scientifically managed state. The Beards view the American Leviathan very approvingly.
5. Judith Sealander, *Private Wealth and Public Life: Foundation Philanthropy and the Reshaping of American Social Policy from the Progressive Era to the New Deal* (Baltimore, MD: Johns Hopkins University Press, 1997), argues that the influence of Carnegie's philanthropies on public policy has been overestimated by most analysts. This may be true if his foundations supported programs that were reflections of current thinking rather than foundation-initiated ideas.
6. John Maynard Keynes, *The General Theory of Employment, Interest, and Money* (New York: Harcourt, Brace & Company, 1936).
7. Karl and Katz, "The American Private Philanthropic Foundation," cited earlier, argue that the foundation system seemed to break down during the Vietnam war.
8. See Joseph G. Peschek, *Policy-Planning Organizations: Elite Agendas and America's Rightward Turn* (Philadelphia, PA: Temple University Press, 1987) for a discussion of conservative think tanks.

9. Ellen Condliffe Lagemann, *The Politics of Knowledge: The Carnegie Corporation, Philanthropy, and Public Policy* (Middletown, CT: Wesleyan University Press, 1989), p. 216.

10. Horace Coon, *Money to Burn: What the Great American Philanthropic Foundations Do with Their Money* (London: Longmans, Green and Co., 1938), ch. 5.

11. These quotations are from materials mailed to me at the economics department at Florida State University in 1996.

12. This list of programs is from *The Foundation Directory, 1994 Edition* (New York: The Foundation Center, 1994).

13. *The Foundation Directory, 1994 Edition.*

14. The Rockefeller Foundation, *1994 Annual Report* (New York: Rockefeller Foundation, 1995).

15. Information on these foundations is from *The Foundation Directory, 1994 Edition.*

16. Thomas R. Dye, *Who's Running America? The Conservative Years,* 4th ed. (Englewood Cliffs, NJ: Prentice-Hall, 1986) makes these points and backs them up with a study of those in prestigious positions.

17. Mary Anna Culleton Colwell, "The Foundation Connection: Links Among Foundations and Recipient Organizations," in Robert Arnove, ed., *Philanthropy and Cultural Imperialism* (Boston: G.K. Hall, 1980), and by the same author, *Private Foundations and Public Policy: The Political Role of Philanthropy* (New York: Garland Publishing, Inc., 1993).

18. Karl and Katz, "Foundations and Ruling Class Elites," cited earlier, p. 31.

19. One of the suggestions from a conference on educating foundation managers was that universities could develop a curriculum in foundation management. The conference proceedings are published in Michael O'Neill and Dennis R. Young, eds., *Educating Managers of Nonprofit Organizations* (New York: Praeger, 1988). This would create an even closer tie between foundations and academics. Of fourteen contributors to the volume, only two had never held an academic appointment, and ten of the fourteen had academic appointments at the time the conference volume was written. This is not surprising because academic institutions reward publication, but because ideas about foundations are developed and disseminated in publications such as this, it further illustrates the links between foundations and academic institutions.

20. Lagemann, *The Politics of Knowledge.*

21. Ben Whitaker, *The Foundations: An Anatomy of Philanthropy and Society* (London: Eyre Methuen, 1974) p. 153.

22. Karl Marx, *Capital* (New York: Modern Library, 1906; originally published in 1867).

23. Abba Lerner, *The Economics of Control* (New York: Macmillan, 1944).

24. Friedrich A. Hayek, *The Road to Serfdom* (Chicago: University of Chicago Press, 1944).

25. Milton Friedman, *Capitalism and Freedom* (Chicago: University of Chicago Press, 1962), and Milton and Rose Friedman, *Free to Choose* (New York: Harcourt Brace Jovanovich, 1980).

6

Donor Intent

Reflecting on the history of America's most prominent foundations, it is apparent that the actual activities of those foundations have often been at odds with the intentions of the donors who created the foundations. Donors earned their fortunes in a market system they firmly believed in, yet after their deaths, their money went toward the promotion of ideas to undermine that system. Even when foundation activities did not have strong ideological content, they often were at odds with the intentions of their donors. The contrast between the philanthropic activities of Carnegie and Rockefeller, the men and the foundations, is striking, and it is even more certain that Henry Ford would have had strong objections to the activities of the foundation that bore his name. In these three cases, however, the foundations were given broad and general mandates, and it would be easy to argue that the foundations have pursued the mandates of their donors, at least in the eyes of the foundations' trustees and managers. Other foundations have more specific mandates, but these more specific mandates raise additional questions. Conditions change, and donors are not in a good position to forecast the best application of their philanthropy decades into the future. How closely should foundation activities adhere to the originally stated intentions of their donors?

The concept of donor intent for nonprofit foundations is a slippery one for several reasons. First, donors do not all have the same intentions. Many observers conjectured that Rockefeller established his foundation in an attempt to rehabilitate his reputation with the general public, and perhaps to win some sympathy with the U.S. Congress in their

135

dealings with Standard Oil. The Ford Foundation was established, at least in part, to avoid the payment of income taxes, and to enable the Ford family to maintain control of the Ford Motor Company. The Fords are not alone in responding to the tax laws; most contributions to non-profit foundations today are influenced to some degree by tax laws. And Rockefeller was not alone in wanting to enhance his reputation through charitable activities. While many donors wish to remain anonymous, or maintain low profiles, others make an active attempt to link their reputations with the charitable causes they support. But one would be reluctant to evaluate the success of foundations based on their ability to avoid tax payments for donors, or to enhance the donors' reputations. Surely the donors had secondary motivations, and hoped that the expenditures from their foundations would be put to some good purpose. So that purpose, even if secondary, would be the donor's intent with respect to the dispensation of the funds.

Once one realizes that putting the money to good purposes can be but one of many reasons for establishing or contributing to a foundation, one sees the potential importance of the accountability issues that face foundations. If what the money is spent on is only one of many purposes of giving the money to begin with, donors will have even less incentive to see that the money is spent as they intended. A donor who provides money for a university building to be named for him might care mostly that his name lives on through the building that is a monument to him, and may have little interest in whether the space is efficiently used, or even needed. Whether the building is cost-effective is of secondary importance to the donor, and this will be even more true if some public money is added to the donor's contribution. The contribution may have been made only because the money would have been eaten up in taxes anyway, and the donation allows the donor to receive some recognition.

When tax laws influence donations, they have the effect of creating an impediment to having the money spent in a manner consistent with the wishes of the donors, because donors have little incentive to monitor the expenditures. A donor who foregoes paying taxes in order to make a donation will be less concerned about how the funds are spent than the donor who foregoes building a vacation home, or passing money on to her heirs.

A second problem with the concept of donor intent is that often the stated intentions of donors are quite vague. The stated goal of the

Rockefeller Foundation is "to promote the well-being of mankind throughout the world." What types of activities would not apply to this lofty but elusive goal? Henry Ford believed that the best way he could use his money to help those less fortunate than he was to invest it, in order to create good jobs that would raise the standard of living. Despite his endowing the Ford Foundation, Henry Ford himself surely believed that his money invested in the Ford Motor Company did more to promote the well-being of mankind than the wealth he left to the Ford Foundation. When donors do not clearly articulate their intentions, there is always a question regarding how closely a foundation's activities reflect the intentions of its creators.

Alan Pifer, who was president of the Carnegie Corporation when Congress was considering sweeping changes in the tax laws affecting foundations in 1969, noted,

> Mr. Carnegie believed that Carnegie Corporation would be best administered over the long run if he did not bind the trustees too closely by the terms of his gifts. He selected the most able men of his day to constitute the original board of trustees and placed in their hand sole power to select their successors, on the assumption that able, public-spirited men would select equally good men to succeed them. No evidence has ever been adduced to indicate that the public interest might have been better served by some other system of governance than this self-perpetuating board. The successive members of it, all of whom have served without compensation, have given their time generously and have brought to the management of the foundation a wide range of experience and talent. In the 58 years of the foundation's history there has not been a single instance of any part of its income incurring to the private benefit of any member of the Carnegie family, any trustee, any employee or any other individual except for services rendered. No consideration has ever existed in the foundation's affairs except furtherance of the greatest possible benefit to the public.[1]

There is little reason to question the intentions of Carnegie when he established his foundation, but it is interesting to note his willingness to let those who were left in charge of the foundation determine its direction. Chapter 8 considers the accountability of nonprofit foundations in more detail, but it is apparent that in some cases, like the prominent Rockefeller and Carnegie foundations, the donors intended to leave the trustees of the foundations largely unaccountable. In cases like this donor intent must be judged not on whether the specific activities of the foundation are in line with the donor's preferences, but rather on whether the results produced by the foundation enhance the well-being of mankind. Whatever the intentions of the donor, the lack of accountability is sure to have a major effect on the correspondence between donor intent and foundation activities.

The vague intentions of some donors notwithstanding, when accounting firm Arthur Andersen & Co. described foundations, it noted, "A private foundation is a charitable organization that generally has been established by an individual donor for the purpose of controlling, to the fullest extent possible, the use of his charitable dollars." [2] Thus, the view of an accounting firm that has foundation giving as part of its business is that donor intent is an important reason why individuals establish, or contribute to, foundations rather than other charitable organizations. This view notwithstanding, a major question regarding foundation policy is the issue of donor intent. It plays a role in government policy toward foundations, but it lies at the heart of the policies that foundations themselves follow.

Foundations with Clearly Articulated Donor Intent

When foundations have a vague statement of donor intent to guide them, the lack of accountability of foundation trustees and officers can lead foundations in directions that may not be in the public interest. Foundations with more clearly articulated statements of donor intent may run into more serious problems. Sometimes the problems arise because there is a question as to whether the initial intent of the donor was really in the public interest. At other times problems can arise when changes occur that were unanticipated by the donor, removing the problem that the donor wanted to help solve from the public interest. In other cases, the conception of the public interest might change over time. Some examples can help illustrate.

In the first half of the nineteenth century, St. Louis resident Bryan Mullanphy saw a large number of homesteaders, traveling in covered wagons, become stranded in Missouri. They were passing through St. Louis to settle in the West, but found themselves without sufficient resources either to continue their journeys or to return to their former homes. Concerned about their plight, Mullanphy established a fund in 1850 to help worthy travelers to continue on to find new homes. Mullanphy perceived a genuine need and left an endowment to deal with it, but since Mullanphy's bequest, there have been increasingly fewer homesteaders passing through St. Louis in covered wagons. The endowment continued to grow, and might have been profitably used to help modern automobile travelers with problems in St. Louis,[3] but once the needs for which the endowment was originally established did not appear so pressing, a number of people challenged Mullanphy's will, and about three-quarters of the endowment was eaten up in legal expenses to try to preserve Mullanphy's original intent. In the end, the courts decided that the remaining funds could be spent to help all kinds of travelers in St. Louis, but the result of Mullanphy's very specific recorded intentions was that most of the money went to lawyers rather than travelers.

Mullanphy's bequest was not unique in running into problems because of a closely specified purpose for which the money was to be used. Early in the twentieth century, a New Jersey woman wanted to leave a bequest to fund book purchases for a church library, and stated in the will that the books were to be purchased for the library in the belltower of a specific church. Her bequest was in the form of stock in the New Jersey Zinc Company, which at the time of her death paid a modest dividend out of which purchases were to be made. Activities associated with the onset of World War I greatly increased the profitability of the New Jersey Zinc Company, and in 1915 the company increased the dividend by 50 percent and paid a 50 percent stock dividend. In 1916 there was another stock dividend of 250 percent, along with a sizable increase in other dividends. Within a year the belltower library was so full of books that no more books could be added. The courts of New Jersey preserved the stated intent of the donor, however, and ruled that books purchased from the endowment had to be placed in the tower library, and that the funds could not be spent for any other purpose, including building a new library.

In 1806 "The Sailors' Snug Harbor" was incorporated based on a bequest from Captain Robert Richard Randall. Captain Randall left the Sailors' Snug Harbor a sizable sum of money and a large tract of land on Manhattan, where he intended that a home for "aged, decrepit, and worn out sailors" would be built, and financed through his endowment. The trustees decided that the Manhattan land left by Captain Randall was too valuable to build a home on, so saved the Manhattan property and in 1831 purchased a tract of 100 acres on Staten Island, on which the home was built and opened in 1832. Income from renting the Manhattan property has since provided a substantial sum of money for the Sailors' Snug Harbor, much of which has been eaten up in administrative expenses. Captain Randall endowed his organization with the most honorable of intentions, but without any accountability his estate has been administered inefficiently, and he certainly did not foresee the widespread availability of pensions, the establishment of Social Security, and the availability of Medicare and Medicaid that today largely fill the need Captain Randall wanted to provide for nearly 200 years ago.

A similar case is that of the 1831 endowment by Stephen Girard for an orphanage in Philadelphia, called Girard College. Girard wanted to endow an orphanage to care for 300 fatherless white legitimate boys between the ages of six and ten who are able to produce birth certificates and the marriage certificates of their parents in order to prove their eligibility. There they would be housed until reaching the age of between fourteen and eighteen. Girard gave detailed instructions on how the orphanage buildings were to be constructed, including the dimensions of the rooms. Girard further specified that the property be surrounded by a ten-foot wall with two gates.

The physical specifications of the orphanage apparently caused some problems for the architects who were charged with following Girard's directions yet trying to make the buildings habitable. But the physical specifications were not as controversial as other provisions that Girard had made. He further specified that "no Ecclesiastic, Missionary, or minister of any sect whatsoever shall ever hold or exercise any station or duty whatever in said College; nor shall any such person ever be admitted for any purpose, or as a visitor, within the premises of said College... I desire to keep the tender minds of the orphans free from the excitement clashing doctrines and sectarian controversy are so apt to produce." [4] Girard's provisions brought immediate lawsuits from his heirs who attempted to invalidate the entire will based on these provisions. The will was upheld, however.

Subsequently a huge amount of coal was discovered on some of the land that Girard left to help finance the orphanage, providing it with substantial resources to help it continue its mission. But at the end of the twentieth century one can see that Girard's mission is not entirely in line with the times. With much better health care than existed in 1821, far fewer boys are being orphaned, and those that are can often find homes with relatives. Even foster care is preferred to orphanage care. Because children born to single parents are ruled out by Girard's will, and because the orphans must be white, the need perceived by Girard has almost vanished.

As more time passes, the very specific intentions of donors are likely to become even less relevant. The issue has been recognized for centuries. A study done by a Royal Commission of the British Parliament in 1818 turned up a large number of endowments for purposes that, even then, appeared questionable. In 1727 a certain Dr. Woodward established a fund to endow a permanent lectureship at Cambridge for the purpose of teaching his theory of the natural history of the Earth, and to defend it against rival theories by a Dr. Camerarus. The report noted that by 1818 both theories had been discredited. A trust was established to pay ransom for Englishmen captured by Barbary pirates, and another to create a university position at Cambridge for the purpose of teaching that coal gas causes malaria.

In the United States, a Boston hospital maintained a fund to finance wooden legs for Civil War veterans well beyond the end of World War I. Another fund was established to relieve the suffering of people with yellow fever so that they would not need be hospitalized. A former president of the Pennsylvania Railroad endowed a fund in order to aid the daughters of men who were killed while working for the railroad. The railroad president did not foresee that improved railroad safety would severely limit the usefulness of this fund. These are all cases of donors with good intentions who had hoped to direct their estates into activities that they saw as useful. In each case, however, the march of time reduced the usefulness of the money that they had hoped would serve the public interest.

More recently, the Marin Community Foundation was established in 1987. The foundation's origins are in what was originally known as the Buck Trust, created when Beryl Buck, an elderly widow, died in 1973. Mrs. Buck lived in Marin County, California, which is across the Golden Gate Bridge from San Francisco, and is one of the wealthiest areas in the United States. Her will stipulated that the benefits of her foundation be limited to her home county. The will was challenged using the argument that she did not understand the extent of her fortune, and that the money should be used for the benefit of the entire San Francisco Bay area; however, the courts upheld the will limiting the benefits to Marin County, and $447 million was transferred from the Buck Trust to create the Marin Community Foundation.[5]

The problems associated with trying to balance the concept of donor intent with the goal of promoting the public interest has been long recognized, and more than a century ago Amos Warner argued against

allowing complete discretion to foundation trustees because foundations tended to be too injudiciously administered by the "dead hand."[6]
Warner gives detailed accounts of monasteries established in Britain
that used the incomes from their endowments to try to battle poverty,
but under lax management and little accountability—the same types of
problems that are being discussed with regard to foundations today. A
major difference in the twentieth century is that earlier foundations were
used almost entirely to aid the poor, making it relatively easy to evaluate the success of a foundation in accomplishing its stated goals, while
contemporary foundations see a much broader mission that makes it
harder to evaluate their performance.

The problems of accountability in the operation of foundations are
serious when donors leave vague or overly general directions regarding
the disbursement of foundation funds. Yet, as this section illustrates, a
new set of problems arises when donors are very specific about their
intent. The problem here is that it is very difficult for people to foresee
how their money might be spent for the public interest decades or even
centuries in advance.

Donor Intent and Family Trustees

One way to keep foundations truer to the intentions of the donors is
to install a self-perpetuating board of trustees that draws heavily on
members of the donor's family. That way, the donor can have some
assurance that his family's intentions, if not his own, will be personally
represented in his foundation's activities. While this might further the
principle of donor intent, not everyone takes the view that donors should
have such influence over their foundations, calling into question the
legitimacy of the whole concept of donor intent. For example, in 1973
the Danforth Foundation made substantial grants of $60 million to Wash-
ington University and $20 million to St. Louis University. At the time,
William H. Danforth was the chairman of the board of trustees of the
Danforth Foundation and also the chancellor of Washington University. Also, the Danforth Foundation board of trustees was dominated by
members of the Danforth family. Critics of the grants did not take issue
with the merits of the grants, but did argue that the grants represented
an arbitrary exercise of Danforth family interests. If the money originally came from the Danforth family, why should the family not be
able to determine how the foundation's money is allocated? Yet the

foundation's president and four foundation staff members resigned because of these grants.

Several reports, including one completed in 1965 by the Treasury Department, have recommended that family control over foundations be lessened or eliminated. The Treasury proposal suggested that twenty-five years after a foundation is established, its trustees be made up entirely of individuals who have no connection with the original donor. Clearly, this would be a way of lessening the effect of donor intent on foundation activities, so it is obvious that not everyone believes that foundation expenditures should remain true to the intentions of the donor.

The problem of family control, if it is a problem, will gradually take care of itself, because as time goes on, even direct descendants of the donors will have a smaller and smaller connection to them. Why would laws be needed to take care of what nature will eventually take care of anyway? One line of reasoning is that if heirs remain in control of the foundation, the foundation in effect serves as a vehicle for allowing the donor to pass wealth on tax free to the control of the heirs. But this effect is mitigated by the fact that there are restrictions on the ways in which foundations can use their resources. If the laws on self-dealing, limited stock holdings, and so forth are followed, then the foundation should be as committed to public purposes as other foundations whose trustees have no connection to the original donor.

Indeed, foundations whose trustees are descendants of the original donor may even be more committed to using the foundation's resources effectively because of their relationship with the donor. Furthermore, the heirs of the donor are likely to be wealthy in their own right, and serving as foundation trustees might be good training for them as they consider how they might want to use their own wealth. And as long as the foundation's resources are used for public purposes, it seems reasonable to allow the family that established the foundation to have a substantial say in which public purposes are funded. Nevertheless, this is an area in which there are strong differences of opinion.

Donor Intent and the Rockefeller Foundation

In the opening section of this chapter the Rockefeller Foundation was cited as an example of one with a vague intent. The stated goal of the Rockefeller Foundation is "to promote the well-being of mankind throughout the world," which conveys very little about the way in which

John D. Rockefeller intended the money he contributed to his foundation to be spent. This does not mean that Rockefeller had no ideas on the subject, however. Indeed, by Rockefeller's actions prior to his death, there is clear evidence regarding the types of activities that he believed would promote the well-being of mankind. Prior to the establishment of the foundation, Rockefeller contributed substantially to fund medical research, and donated money to a number of medical specific causes, including funding programs to help eradicate hookworm, malaria, and yellow fever. Rockefeller also contributed money to educational institutions, including a substantial amount to the University of Chicago. Rockefeller liked to fund programs that showed clear promise that if money were spent on them, results could be achieved.

His financing of the fight against hookworm in the United States is a case in point.[8] Rockefeller gathered a small group of leaders in the medical profession to meet with him to suggest ways in which his money might be used in a beneficial way. Rather than asking in a general way how his money might be used, he asked specific questions. He asked them if there was some malady that affected a large number of people for which there was a cure that would be completely effective. He was not interested in general issues regarding public health, but rather wanted to provide specific treatment that would be effective, and that would provide clearly visible results through large-scale demonstration projects. His consultants advised him that hookworm fit his description. His money could be used to eradicate the disease, the results would be tangible and visible, and the expenditures could be accounted for to assure that no money would be wasted. Rockefeller agreed.

The Rockefeller Sanitary Commission was established with a professor from the University of Tennessee at its helm. The commission set up demonstration projects and convinced Southern states that there was a problem, and that it could be solved. More than half a million cases of hookworm were treated with Rockefeller's money before governments picked up the project in the United States and throughout the world. Rockefeller felt the satisfaction of success, and his hookworm project provided a model for his future philanthropic activities. The hookworm project was undertaken from 1910 to 1914, so began prior to the establishment of the Rockefeller Foundation, and Rockefeller intended for the foundation to pursue similar projects. His battle against hookworm provided a model for the foundation's funding of programs to fight malaria and yellow fever.

Rockefeller's own philanthropic activities showed that he was interested in financing activities that attacked well-defined problems, and problems that showed promise of being solved if money were spent on them. He liked projects that could show people how they could help themselves, and he liked projects that would have clear and visible benefits to show as results. Perhaps he liked the visibility of the beneficial results because that would further enhance his own public image, but just as likely he preferred such projects because it was easy for him to see that others were not squandering his money, but rather were truly putting it to good use for the benefit of mankind. Thus, the vague statement of the intent of the Rockefeller Foundation takes on a more focused vision when coupled with an analysis of Rockefeller's own charitable activities.

Donor Intent and the Carnegie Corporation

Like the Rockefeller Foundation, the Carnegie Corporation also leaves a great deal of discretion to the trustees of the foundation. To get some feel for the nature of Carnegie's intent, it is worth considering his own words describing the foundation's purpose. Carnegie established his foundation

> to promote the advancement and diffusion of knowledge and understanding among the people of the United States, by aiding technical schools, institutions of higher learning, libraries, scientific research, hero funds, useful publications, and by such other agencies and means as shall from time to time be found appropriate therefor [sic]. My desire is that the work which I have been carrying on, or similar beneficial work, shall continue during this and future generations. Conditions upon the earth inevitably change; hence, no wise man will bind Trustees forever to certain paths, causes, or institutions. I disclaim any intention of doing so. On the contrary, I give my Trustees full authority to change policy or causes hitherto aided, from time to time, when this, in their opinion, has become necessary or desirable, they shall best conform to my wishes by using their own judgment... My chief happiness as I write these lines lies in the thot [sic] that, even after I pass away, the welth [sic] that came to me to administer as a sacred trust for the good of my fellow men is to continue to benefit humanity for generations untold, under your devoted and sympathetic guidance and that of your successors, who cannot fail to be able and good men.[9]

This statement provides substantial insight into the intent of Andrew Carnegie as he endowed his foundation. Carnegie referred to his prior philanthropic activities as a model for the ways in which he wanted his money to be used, but at the same time realized that over time the most worthy causes might change. With a competent board of trustees, Carnegie believed that the foundation would be in a better position to pursue the public interest by giving the trustees substantial discretion than if they were bound closely by his instructions. While one might argue in the abstract about whether Carnegie Corporation grants were made following the intention of the donor, in practice it would be difficult to cite specific cases in which one could know that donor intent was violated, because Mr. Carnegie intended for his trustees to use their best judgment.

Nonprofit Status and Agency Cost

One reason to be concerned about donor intent is that a foundation is established by a donor's endowment with the idea that the foundation's trustees will act as an agent of the donor in order to use the money in the way the donor specifies. This might mean funding some specific cause, or as in the cases of the Carnegie and Rockefeller foundations, it might mean finding good things to do with the money to improve the human condition. Nevertheless, trustees act as agents of the donor. One potential problem with any principal-agent relationship is that the agent may not always act in the best interest of the principal. Thus, the management of a foundation may not spend the foundation's resources in a manner that carries out the intent of the donor. The most obvious potential problem is that the foundation's expenditures will go toward benefits for the foundation's employees and management, rather than for the purposes intended by the donor. The nonprofit status of foundations helps to control this potential problem because a foundation's management will not be able to (legally) appropriate the foundation's assets for private use.

To understand the nature of the potential problem in more detail, consider a customer buying a product from a for-profit firm in the private sector. The customer tenders money to the firm in exchange for the firm's product, and is in a good position to evaluate the benefits produced in exchange for the payment tendered. The customer cares only for the value she receives in exchange for the money, and except in unusual circumstances, does not care in the least what the firm does with the money paid by the customer. Given the choice of buying from one of two firms, the customer cares only about which firm provides the best product for the money. If one firm makes a 5 percent profit on the sale and the other makes 20 percent, this is not relevant to the customer, who would gladly buy from the more profitable firm if the product was a better value.

The same is not true for a nonprofit foundation. With a foundation, the product that is produced is not directly consumed by the donor, but the donor is interested in knowing that the money was used for the purpose the donor intended. Even if nonprofit organizations provide good benefits relative to their expenditures, donors are still concerned when those who run the foundations seem to be reaping substantial personal gains from the foundation's activities. For example, in the early 1990s when William Aramony, as president of the United Way of America, was accused of financing a lavish personal life-style out of the revenues of United Way, there was a public outcry that led to his being terminated from the position and ultimately convicted of wrongdoing. However, when Bill Gates became a multibillionaire through the sales of microcomputer software in the private market, there was no suggestion that he did not deserve the returns he received from creating and selling software.

In Aramony's case there was the legal issue of whether his activities might have violated the law, but the legal issue was minor when compared to the issue of the violation of public trust. Those in the nonprofit sector are held to higher standards than those in the private sector, and even if Aramony had been legally cleared of wrongdoing, the cloud in terms of a violation of public trust would have remained. In Gates's case, there have been questions about whether his business practices were legal, but this is beside the point. If business people act legally and nonfraudulently, the profits they receive from the customers are considered a fair compensation for the services they provide. Customers do not care how the money they spend for products is spent. But with regard to nonprofit organizations, those who provide the funding do care about its dispensation, and do not want those who raise the money to spend it for their own benefit.

In the third sector the ethical issues transcend the legal issues, but are not unrelated. When there is a public perception of unethical behavior, there will also be a push for legislation to try to prevent it. Indeed, there should be, because of the privileged legal status under which the nonprofit sector operates.

The agency problem that donors face in the nonprofit sector is that it is difficult to monitor the activities of foundations once the money is donated in order to be assured that the money is spent as it is intended. Large foundations with many full-time employees undertake so many activities and fund so many projects that a donor could not possibly monitor them all. And because many donations are bequests, it will be even more difficult for donors to monitor the activities of foundations if the donors are dead!

One way that foundations can go part way toward assuring donors that those who operate the foundations will not profit from the donations is to explicitly make the foundations nonproprietary. If no profits will be distributed, then donors can be at least partly assured that their money donated for public purposes will not be siphoned from the foundation for private gain.[10] Of course, the foundation's management could still receive excessively lavish perks from the foundation, as the case of William Aramony and the United Way illustrates. Thus, many foundations ask that their directors serve with little or no pay, and cover only the expenses involved in attending meetings (which still can be lavish). The point is that the nonprofit status of foundations provides a way for donors to receive some assurance that the foundation's management will not profit from the foundation's endowment. Even this does not solve the agency cost problem, however.

Agency Cost and Foundation Grants

The problem of agency cost is apparent when considered in the context of the above examples. Those examples deal with fraudulent or wasteful expenditures, so would be relatively easy to identify, if one wanted to take the time and trouble (and if those perpetrating the fraud and waste were not too skillful in covering their tracks). The agency cost problem becomes much more severe when evaluating the purposes toward which foundation grants are applied, because there often is no clear-cut standard that can be used to evaluate how the money should best be spent. Given the very general statements of donor intent left by Rockefeller and Carnegie, what would be an example of a type of foundation grant that was not in accordance with the intentions of the donors? Yet if the possibilities that foundations might waste money, or might fraudulently use foundation resources, are admitted, it also must be admitted that foundations might expend money in ways that violate the intentions of the donors. The whole idea of donor intent becomes very slippery when one realizes that unless the donor's intentions are stated very specifically, one can never cite specific examples to show how they are violated.

The Duke Endowment provides an interesting case study, because Buck Duke left specific instructions both on how the endowment should be invested and on how the income from the endowment should be distributed. In 1962 the trustees of the Duke Endowment went to court to try to invalidate some of the provisions regarding the way in which the endowment should be invested, but ultimately lost the case.[11] Thus, donor intent had to be preserved in this case, because it was so specifically stated. The terms of Duke's bequest also specified that 32 percent of the income was to go to hospitals, and 10 percent to Methodist churches. This still provides considerable latitude to the trustees, and the reader can be sure that if the trustees went to court to overturn one of the provisions clearly intended by the donor, they would not hesitate to exercise their discretion in areas that were less closely specified by the bequest.

The concept of donor intent thus comes into question, not because there is a debate over whether it is a good idea to recognize the intentions of the donor then, but because of the agency cost problems that make it questionable as to whether it is even feasible to ask foundation trustees to remain true to the intentions of the donor. The trustees do not necessarily have the same interests as the donor, and the institutional structure of foundation governance is such that whenever any ambiguities arise, the intentions of the trustees will dominate the intentions of the donors.

Donor Intent and the Production of Ideas

The discussion of donor intent has to this point been very general, but has led to the conclusion that except when the intentions of the donor are stated very specifically, the concept of donor intent will be very difficult to apply. This study is interested mostly in the ideas that are developed and promoted with foundation grants, rather than foundation activities in general, and when the more narrow subject of donor intent as applied to the ideas promoted by foundations is considered, it is apparent that the concept of donor intent is even less relevant. When foundations finance studies, conferences, activities at think tanks, and research in general, one can have little idea ahead of time what ideas will be produced in the process. These activities fall under the general category of the production of knowledge, and if one knew ahead of time what the product would be, there would be little reason to fund the projects. However, trustees do have the power to direct the results of the studies and conferences they fund to a degree, because they choose the people who participate in them. The relevance of donor intent is questionable, but the concept of trustee intent becomes very relevant.

In some areas, such as medical research, one might have little clue as to the nature of the ideas developed, but can see that any good ideas will in fact further the public interest. In the social sciences, one can be less confident because solutions are often ideologically charged, as the previous three chapters have illustrated by example. Thus, while in the abstract one can see the benefit of studies that might search for ways to produce world peace, or eliminate poverty, or create more efficient urban living areas, in practice the lines of reasoning behind such studies will be based on some specific ideology. The results are likely to be controversial, but more to the present point, the funding decisions are more likely to be made on personal and ideological grounds than on the basis of scientific merit. The intentions of the donor will be reflected only to the extent that the donor's ideology was in rough correspondence with those who presently populate the foundation's board of trustees.

The Relevance of Donor Intent

The concept of donor intent as applied to the financing of the production of ideas through the grants of nonprofit foundations is slippery. The first question is whether donor intent should be followed. If a foundation is in the business of funding the development of ideas, and if the direction of funding is determined by the donor, then perhaps the ideas generated will be antithetical to the public interest. Political contributions are not tax deductible, because people are using the money to further their own ideas in the public policy arena. This is true even though one would hope that the result of democratic elections is the selection of officials who will further the public interest. Foundation contributions to political activities are prohibited, but why should not the production of all ideas fall into the same category as political ideas? Even when politics are not directly involved, questions about the desirability of donor intent are still raised, as in the case of the Danforth Foundation's grants to Washington University and St. Louis University. Perhaps donor intent is not even desirable.

If this is so, then the proposals that have been made periodically to exclude those who are related to the donor from serving as trustees for their foundations would have some merit. Donors should have the opportunity to determine who will serve as trustees, it might be argued, but on the other side one might argue that the selection of trustees is one of the privileges a donor gives up in exchange for the tax-preferred status of a foundation. The status quo allows relatives to be trustees, however, and by having relatives as trustees, the accountability of the foundation to the donor is enhanced. While recognizing arguments on both sides, on net it would seem to be desirable to allow relatives to be trustees, and to try to remain true to the concept of donor intent.

Over time, the connection of the trustees to the donor must diminish until eventually none of the trustees would ever have had the opportunity to have known the donor. This means that however one feels about having the dead hand of the donor guiding a foundation's activities, the donor's influence must continually diminish until it will have no effect outside of those provisions in the donor's bequest that are so specific that the trustees cannot avoid honoring them. Thus, over the long run the concept of donor intent is irrelevant, especially with regard to the production of ideas with foundation grants. Grants are made at the discretion of the trustees, not the donors.

Donor Intent and Foundation Accountability

For foundations that fund limited and specific causes, the stated intent of the donor can remain a major factor in the foundation's activities. As some examples presented earlier in the chapter show, when the donor's intent is very specifically stated, the foundation's expenditures may end up being allocated in a way that everyone could see after the fact would not have been approved of by the donor. Donor intent also can work for a while by appointing relatives of the donor as trustees, although the impact of this must diminish over time.

For foundations with broad mandates, and for those that finance the production of ideas and want to promote the solving of social problems, donor intent is more problematic. One can never know the specific intentions of deceased donors with regard to the production of ideas, but even that is irrelevant when the agency problems involved are considered. There is just no practical way in which the intentions of the donor can be made to take precedence over the intentions of the trustees. Chapter 8 will further examine the accountability problems that exist with nonprofit foundations. Meanwhile, this chapter weighs in with the conclusion that, especially when foundations fund the production of ideas, trustees are not accountable to the intentions of the donors, nor to anyone else.

Notes

1. J. George Harrar, Alan Pifer, and David Freeman, "Effect of the Tax as Seen by Foundations," in *Foundations and the Tax Bill* (New York: The Foundation Center, 1969), p. 61.
2. Arthur Andersen & Co., *Tax Economics of Charitable Giving,* 8th ed. (Chicago, 1983), p. 85.
3. This example and others in this section come from Horace Coon, *Money to Burn: What the Great American Philanthropic Foundations Do with Their Money* (London: Longmans, Green and Co., 1938).
4. Coon, *Money to Burn,* p. 9.
5. Teresa Odendahl, *Charity Begins at Home: Generosity and Self-Interest Among the Philanthropic Elite* (New York: Basic Books, 1990), p. 10.
6. Amos G. Warner, *American Charities: A Study in Philanthropy and Economics* (New York: T.Y. Crowell, 1894), p. 389.
7. John W. Nason, *Trustees and the Future of Foundations* (New York: Council on Foundations, 1977), p. 32.
8. This case is described by Victor Heiser, *An American Doctor's Odyssey* (New York: W.W. Norton and Co., 1936).
9. Warren Weaver, *U.S. Philanthropic Foundations: Their History, Structure, Management, and Record* (New York: Harper & Row, 1967), p. 30. Words that appear to be misspellings in the quotation actually are spelled in accordance with Carnegie's campaign to simplify spelling, another cause that he funded.
10. See Earl A. Thompson, "Charity and Nonprofit Organizations," in Kenneth W. Clarkson and Donald L. Martin, *The Economics of Nonproprietary Organizations* (Greenwich, CT: JAI Press, 1980), pp. 125-138.
11. Joseph C. Goulden, *The Money Givers* (New York: Random House, 1971), p. 48.

7

Trustees and the Direction of Foundations

Trustees have the ultimate responsibility for deciding the direction of foundations. They choose the foundation's management and the way in which the foundation is operated, and bear the final responsibility for the types of activities that are carried out by foundations. Trustees are in one sense like directors of a corporation, because directors also choose managers, operating styles, and activities of firms. Yet this analogy, as accurate as it seems with regard to the day-to-day operations of the organizations, falls short when considering the longer-range missions of corporations versus foundations. The crucial dimension that distinguishes the types of organizations is the public responsibility that foundations have when compared to corporations.

Trustees might also be compared to the elected officials that are ultimately accountable for the operation of governments. Duty to the public interest is in this case a common element that links governments and foundations. They differ because trustees are also bound by the charters of their foundations, and also because trustees do not have the regular evaluation of their activities that elected officials have every time an election is held. The accountability of elected officials provides a check on their use of discretion in their elected offices. Dissatisfied citizens can vote them out of office. Furthermore, elected officials can offer their elections as evidence that the voting public is satisfied with the way in which their actions serve the public interest. No such evidence is available for foundation trustees. Because of this lack of accountability, the evidence based on job performance must be greater on the part of trustees in order to persuade the general public that their actions are, in fact, in the public interest. While superficial similarities might be observed between the positions of foundation trustees and corporate directors, or between trustees and elected officials, ultimately they must be seen as fundamentally different.

Trustees as Managers

The trustees of a nonprofit foundation fill a role similar to directors of a corporation only in matters relating to the day-to-day operation of foundations. The trustees are ultimately accountable for the activities of the foundation, the trustees are in charge of selecting the managers of the foundation (or undertaking those management duties themselves), and the trustees must bear ultimate responsibility for any inefficiencies or improprieties of their foundations.[1] Yet in many ways the role of corporate directors is much more clear cut than foundation trustees, because while both have the immediate management responsibilities for their organizations, the long-run responsibilities of corporate directors center on maximizing corporate profits for the firm's owners. This also provides a convenient bottom line on which directors can be evaluated. If corporate profits are healthy and increasing, then the directors are doing their job.

With regard to trustees of nonprofit foundations there is both a public trust to be upheld and an obligation to remain true to the intentions of the donors that established the foundation. There are no profits and losses on which trustees can be evaluated, and no clearly defined measuring stick that can assess the effectiveness of a foundation.[2] One might attempt to measure a foundation's performance based on how well it has lived up to its own expectations, in terms of furthering the goals of its charter. For example, two of the largest charitable organizations (that are not foundations operated from endowments) are the American Cancer Society and the American Heart Association. Both cancer and heart disease remain major killers in the United States, and despite some promising treatments that have been developed, cures seem as far away today as they did fifty years ago. Thus, both organizations must be judged failures (at this time, anyway) when evaluated against their own goals.

James T. Bennett and Thomas J. DiLorenzo have done a detailed study of health charities and concluded that not only do they spend excessive amounts on fundraising, sometimes disguising their fundraising activities as educational activities, they also operate inefficiently, they report administrative expenses as research (by listing expenses for a person who oversees grants to cancer researchers as research, for example), and that they have little incentive to solve the problems they are raising money for in any event. Many people make their living working for organizations such as this, and if a cure for cancer were found tomorrow, the people working for the American Cancer Society would be out of work.[3] While the organizations Bennett and DiLorenzo examine are charities, not foundations, the potential for abuse is even greater in foundations, because the degree of oversight is smaller, the donors, for the most part, are dead, and there is no need to open up the foundation's activities to outside scrutiny for fundraising purposes.

Perhaps this line of reasoning is too demanding to be applied to foundation trustees, or trustees of any charity. Foundations are working on difficult problems, after all, whether they are searching for a cure for cancer or trying to create world peace, so one should not be surprised if progress sometimes appears slow. One must recognize that the role of a nonprofit foundation is to fill the voids in a society by undertaking activities that are valuable, yet are inappropriate for both government and private firms. If there was a clear bottom line to a foundation's activity, and if that activity did have a reasonable chance of being profitable, then private sector firms would stand ready to act, led by Adam Smith's famous invisible hand. But when projects might be expensive and the chances of success are uncertain, the market is likely to shy away from those activities.

Curing cancer may or may not fall into such a category. Surely a cure, if found, would generate a substantial amount of revenue. But the foundations that are the subject of this study are producing a product that is less likely to be marketed. How would one sell world peace? How would one sell any public policy idea? When goals are difficult to measure and monitor, one management problem is that foundations will define their goals in terms of visible and easily accomplished goals, rather than more the more fundamental and valuable goals that underlie the foundation's mission.[4] Trustees have the responsibility of overseeing the management of their foundations, like corporate boards, but that is a small part of the responsibility of trustees, although it is the most clearly defined part.

The Larger Responsibilities of Trustees

In a broader sense, there are three major groups to which trustees are responsible: donors, the general public, and recipients of the products of foundations. How, exactly, are foundation trustees responsible to these groups, and what should they do to carry out these responsibilities? A good starting point for considering the issue is to draw a parallel between a foundation trustee and a trustee who is appointed to oversee someone's financial affairs. The manager of portfolios in a trust department of a bank might provide an example. In this case, the trustee is entrusted with assets belonging to a principal with the understanding that the trustee will manage those assets for the best interest of the principal. A trustee would be expected to adhere to very high standards of conduct in such cases. As Justice Benjamin Cardozo said, "Many forms of conduct permissible in a workaday world for those acting at arm's length, are forbidden by those bound by fiduciary ties. A trustee is held accountable to something stricter than the morals of the market place. Not honesty alone, but the punctilio of an honor the most sensitive, is the standard of behavior." [5]

One might imagine, for example, two individuals with stock portfolios, one who holds her stocks in an account with a brokerage firm and another who has turned over the management of his portfolio to a trustee. It might be perfectly acceptable for the stockbroker to call the first individual with recommendations that some of her stocks be sold, or that she buy some additional stocks, yet it might be unacceptable for the trustee of the second person's account to undertake those same transactions that were acceptable for the broker to recommend. Why? There could be any number of reasons. The recommended stocks might be risky (but the first individual can choose to accept that risk), or the purchases and sales might run up a substantial amount of brokerage commissions that would result in a transfer of wealth from the principal to the trustee, or the trustee's business might have a financial interest in some of the recommendations. With full disclosure, there would be no ethical problem with a broker making such recommendations, even though there would be an ethical problem if these recommendations were carried out by a trustee.

Trustees of nonprofit foundations have the same ethical limits as trustees in other situations, and they must not only act in the best interest of donors, the general public, and beneficiaries, but must also avoid perceptions of conflicts of interest, avoid profiting themselves from the activities of their foundations—even if the foundations benefit also—and must avoid risky actions that could jeopardize their foundations' public purposes. They are bound, as Justice Cardozo said, by stricter moral standards than those of the marketplace. In the abstract, one can hardly object to these ethical responsibilities of foundation trustees, but how, exactly, do they meet their responsibilities? Their first responsibility is to their donors. The issue of donor intent is important enough, but is not easy to sort out, as the previous chapter illustrated. What about their responsibility to the general public, and to the intended beneficiaries of foundation resources?

Responsibility to the General Public

The public trust placed in nonprofit foundations stems directly from their tax-privileged status. If foundations were not given special privileges under the tax code, then one would be hard pressed to come up with an objection to allowing foundations to expend their resources just like any other private organization. Because foundations do have tax-privileged status, the taxpaying public, which bears more of the tax burden in exchange for the reduction in the burden borne by foundations, has a right to ask in exchange that foundations have a public purpose and that their activities in the public interest more than compensate the general public for the loss in tax revenues. But what, specifically, should foundation trustees be required to do to maintain this public trust?

The public expects three things from foundation trustees. First, as Justice Cardozo said, it expects them to act with the highest level of propriety, and holds them to higher standards than those of the marketplace. It expects that trustees will not profit from their position as trustees, even if the foundation benefits also. The facts are important, but appearances are important also. Second, it expects trustees to carry out the intentions of the donors who established the foundations. Third, it expects them to ensure that the foundation actually benefits the intended beneficiaries. The first expectation, that trustees act with propriety and give the appearance of doing so, is the most straightforward. The expectations that the intentions of the donors are adhered to and the welfare of the intended beneficiaries is furthered are more vague.

Responsibility to the Foundation's Beneficiaries

Trying to define the trustees' responsibility to a foundation's intended beneficiaries is a slippery undertaking, partly because it is unclear who those beneficiaries are supposed to be. The first place to look is to the intentions of the donor, but many statements of donor intent are left intentionally vague. When foundation resources are supposed to be used for the benefit of mankind, who, exactly are the intended beneficiaries? Should such a foundation's trustees be considered in breach of their responsibilities if there are some people on Earth who have not seen their welfare enhanced because of a foundation's activities? This would, undoubtedly, be viewed as extreme. Consider a more specific case of a foundation established to undertake cancer studies, or to undertake studies to further world peace. In both cases the foundation's intended beneficiaries might be viewed as mankind in general, and both a cure for cancer or the creation of world peace would have generally recognized benefits. Most such studies do not cure cancer or produce world peace, however. Are there no beneficiaries? Even here, the researchers who did the studies are likely to be beneficiaries, because they received foundation grants. Should researchers themselves be viewed as beneficiaries of foundation grants? Clearly, they benefit.

Foundations themselves may find themselves looking at a grant's beneficiaries in this way, because the researcher most likely applied for a foundation grant to initiate the grant-making process, and because writing a grant application is an activity costly to the researcher, the mere fact of an application indicates that the researchers would view themselves as better off if the grant were made. Thus, foundations can benefit researchers by giving them grants. The public may or may not benefit, but the researcher certainly does. Applying for grants has become a major activity and a major source of revenue for universities, independent think tanks, and consulting firms. Thus, many foundations interact with those making grant applications, not the general public that is supposed to benefit from the foundation grants.

A comparison of organizations that make research grants with organizations that directly provide benefits for the needy is instructive. When food, clothing, and shelter are provided for indigent people, there is some way to account for the benefits to the general public from a foundation grant. When a study is undertaken on the causes of poverty, the researchers, with whom the foundation directly interacts, are made better off by the income they earn for doing the study, but the benefit to poor people is, at best, indirect. Indeed, in the social sciences it is not uncommon for different studies to arrive at conflicting conclusions, suggesting that the results of both studies could not be in the public interest.[6]

Maybe grants that benefit researchers do benefit the general public by keeping alive lines of research, and by increasing the incomes of those who pursue research in certain areas in order to keep them active in research and to encourage others to follow. The point is that it is not at all clear who benefits from foundation grants, or who is supposed to benefit. When looking at the beneficiaries of grants, at least part of the question goes back to donor intent. Trustees are in the difficult position, then, of having to oversee a grant-making process in an environment where it is not clear who should benefit from the grants, or who does benefit from them. Measurement of benefits is often difficult, and this is one of the main reasons why the image of integrity is so important for foundations and their trustees. The public has placed a trust in trustees, and when results are difficult to measure, it is especially important that the actions of foundations make it unquestionably clear that foundations are exerting a sincere effort to further the public interest.

Self-Perpetuating Boards of Trustees

One issue that has been of continual interest to those who observe foundations is the methods by which trustees are selected. Trustees may be selected in a variety of ways. In many cases in which a corporation has provided the foundation's endowment, corporate officers will be charged with the responsibility of selecting the foundation's trustees. Other foundations have their trustees selected by officials in outside organizations. Mayors or judges may be involved in the selection of trustees for foundations with a local focus.[7] By far the most common means by which the trustees are selected for foundations is by having the remaining trustees select replacements for those who leave the board.[8]

A self-perpetuating board of trustees has several advantages. Trustees will be selected by those individuals who are most knowledgeable about the activities of the foundation and about the activities of the board. The procedure is simple. Furthermore, trustees are more likely to select fellow trustees who are compatible, thus helping facilitate the collective decision-making process for the board. Several disadvantages are also apparent. By selecting trustees with whom they are comfortable, the foundation may be insulated from critical evaluation, further aggravating the lack of accountability that is the hallmark of nonprofit foundations. Furthermore, self-perpetuating boards are likely to lack the diversity of a board appointed by other means. In part this reference to diversity might mean ethnic diversity, but even when ethnic diversity is present there will be likely to be a lack of class and professional diversity.

One would have less reason to be concerned about a lack of diversity among corporate directors, or even elected officials. Although a democratic society would want to avoid policies that would effectively disenfranchise minorities, elected officials are accountable at the ballot box. Following a different line of reasoning, corporate directors are responsible for the performance of the corporation, and diversity should be a minor issue. But for foundations that are charged with furthering a vaguely defined public interest, a board of trustees selected from a very narrow subset of the population might not be in a good position to recognize the public interest as viewed by the broader population.

The problem of homogeneity among trustees can be aggravated when a super-majority of a self-perpetuating board is required to approve new members. Many foundations require merely that a majority of the trustees approve any new trustee, but some require a super-majority such as two-thirds, or in some cases even unanimous approval of the existing trustees.[9] Having a larger majority requirement to approve a new trustee is equivalent to saying that a candidate may be rejected by the disapproval of a smaller minority of the existing trustees, which would be likely to make the trustees even more exclusive a group.

Self-perpetuating boards of trustees can bring with them a number of drawbacks, but perhaps the most severe drawback is that self-perpetuating boards further aggravate the problem of the lack of accountability that plagues nonprofit foundations. This is yet another area in which a change in public policy might be warranted.

The Turnover of Trustees

One can see arguments for both stability and turnover in a board of trustees. Stability provides a group of experienced trustees and provides continuity for a foundation. Turnover provides fresh ideas and a better possibility for a critical look at the foundation's past activities. Surely newcomers will be more able to criticize the work of their predecessors than individuals will be to look critically at their own work. Of course, it is possible to achieve both stability and turnover if trustees serve for long terms, but their terms are staggered.

The length of terms of trustees varies considerably, and sometimes is left vague in a foundation's charter. In some cases trustees are appointed for life, while in other cases they are appointed for one-year terms.[10] Longer terms of three to ten years are also common. When directors serve for one-year terms, reappointment is almost always a formality—so much so that at times trustees may forget to reappoint themselves. Any time when a board is self-perpetuating, it may be difficult for directors not to reappoint a member who wants to be reappointed, but because the typical director serves with little or no compensation, unless there is an obvious reason not to reappoint a director, this may not be a problem. When trustees serve longer terms, it is more likely that the end of the term provides a trustee with a good reason to decide against serving for another half decade or so, whereas it may be too easy to stay on for just another year.

Many foundations have mandatory retirement ages for their trustees. The Rockefeller Foundation requires trustees to retire at age sixty-five, and the Ford Foundation has a mandatory retirement age of seventy. At its inception, the Carnegie Corporation had no mandatory retirement age, and many trustees continued on the board into their eighties and even nineties. In 1960 the Carnegie Corporation instituted a mandatory retirement age of seventy-two, which was lowered to seventy in 1971.[11]

Turnover of trustees is one area in which rules governing the service of individual trustees may not necessarily work out in the best interest of the governance of the foundation. Should a particular trustee retire from the board, or should be board reappoint the trustee if his term is up? When looked at from the point of view of the public interest, part of the answer depends upon the trustee in question, but part also depends upon the composition of the rest of the board. In a board of elderly trustees all with long service, turnover would provide the double benefit of providing new blood to the board and also giving a new trustee some experience with a board that itself has substantial experience. But if the same trustee is the only one on the board with substantial experience, replacing the trustee could eliminate valuable experience from which the newer trustees could learn. Common sense would suggest that trustees should be of different ages so that all would not retire (or die) at about the same time, leaving an inexperienced board. So the issue of when a trustee should be replaced is not as simple as looking at the trustee alone. The entire composition of the board must be considered.

Quite likely a trustee's own decision will also depend upon the composition of the board and the individual who is likely to replace the retiring trustee. Surely many trustees like the personal power that comes with the position, but they also want to use the position in order to further what they view as the appropriate mission of the foundation. If the other trustees think like the one considering retirement, and if the likely replacement (who might be chosen prior to a trustee's retirement) is sympathetic to the retiree's point of view, then it will be easier for a trustee to make the decision to retire. Because of the self-perpetuating nature of boards, however, all trustees will consider each other when their terms expire, making it likely that each individual trustee will make the final decision about when he or she will step down, and that decision is likely to be made as much reflecting the individual trustee's interests as the interests of the foundation.

One must recognize that while trustee turnover must be an important policy concern for foundations, there is not necessarily a public policy issue. Just because foundations might work better with different policies on turnover does not mean that the government should try to implement standards in the area. Good policies will be imitated by other foundations, not necessarily because existing foundations will change their policies but because new foundations will be organized to imitate the policies that appear most effective. Thus, there is an advantage to allowing foundations to adopt a variety of policies even if it would appear to an outside observer that one policy is better than another.

Diversity Among Trustees

When choosing foundation trustees, one should want to select individuals with wisdom and experience, people with social status that will reflect well on the reputation of the foundation, and of course, individuals with the time, interest, and philanthropic inclinations to provide competent service to the foundation. This list of desirable qualifications implies that foundation boards will not have diversity in their trustees in a number of dimensions. There is a tendency to think of diversity in terms of ethnic, gender-specific, regional, or religious terms, and foundations have both recognized the value of such diversity and acted on it in recent years.[12] Prior to World War II foundation trustees tended to be white males in their fifties and sixties, living in the Eastern United States, and coming from Protestant religions. Today there is more regional and religious diversity, and it is more common to find women and ethnic minorities serving as foundation trustees. Despite the outward appearance of diversity, the qualifications of the job dictate that trustees are drawn from an older, wealthier, and more educated group than the population as a whole, and that under the surface there is a substantial homogeneity among trustees.[13] Is this appearance of diversity enough, or should foundations dig deeper to find trustees that are more representative of the general population?

There may be good arguments for diversity in gender, ethnicity, religion, and region. People with diverse backgrounds can bring perspectives to boards of trustees that may be difficult for a more homogeneous group to see. Yet the argument for diversity can be overdone. Foundation trustees are not supposed to represent the general public in the same way that elected members of the House of Representatives do. Rather, they represent the intentions of the donors, and attempt to use foundation resources for the well-being of the beneficiaries selected by the donors. They are supposed to keep in mind the public interest, but this must mean only to try to do good things with the foundation's resources and to try to avoid harm, not to try to spread benefits to everyone. Foundations have limited missions. There is no particular reason why boards of trustees should incorporate a diversity that reflects the population as a whole, or even a subset of the population.

In addition, if trustees are supposed to manage a foundation's activities, a certain unity of opinion among board members ought to be desirable. If the trustees are divided along ethnic, professional, or religious lines, then consensus will be hard to come by. Yet consensus is desirable both for the unity and morale of the foundation and to enhance the foundation's operations. Trustees, especially when they are self-perpetuating, tend to be friends and acquaintances, which will help create consensus. Foundations, unlike governments, are not charged with benefiting all members of society equally, and homogeneity among foundation trustees should not be as much an issue as, for example, homogeneity among government officials.[14]

Should Trustees be Compensated?

Most foundation trustees serve without compensation, although there is a systematic bias so that the larger the foundation, the more likely it is that compensation will be paid to trustees.[15] The arguments in favor of compensation are that trustees might feel more of an obligation to work harder for the foundation if compensation were paid, and that some compensation for their hard work should be given as a tangible expression of appreciation for the efforts of trustees. Would better trustees be attracted with compensation? Perhaps, but the motivation to serve on a board of trustees should be primarily philanthropic, not monetary. Compensation might even compromise the quality of trustees.

Serving as a trustee takes away time from other activities, which, as noted earlier, limits the selection of trustees to a subset of the population.[16] People who are working two jobs to make ends meet will not be in the pool of people considered for trusteeship, but there is a continuum of people from those who work hard because they need the money to those sufficiently well off that additional income means little. Trustees of community organizations, hospitals, colleges and universities, and museums are not compensated, and they have considerable responsibility and devote considerable time to their organizations. Should foundations be different? If serving as a foundation trustee is a philanthropic activity rather than a vocation, then an argument can be made against compensation, even while recognizing that this will limit the pool of potential trustees.

The Foundation Staff

The largest foundations have a full-time staff that runs the day-to-day operations of the foundations, but the typical smaller foundation has no professional staff. A full-time secretary may be necessary, and after 1969 foundations need accounting and legal services more than before, but these activities can be contracted out. In many cases a foundation's trustees also serve as the foundation's management. One can easily see how a foundation, as a grant-making organization, can operate in this manner. The trustees are ultimately responsible for the foundation's activities, so they must oversee the grant-making process and set the direction of the foundation in any event. A professional staff might help to sort through the applications and determine which are more worthwhile to support than others, but the trustees are the ultimate decision makers. What would a professional staff have to offer?

A full-time professional staff might be in a better position to evaluate proposals, and also might be in a better position to help applicants design effective proposals and programs. If programs would be better with staff input, this can be a major reason to retain a staff. Foundation staff personnel also might be able to provide assistance to applicants whose applications are rejected. They still might have worthy causes and funding potential elsewhere. A foundation's activities can be enhanced by its staff both because better projects are chosen for funding and because the projects themselves are improved by the input of the foundation staff.[17]

With these advantages come disadvantages of staff also. The most obvious is that it costs money to hire a staff, and money spent on staff is money not spent on programs. But other less obvious drawbacks remain. A full-time staff, because of its information advantage, may in effect remove the trustees from power by making decisions for them. Furthermore, because the staff will have some control over which grants are funded, they may steer applicants in a certain direction and have a negative impact on the activities of applicants. Henry S. Pritchett, former president of the Carnegie Corporation, said in the foundation's 1922 annual report, "Somebody must sweat blood with gift money if its effect is not to do more harm than good." [18] Because a foundation staff necessarily takes some power away from the trustees, there is the potential that some staff activity might work against the public interest.

Even when a foundation is so large that it needs a permanent staff, it is often difficult to tell how big the staff should be. A private firm will want to increase its workforce as long as additional employees add more to the bottom line than they cost, but with no clear-cut measure of profit in a foundation, there will always be some ambiguity with regard to whether additional employees will help or hinder the operation of a foundation.

Foundation Networks

Because the pool of potential foundation trustees is relatively limited, because some experience in the work of foundations is desirable, and because those who serve as trustees must have a sense that foundations do pursue activities in the public interest, one would not be surprised to find that there is a network of individuals who serve as foundation trustees. Often, individuals serve as trustees for more than one foundation, and often there is a link between the trustees of a foundation and the organizations to which foundations make grants. In a series of studies done on foundation trustees Mary Anna Culleton Colwell found that about half of the trustees for twenty large foundations also served as trustees of other foundations in that same group.[19] Some foundations had more overlap among their trustees than others. The Ford Foundation had twenty-one trustees in the study, of whom eight served on other foundation boards, whereas the Rockefeller Foundation's nineteen trustees over the time period included fifteen who were on other boards. Laurance S. Rockefeller served as a trustee on eight boards during that time, including the Rockefeller Foundation, six other foundations established by the Rockefeller family, and the Alfred P. Sloan Foundation. Among the twenty foundation boards examined in that study, the Rockefeller Foundation had at least one trustee who also served as a trustee on twelve other foundations, and the Carnegie Corporation had trustees who served on eight others. Among large foundations, there is a small network of people who determine how those foundations spend their money.

There is also a substantial overlap between the nonprofit foundations that make grants for public policy studies and the organizations that receive grants. The same sample of twenty grant-making foundations and thirty-one recipient organizations showed that eighteen of the recipient organizations had board members who were also trustees of those large grant-making foundations.[20] An examination of the boards of three influential public policy think tanks, the Brookings Institution, the Hoover Institution, and the Council on Foreign Relations, shows that for each organization, more than half of the organization's board members serve as trustees for grant-making foundations. While some foundations have policies that prevent trustees who are affiliated with a grant applicant from participating in the decision as to whether the grant should be funded, others do not. Even when such policies are in place, it is easy to see how such overlapping boards can facilitate the making of grants.

Foundation networks are formed in more indirect ways as well. Trustees of a foundation may work as advisors to other foundations or recipient organizations, or may even be employed by them to write studies or do other work. There is also a close association between foundation trustees and corporate directors. Of ninety-eight foundation trustees examined in one of Colwell's samples, fifty-seven of them were directors of a major American corporation.[21] Links also exist through social clubs and other organizations. With a small pool of potential trustees to choose from, one would expect that there would be homogeneity among trustees, but Colwell's studies have documented that the same people hold many positions as trustees of grant-making foundations and recipient organizations, and at other times may hold important government posts. In many cases, trustees are making grants to themselves.

When considering the impact of foundation networks on ideas, one must take into account that the networks extend substantially beyond the grant-making foundations. Foundation trustees are often influential business people, they often are affiliated with organizations that receive foundation grants, and they may play a direct role in the creation of public policy. Thus, accountability becomes a major issue. At the end of the twentieth century Americans can see the importance of fundraising in political campaigns, and the role of money in politics has caused a substantial amount of debate. Yet through foundation networks, individuals who are inside the system are able to fund the promotion of their ideas without any kind of appeal to the general public, and without any accountability. In addition, because policy ideas funded by foundations may have the appearance of being more objective, the ties within the foundation network that produce policy studies may warrant closer examination. Ideas that appear objective due to foundation connections may have very ideological origins.

The Role of Trustees

Trustees bear the ultimate responsibility for the functions of their foundations. The discussion in this chapter has raised a number of policy questions, and has shown that there may be a gap between the activities of trustees in some ideal world and the way in which trustees operate in the real world. The standards to which trustees are held are—and should be—higher than those for individuals in the private sector, so any analysis must consider not only the actual activities of trustees but also the public perceptions.

There are several areas in which public perceptions with regard to trustees may cast suspicion upon the third sector, including the nature of self-perpetuating boards, the issue of family control, the relative lack of diversity among trustees, and the overlap between trustees and the organizations to which they make grants. When considering the role of foundations in the creation of ideas, the interrelationships between foundations and the organizations that receive foundation grants stands out as the most serious problem. Trustees provide the direction for foundations, but if they also have a direct link to the organizations that receive their grants, they are in a position to fund their own ideas with no accountability to the public and no market or electoral check on their activities, as would occur in the private and public sectors.

Because the issue is important, the next chapter considers the lack of accountability in the third sector in more detail. The subject deserves attention because foundations have a substantial amount of discretion in their activities, and have no oversight. Such discretion gives foundation trustees the opportunity to initiate grants that reflect their own interests as much as the general public interest. If trustees are public spirited, the interests of foundation trustees might be congruent with the interests of the larger society. A problem emerges when the same individuals are on both the giving and receiving ends of the grants. Then foundations can fund the trustees' own causes and programs, and the foundation's assets become an extension of the trustees' wealth.

Elaborate safeguards are designed to make sure that this type of conflict of interest does not occur in the public sector. Public officials are prevented from receiving many types of outside income that would be legitimate in the private sector. Close attention is paid to prevent any favors that government agencies might do to aid public officials. Yet public officials ultimately are accountable at the ballot box, so that if the public perceives inappropriate activities or favoritism, even if it is legal, the public has the right to remove them from office. Not only is such accountability absent from the third sector, activities that would constitute a clear conflict of interest in the public sector routinely occur in the nonprofit sector.

When considering the relationship between trustees and the ideas that are developed with foundation grants, ideally one would like to think that trustees would choose among the most promising applications in order to produce studies, conferences, and reports that would further the public interest. Often there is a very close relationship between the trustees and the ideas that are generated, however. Because there is no clear bottom line for evaluating foundations, and because of the many questions that may arise about trustee activities, it is easy for trustees to exert little oversight over foundation staff, and to develop a comfortable relationship with the foundation's favored beneficiaries. The oversight activities of corporate boards have sometimes been questioned for being too lax, but there is even more reason to question foundation boards on these grounds.[22]

Trustees may be an extension of the donors, or may even be the donors themselves for a period of years. Family relationships among trustees were one of the issues raised in this chapter. Over time trustees will have an increasingly remote connection with the original donors, however, so the ideas of the donors will become increasingly remote in relation to the ideas financed by their foundations. The previous chapter showed that there are complex issues related to the concept of donor intent. After considering in more detail the role of trustees in this chapter, the next chapter examines the accountability issue and looks at the incentives facing those who run America's foundations.

Notes

1. See Arnold J. Zurcher, *The Management of American Foundations: Administration, Policies, and Social Role* (New York: New York University Press, 1972), ch. 3.
2. Zurcher, *The Management of American Foundations*, p. 77.
3. James T. Bennett and Thomas J. DiLorenzo, *Unhealthy Charities: Hazardous to Your Health and Wealth* (New York: Basic Books, 1994).
4. Peter F. Drucker, *Managing the Non-Profit Organization* (New York: HarperCollins, 1990) discusses this type of problem, and provides some guidance but no real solutions.
5. John W. Nason, *Trustees and the Future of Foundations* (New York: Council on Foundations, 1977), p. 79.
6. Critics of this statement will charge that informed discourse on important subjects will eventually lead to a consensus of opinion, so that even studies with conflicting conclusions can be valuable as contributions to an intellectual debate that eventually will be resolved.
7. Zurcher, *The Management of American Foundations*, p. 36.
8. Nason, *Trustees and the Future of Foundations*, p. 48.
9. M.M. Chambers, *Charters of Philanthropies: A Study of Selected Trust Instruments, Charters, By-Laws, and Court Decisions* (Boston: D.B. Updike, 1948), p. 18.
10. Nason, *Trustees and the Future of Foundations*, p. 51.
11. Nason, *Trustees and the Future of Foundations*, p. 52.
12. Nason, *Trustees and the Future of Foundations*, ch. 6, discusses the issue of diversity among board members.
13. Thomas R. Dye, *Who's Running America? The Conservative Years*, 4th ed. (Englewood Cliffs, NJ: Prentice-Hall, 1986), p. 243.
14. Zurcher, *The Management of American Foundations*, pp. 35-36.
15. Nason, *Trustees and the Future of Foundations*, p. 75.
16. Zurcher, *The Management of American Foundations*, p. 39.
17. Zurcher, *The Management of American Foundations*, p. 37.

18. Nason, *Trustees and the Future of Foundations,* p. 63.
19. Mary Anna Culleton Colwell, "The Foundation Connection: Links Among Foundations and Recipient Organizations," in Robert Arnove, ed., *Philanthropy and Cultural Imperialism* (Boston: G.K. Hall, 1980).
20. Mary Anna Culleton Colwell, *Private Foundations and Public Policy: The Political Role of Philanthropy* (New York: Garland Publishing, Inc., 1993), p. 88.
21. Culleton Colwell, *Private Foundations and Public Policy,* p. 99.
22. Melissa Middleton, "Nonprofit Boards of Directors: Beyond the Governance Function," Chap. 8 in Walter W. Powell, ed., *The Nonprofit Sector* (New Haven, CT: Yale University Press, 1987), concludes that trustees are often lax in their oversight.

8

The Accountability of Nonprofit Foundations

In the nineteenth century when nonprofit foundations were relatively limited in scope, when they applied their funds to clearly defined public purposes, and when there were no tax incentives to influence the activities of foundations, public accountability of nonprofit foundations was not of much concern. The situation changed in the twentieth century after the establishment of large general-purpose foundations, and after the tax code could prompt donors to create nonprofit foundations for the private benefit of their heirs. Prior to the twentieth century, foundation trustees had the responsibility for safeguarding the foundation's assets to ensure that they were used for the clearly defined purposes specified by the donor, that resources were not wasted, and, of course, that they were not diverted for the personal benefit of those managing the foundations. In the main, this meant that trustees and managers were accountable for honesty and diligence. Two things have changed the nature of accountability in the twentieth century: the broadening of the scope of foundation activity, and the applicability of tax law to foundation activity.

Accountability in part means obeying tax laws, but twentieth-century tax law implies more than that. Because foundations can be used for tax avoidance, accountability also means managing foundations in such a way as to avoid the appearance of impropriety. Partly this is to preserve the reputation of foundations as institutions that promote the public welfare, rather than as tax shelters, and partly this is to prevent Congress from taking actions such as those in 1969 to curb perceived abuses. The broadening scope of foundation activity also imposes addi-

171

tional accountability requirements on foundations, because foundations now must demonstrate that their varied activities really are in the public interest. Could a conference on world peace really just be a boondoggle designed to benefit the participants? Even the appearance that this might be so could hurt the reputation of not only the sponsoring foundation, but foundations in general. The conference money could have been used to buy medicine for the poor, after all. One must recognize that appearances are, indeed, important for foundations, both to maintain a favorable public perception and to forestall additional legislative inquiries.

The potential concerns are many. One might worry, as in the case of the Ford Foundation, that the real intention of the donor is to avoid paying taxes and pass along wealth and corporate control, untaxed, to his heirs. In this case the Treasury would be deprived of the revenues, and there may be larger issues regarding the social control of wealth, if inheritance taxes are viewed as having social purposes by fostering equality in addition to raising revenues. One might be concerned that the tax-exempt organization is a vehicle for channeling untaxed benefits to those who are on the foundation boards, or who are employed by the foundations. Without the discipline provided by the market system, as in corporate America, foundations have nobody to answer to when justifying their use of funds. Third, one might be concerned that the activities of foundations work against the public welfare. This issue becomes more relevant when realizing the extent to which there is a lack of accountability of foundations to anybody. While all these aspects of accountability are important, this study focuses on the problems of accountability as they relate to the activities pursued by foundations and the ideas generated by their work.

When the George Peabody Fund was established in 1867 for the purpose of furthering education in the American South, it broke new ground because Peabody's instructions required the foundation to report to and be accountable to the general public.[1] Accountability did not become a significant issue until the twentieth century, however. This chapter will look at some of the debate over the twentieth century regarding public accountability of foundations. The chapter will also compare the accountability of different types of organizations to see where foundations fit in. But first, the chapter will consider why accountability is an issue, how it relates to the production of ideas, and will reflect on the incentives facing those who run America's foundations.

Accountability and Ideas

When foundations entered the realm of social science in the twentieth century, and began financing the production of ideas, accountability took on a broader meaning. For the ideas produced with foundation funding to have credibility, foundations must assure the public not only that they are not using resources in a fraudulent manner, but that the results they are producing are the result of objective scholarly research —unbiased and nonpartisan. Chapters 10 and 11 discuss possible policy changes that might be made with regard to foundations, but to evaluate public policy toward foundations one needs to have some idea about what should be expected from them. Ultimately, the answer is that they are expected to act in the public interest. That means not only adhering to the letter of the law, but also recognizing that foundations should, by their nature, be held to higher standards than those in the private sector. That means not only preventing fraud and abuse, and making sure foundation resources are not squandered, but also behaving in such a way that the propriety of the foundation's activities, its trustees and its officers is beyond question. This volume does not deal primarily with those issues, however, but with the ideas produced by foundations.

The same criteria for accountability can be carried over to the production of ideas. Foundation trustees undoubtedly have their own biases with regard to public policy, and considering the charge given to the trustees of foundations such as Carnegie and Rockefeller, it would be difficult to fault them for directing foundation resources toward opportunities that they personally believe would have the most beneficial impact. At the same time, funding what would appear to be propaganda designed to support a viewpoint or further a political agenda would appear to violate the public trust. Such activities may be illegal following the 1969 reforms, but legality is beside the point. Foundations tell the public that they have a responsibility to further the public interest, so appearances are more important than legal technicalities.

Foundations can—and do—take steps to give the work they finance the appearance of legitimacy. By funding reputable scholars and having fair and objective reviewing processes that determine who gets foundation grants, the appearance of credibility can be enhanced. The production of academic research can provide a good model for foundations. Academics have their own biases, but there are also academic standards that are upheld by having proposals and methods reviewed by other academics with established reputations. Articles in academic journals are published only after having undergone this type of peer review process. Foundations use similar methods, but the appearance of objectivity can be enhanced if reviewers are selected based on scholarly credentials rather than on ideological orientation.

By their nature, foundations should meet standards that are higher than other organizations, and even than other nonprofit organizations. People can contribute money toward organizations that support particular causes, and such organizations are by their nature not expected to retain the appearance of objectivity. Foundations argue that they act in the public interest, creating a higher standard of accountability to the public. Of course, all organizations are accountable to the public to varying degrees, including private firms, so it is worth exploring the nature of accountability in more detail to see more precisely the standards that should apply to foundations.

To whom are organizations accountable? To whom should they be accountable? Should private sector firms be accountable to different groups, or in different degrees, than nonprofit foundations? A good way to deal with these questions is to see how for-profit firms are accountable to their customers, to their stockholders, to the government, and to the general public, and to contrast for-profit firms with nonprofit foundations. The comparison shows that for-profit firms are accountable to all of these groups to varying degrees. When the cases are examined, there is good reason to want nonprofit foundations to be held more accountable than private firms, yet in all respects they actually have less accountability.

The Customers of Foundations

Private sector firms are in business to sell goods and services to their customers, and the first level of accountability is to their customers. Customers, as consumers of the goods and services they purchase, are in a good position to evaluate the effectiveness of the firms with which they deal, and if firms are not responsive to their customers, they will lose those customers to other firms that are more responsive to customer demands. This competition among firms creates incentives for all firms to provide the best value they can to their customers.

Nonprofit foundations do not have customers in the same way that businesses do. Businesses produce benefits for their customers in exchange for payment, but foundations receive funds from donors with the stated purpose of providing benefits for others. Thus, donors can be considered customers only in the loosest sense that they are spending their money with the hope of providing some benefits, but because the benefits will go to others, donors will not be in a good position to evaluate the cost-effectiveness of a foundation's expenditures. The real analog to private sector customers is the group for which the foundation is supposed to provide benefits.

The intended beneficiaries are different from one foundation to another. Consider two foundations at opposite ends of the accountability spectrum: the Duke Endowment and the Rockefeller Foundation. The income from the Duke Endowment is intended to benefit universities, hospitals, and a few other institutions, and when the endowment was created the shares going to each beneficiary were specified. Duke University gets 32 percent of the endowment's income, hospitals in the Carolinas get 32 percent, orphanages in the Carolinas get 10 percent, Davidson College and Furman University each get 5 percent, Johnson C. Smith University gets 4 percent, 10 percent is earmarked for the construction and maintenance of Methodist churches in North Carolina towns with populations below 1,500, and 2 percent is to go for the care of retired preachers, their widows, and their orphans.

Because the Duke Endowment has such specific instructions for the disbursement of its income, the named beneficiaries have an incentive to watch over the management of the endowment to see that it provides them with the maximum benefit possible. Duke University, for example, is entitled to a substantial and specific share of the endowment's income, so it will be very interested in monitoring the performance of the endowment. In cases such as the Duke Endowment, there is something resembling accountability to the customers of the foundation because the donor left clear intentions regarding who was supposed to benefit from the establishment of the foundation. The accountability is not as severe as would exist in the marketplace, however, because if the Duke Endowment underperforms relative to other endowments, there is no market penalty, and the endowment will not go out of business or lose its customers. However, the managers and trustees of the Duke Endowment will find it harder to engage in fraudulent activity, and to siphon off endowment funds for their own personal benefit, because the beneficiaries have an incentive to monitor the activities of the foundation in order to maximize their own benefits.

At the other end of the spectrum is the Rockefeller Foundation, which has as its statement of purpose, "To promote the well-being of mankind throughout the world." While it is easy to imagine a close relationship between the Duke Endowment and Duke University, and it is easy to imagine university administrators keeping an eye on the management of the endowment, it is just as difficult to imagine "mankind throughout the world" monitoring the activities of the Rockefeller Foundation. Indeed, just the opposite is true. Whereas the beneficiaries of disbursements from the Duke Endowment are entitled to their shares, beneficiaries from the Rockefeller Foundation receive benefits only if the foundation grants them an award. Thus, potential recipients make applications to the Foundation with the hope of receiving a grant, and if they do they are indebted to the foundation's management for the grant. In such a situation, recipients are not likely to be critical of the way in which the foundation is managed. Indeed, criticism will make them less likely to get a foundation grant, so scrutiny of the foundation's operations can provide no benefit. And because grants are made to those that the foundation views as worthy of support, there is only a loose connection between the performance of the foundation and the flow of benefits to the foundation's beneficiaries anyway.

Private firms are accountable to their customers, and customers are in a good position to evaluate the performance of the firms they interact with. Foundations are less accountable because the individuals and groups who receive the foundation's benefits are not the individuals who finance them. In some cases, like the Duke Endowment, there are beneficiaries who have an incentive to exercise oversight, but in others, like the Rockefeller Foundation, there is no clear-cut group of intended beneficiaries who will exercise oversight. Without the policing action of the market, foundations have much more latitude in their activities.

Accountability to the General Public

Private firms have relatively limited accountability to the general public, and with good reason. They exist to satisfy the demands of their customers. They have the responsibility to obey laws and to pay taxes. Publicly traded corporations have additional financial disclosure requirements. Additional requirements could be enumerated, but when operating within the bounds of the legal system, the accountability of private firms to the general public is relatively limited.

Nonprofit foundations are accountable to the general public in all the ways that private firms are, and more. They must limit the scope of their activities and comply with government regulations as a condition of their tax-preferred status, but the conditions set out by donors when foundations are established also create a responsibility to the general public. Organizations like the Rockefeller Foundation have a stated responsibility to mankind throughout the world, but even foundations with more limited missions like the Duke Endowment have a public responsibility to their stated beneficiaries. Their tax-preferred status was granted on this condition.

The general public has a relatively limited ability to monitor whether nonprofit foundations are living up to their public responsibilities. While most foundations issue annual reports, it is relatively difficult to verify that the foundation actually is pursuing the activities they are claiming to pursue in their reports. Some transgressions are common but obvious. Some nonprofit organizations will claim as a part of their mission that they undertake educational programs and disseminate public information about their cause. In fundraising solicitations they will show that a substantial portion of their funds are educational, and that only a small amount of their funds go toward fundraising. What they fail to mention is that enclosed with their request for a donation is some information about the charity and the cause that it is trying to further, and that because of that enclosed information, the solicitation you received is a part of the organization's educational budget, not its fundraising budget.

Yet another common transgression is to report the costs of administrators who make grants for certain purposes as an expenditure for that purpose. For example, a foundation that makes grants for medical research may have a staff of administrators who make research grants. Rather than calling that staff administrative overhead, they will categorize expenditures on the staff as medical research, because they are the staff in charge of the medical research grants. Budget categorizations of this type make an organization appear to spend much less of its money on fundraising and administrative overhead than it actually does.[3]

Nonprofit foundations have public missions, so in principle they are accountable to the general public for their actions. Yet in practice there is no way for the general public to hold foundations accountable. In contrast, private firms do not serve public purposes, so there is no reason to hold them so accountable. Ironically, we tend to be more concerned with the public accountability of private firms than nonprofit foundations. Legally enforced standards are set for radio and television broadcasters, some products (such as prescription drugs) are sold to the public only on a limited access basis, and the government enforces quality standards for products as diverse as automobiles, hot dogs, and baby cribs. If private firms are held to severe standards, what standards are imposed on nonprofit foundations that are presumably chartered for public purposes? Outside of restrictions on overtly political activities, there are few standards on their products. This is, undoubtedly, because what they produce is relatively abstract when compared to the goods and services we buy in the private sector.

Accountability to the Government

Private firms, like nonprofit foundations, are accountable to the government because they must obey the laws. The primary difference in accountability comes from the tax-preferred status of foundations. Whereas private firms pay taxes on their incomes, nonprofit foundations are financed through tax-free contributions and do not earn taxable income. Were it not for their special status, foundations and their donors would owe substantial tax payments as a result of their operations.

The accountability of private firms means that they must document their income and expenses in detail, showing their profitability. Publicly traded firms are required to make even more financial disclosures. The government uses this information to raise tax revenue from firms, but as a side effect the information also is beneficial to investors who can evaluate the effectiveness of firms. Even a profitable firm can be bought out, and its management can lose control, if others in financial markets decide that the firm is not as profitable as it could be.

Nonprofit organizations, because they are largely exempt from the obligation to pay taxes, are not subject to the same government scrutiny. The government may be more interested in their activities, in order to verify that the organization merits nonprofit status, but it is less interested in the way that the firm actually receives and disburses funds. For example, any profits that a book publisher makes on the sales of books is taxable income, whereas when nonprofit foundations sell books, they are disseminating information but not earning taxable income. These tax issues, taken up in chapter 4 as they relate to the activities of foundations, are also relevant to the issue of accountability.

Accountability to the Donors

Donors have relatively little information regarding what happens to their donations when they contribute to a nonprofit organization for philanthropic reasons. That is true whether one is endowing a foundation or whether one is sending a contribution to CARE. One reason why nonprofit status is important to philanthropies is that it provides donors with some assurance that their donations are being used for charitable purposes rather than going toward the enrichment of the firm's management. When buying computer software one exchanges money for a product, and both buyers and sellers view the transaction as worthwhile. If, in the process, Bill Gates becomes a billionaire, we have some notion that he earned his billions. But if foundation managers, or others associated with charitable organizations, profited from charitable activities, we would view that activity as a violation of the public trust. Nonprofit status does not guarantee that donations will be spent wisely, but it does indicate that managers have no claim on the organization's revenues beyond the wages they earn for their labors.[4]

The accountability problems suggest a reason why people choose to volunteer their time, rather than money, even when donations of time are not tax deductible. When money is donated it is difficult to see whether that money is being used for a purpose for which the donor would approve, but by donating time the donor is in a good position to judge the effectiveness of the donation. Thus, donating time helps the donor monitor the activities of the recipient organization and better evaluate the way that the donation is used.

The donors who fund nonprofit foundations are probably more accurately viewed not as customers of foundations, but as stockholders. Like stockholders in the private sector, they provide the capital that enables the organizations to invest in activities to further their missions, but unlike stockholders they expect their return to be in the form of the socially beneficial activities of foundations rather than in the form of dividends. On close examination, donors are neither customers nor stockholders, but the analogy between stockholders and donors holds enough parallels that it provides insight into some of the accountability problems that exist with foundations.

Separation of Ownership and Control

In a classic study of the corporate form of organization, Berle and Means discussed the problem of the separation of ownership from control in corporations.[5] In brief, the problem is that the owners of a firm are not the individuals who manage it, so those who are the firm's decision-makers may not always act in the best interest of the firm's owners. This idea has been generalized by more recent work, and the problem applies much more broadly than just to corporations. The key problem Berle and Means focused on is often described by economists as one of agency cost,[6] and arises any time one individual, called the principal, relies on another, called the agent, to further his interest.

An investor using the advice of a stockbroker is an example of a principal, and the stockbroker is the principal's agent. If the broker gets paid on commission, the broker has an incentive to buy and sell stocks to boost commission income, but has much less of an incentive to make the investor money. Thus, a principal-agent problem arises in which the agent (the broker) has interests different from the principal (the investor) and the agent therefore may not always act in the best interest of the principal. When getting automobile repairs, an uninformed consumer may just ask the mechanic to fix whatever is wrong with the car, placing the owner and mechanic in a principal-agent relationship. In this case, the mechanic has an incentive to misstate the problems the car has in order to boost his income, which creates agency cost. The examples could go on, but the idea should be clear. When one individual (the principal) relies on another (the agent) to act in his best interest, the incentives may be such that the agent can profit from acting in a way that is not in the best interest of the principal, creating agency cost. The idea is that if the principal were as informed as the agent, and made his own decisions instead of relying on the agent, the principal would have made different decisions, and been better off as a result, than when the agent makes decisions for the principal.

With regard to the corporate form of organization, stockholders invest in a firm with the hope of receiving a flow of income from the firm's profits. They are the principals. The firm is run by managers, who act as agents for the stockholders. But because the managers are not the owners, they may make decisions that benefit management rather than the stockholders. Thus, the separation of ownership from control gives rise to an agency cost.

In the private sector there are a number of factors that work to reduce agency costs. First, although managers are not the firm's owners, they often do have a significant amount of their wealth tied up in the firm. Thus, they do stand to benefit financially from the firm's profits. Second, in order to encourage management to take account of the interests of stockholders, firms often provide stock ownership plans in which managers (and sometimes all employees) receive some of their compensation in the form of stock options that can be exercised in the future. For example, a stock option might enable an employee to buy the company's stock one year from its issuance, at a price well below its current price. Thus, any increase in the stock's price before the option is exercised benefits the employee with the stock option just as much as any stockholder. This gives employees and managers an incentive to further the interests of the stockholders.

Yet another factor comes into play just because the stock can be bought and sold. If management is not overseeing the firm in a manner that will maximize the value of the firm, the firm can be bought out and the new owners can install new managers to increase the firm's value. A stock market provides a ready indication of the relationship between the assets of a firm and its expected future profitability.

All of the agency problems that exist with private firms exist with nonprofit foundations. The donors, like stockholders in a for-profit firm, are hoping for a return on their investment, but the return that foundation donors hope for is much less tangible, and is not valued on the market. There is no stock price that can be referenced to judge the foundation's performance, and there is no way to vest the managers of the nonprofit foundation with a partial interest in the profitability of the foundation. Foundation managers often do receive substantial benefits from their positions, but these benefits are independent of the performance of the foundation, and the performance of the foundation is hard to evaluate anyway.

Although agency problems do exist with for-profit firms, the fact that a firm is continually valued on the stock market provides a good way for stockholders to judge the degree to which managers are furthering the interests of stockholders. No such convenient indicator exists for nonprofit foundations, so there is no good way for donors to tell whether their money is being put to good use. Furthermore, judging the performance of a nonprofit foundation by the value of its good works is always going to be more nebulous than judging the performance of a corporation based on a relatively easy-to-measure indicator like profitability. While the separation of ownership from control may create some inefficiencies in the for-profit sector of the economy, it is a much more severe problem in the nonprofit sector, and is a major reason why foundations lack accountability to their donors.

The Free Rider Problem and Accountability

The free rider problem occurs when some individuals are able to benefit from the activities of others, and thus receive a free ride. When the possibility of free riding exists, everybody has an incentive to let others produce benefits for them, so too few of the benefits get produced. When free riding is possible, an argument is often made for government production of the good in question, but free riding is possible in the private sector as well.

The free rider problem provides a standard justification for government involvement in charitable activities. The argument goes like this. Most people want to see help provided to those who are least fortunate in their society. The interest of the givers is to see that those who have trouble taking care of their own needs have their welfare improved through charitable activity. The free rider problem arises because if one person makes a charitable donation, it improves the well-being of less fortunate individuals and in that way makes every potential donor better off. The goal of the donor, in this case, is not to give away money, but to improve the lot of those worst off, and if others donate to charity, the free rider can see the improvement in the recipients without having to make any personal donations.

This problem may be relevant to the level of donations to charitable foundations, and donations may be undersupplied for that reason. Indeed, many so-called charitable contributions go toward items like concert halls, art galleries, and historic preservation: things that wealthy people like but that provide minimal benefits to the needy. Foundations that supply ideas rather than direct benefits to the needy may actually receive excessive contributions for this reason. The donors receive the tax benefits of being charitable, and can feel like they are donating to a worthy cause, even though it is one that provides little benefit to those who need it the most. But the supply of funds for charitable activities is somewhat beside the point here. The free rider problem also can have a major impact on the accountability of nonprofit foundations.

The agency problem that exists because of the separation of ownership from control in for-profit firms occurs because stockholders do not want to devote the time to managing the firm themselves. Thus, they have less information about the management's activities and the firm's performance than they would if they were fully informed. Stockholders have a direct financial interest in the performance of the firm, however, which gives them a good personal reason to be informed. But because all stockholders will benefit from any monitoring that any one stockholder does, stockholders have an incentive to exert too little oversight, instead free riding on the oversight exercised by other stockholders.

Stockholders with large blocks of shares, and those who derive a major part of their income from the shares of one company, have more of an incentive to exert oversight. The best example of this is Bill Gates, the largest shareholder of Microsoft, who in 1996 owned nearly one quarter of the company's stock. Owners of Microsoft shares can confidently free ride rather than become informed about the company's management, because Mr. Gates, as the company's largest shareholder, has such a strong incentive to remain informed. In addition to this high-visibility example, many other companies have large shareholders who exert oversight, while smaller investors free ride.

While stockholders to have some incentive to free ride on the oversight of others, they do have a direct financial incentive to be informed, and if they have doubts, they can sell their shares. Because there are many companies from which to choose on the stock exchange, one does not need to harbor many doubts about a company before selling the stock and investing in another company seems like a good strategy. Thus, the direct financial incentives of stockholders helps to limit free riding on oversight, even when it is recognized that the main way in which small stockholders exercise their oversight is by selling shares of the company in question.

With regard to nonprofit foundations, much less information is available about the foundation's performance, as previously noted. This makes free riding on the oversight of others relatively more attractive when compared to the for-profit sector. But more important, donors to nonprofit foundations have no direct financial incentive to exercise any oversight. For-profit firms provide a monetary return to their investors, creating a clear incentive for oversight, whereas nonprofit foundations return their donors nothing except the feeling that they are doing something good with their money. Thus, unlike private firms, they will be financially no worse off if, once the donation is made, they make no attempts to see how effectively their money is being used. All donors, no matter how large, have this same incentive to free ride on the oversight activities of others, so the free rider problem creates a nonprofit foundation sector that is remarkably free of donor oversight.

Indeed, when the Rockefeller Foundation was established, Rockefeller purposefully designed the foundation in such a way that he would have no control over the disposition of the foundation's resources. This autonomy makes the foundation appear to have much more in the way of humanitarian motives, and especially in Rockefeller's case makes it appear much less likely that the foundation would be another way in which the donor could further his own personal interests. However, it also keeps the donor from exerting any oversight. Once the money has been given away, there is no personal financial incentive for oversight in the same way that there is for one's personal investments. But if even the biggest donors, like Rockefeller, free ride on oversight, who is overseeing the disposition of the foundation's donations? Nobody is. And the free rider problem explains why no donor has the incentive to.

If foundations that continually receive donations have potential free rider problems that lead to a lack of accountability to donors, there is absolutely no accountability for foundations like Rockefeller, Carnegie, and Ford, that receive their entire incomes from earnings on an endowment from individuals who have died long ago. One can talk about degrees of accountability to donors, but in the case of many of America's largest foundations there is absolutely no accountability.

Nonprofit foundations are not unique in having accountability issues. For-profit firms are accountable to their customers, to their stockholders, to the government, and to the general public, but in many cases agency problems and free rider problems may create a problem in which firms are not as accountable as one would hope.[7] Accountability problems with for-profit firms have been a concern of economic theorists, but when comparing for-profit firms with nonprofit foundations, we see that all of the accountability issues that exist with for-profit firms also exist for nonprofit foundations. Furthermore, there are better mechanisms to ensure accountability in the for-profit sector than in the nonprofit sector. There are legitimate reasons for being concerned about the lack of accountability of private sector managers, but all of these factors apply even more seriously to nonprofit foundations. The accountability issues with regard to for-profit firms are all more significant for nonprofit foundations, and in addition, there are other reasons why nonprofit foundations are even less accountable than private firms.

Public Accountability of Nonprofit Institutions

The accountability problems arising from the separation of owner-ship from control in corporations exist in nonprofit institutions as well, but with nonprofit institutions, other potentially more significant prob-lems arise. If profits serve to monitor the performance of private sector corporations, nonprofit institutions are missing this vital check. The discussion to this point has focused on trying to see who has the incen-tive to monitor nonprofit foundations, and on trying to see to whom nonprofit foundations might have to answer for their activities. In both cases, nonprofit foundations were shown to be less accountable than for-profit firms. However, even if one wanted to hold nonprofit founda-tions accountable for their activities, there is a major question of how one would measure the performance of foundations in order to evaluate them.

Other organizations that deal primarily in the world of ideas face some sort of market test that provides a basis for evaluation. Colleges and universities must be able to attract students in order to survive, so while one might rightfully view the output of a university as intangible and hard to measure, the public's evaluation of a university's output can be gauged by the number and quality of the students it accepts, and on the performance of its graduates. Authors and publishers rely ulti-mately on the market to sell their works, providing a market test, but a study funded by a foundation grant offers little that can aid the public in evaluating its quality, or the degree to which the study furthers the public interest. Thus insulated, foundations are free to make their grants based on whims, personal preferences, or any other criteria without any indicator of the efficacy of the grant. Indeed, sometimes exactly the opposite of market indicators might be used, as is the case when foun-dations justify funding a particular type of study because there is no other means of support for it. If this is so, then what indicator is there, besides the preferences of a foundation's management, that the funded activity is in the public interest?

This analysis of the accountability of foundations is in no way in-tended to suggest that foundation managers and trustees are not dili-gent individuals interested in pursuing the public interest. Rather, it implies that if foundations do not make effective use of their resources, there is no good way for the general public to tell, and perhaps just as seriously, there is no good way for foundation managers themselves to tell. If two automobile companies produce cars that have similar prices, how might one tell if one car is better than the other? Sales figures provide a good indication, and automobile companies themselves know this, and imitate the features of their competitors' cars that they believe make those cars desirable to consumers. If two foundations finance studies with grants of about equal size, how would one evaluate the degree to which those studies further the interest of mankind? That is a tougher question, and the criteria must be vague.

Nonprofit institutions lack accountability because few people have the incentive to hold them accountable, because trustees and managers do not have to depend on the quality of their output for their income, and because their products are inherently difficult to evaluate.

Public Accountability of Nonprofit Foundations

Nonprofit foundations share the accountability problems of other nonprofit institutions, but there are additional concerns about the accountability of endowed institutions. With no donors to answer to, and no need to solicit future funds, the trustees of nonprofit foundations are answerable to nobody. They must, of course, obey the laws that allow them to maintain their nonprofit status, or risk legal sanction, but beyond this, there is little to check their activities. Mindful of this potential problem, donors, and foundations themselves, have taken some steps to try to preserve the intentions of the donors in the activities of the foundations. Foundation trustees often serve without compensation, and boards of trustees are often self-perpetuating, meaning that when a member leaves the board, the remaining members appoint a replacement. Because some status is involved in being on such a board, foundations can hope to have a good slate of candidates among which to choose, and if a good board is selected initially, there is the hope that its quality will perpetuate itself.

Still, there is woefully little accountability for nonprofit foundations that rely only on their endowments for income. There is no fundraising activity, no way for past donors to exert any control, and almost no governmental or legal control over the foundation's activities. One can hope that the foundation will act in the public interest, but there is absolutely no sanction or penalty that will be brought to bear against foundations that do not. Indeed, some evidence suggests that if the opportunity arises, the management of a nonprofit organization prefers to set itself up as an endowed foundation rather than an organization relying on continual fund-raising, partly to avoid the chores of fundraising, but also partly to provide the foundation with more independence and less accountability.[8] The nonprofit foundation that operates entirely from endowment income answers to nobody.

Corporate Philanthropy Versus Nonprofit Foundations

Corporations often take an active interest in charitable activities. They participate in United Way fundraising drives, they provide grants to local communities for activities as diverse as beautification of local areas, assistance of local schools, and the sponsoring of recreational activities. Corporations are major supporters of universities through general gifts, through the matching of employee contributions to universities, through the funding of professorships in order to improve the quality of a university's faculty, through the funding of scholarships for students, and through the provision of research grants. Some of these activities are related to the corporate bottom line only to the extent that corporations will fare better when they are located in better communities. Other activities are more directly related to the mission of the donor corporations.

One can easily see why corporations that recruit workers from the ranks of college graduates would be interested in improving the education that those graduates receive. Thus, donations to universities can be a good investment for a corporation. By funding professorships, goodwill may be created so that professors steer their better students toward those donors that have established a relationship with a university. One would expect engineering firms to make their contributions to engineering schools, accounting firms to make contributions to business schools. and so forth. Donations made in this way also enhance the accountability of the recipient to the donor. Firms that hire accountants will be in a good position to evaluate how effectively their donations are being used, providing an incentive for the recipients to demonstrate to donors that the money is well used in order to attract future donations.

Research grants to universities will function in much the same way. Researchers will submit proposals, and the firms making the grants typically will be in a good position to evaluate how effectively research money is being spent. In many cases donors may be hoping for specific results from the research that will be of direct use to the donors. The big advantage of this type of corporate philanthropy is that the recipient has a substantial amount of accountability to the donor.

One can hardly argue that there is any disadvantage to this type of arrangement, because both the donor and the recipient agree to the grant. In a larger sense, however, if these types of arrangements dominate, it might turn out that, as an example, university research could become overly focused on questions of corporate interest and on issues that bear some immediate relationship to the bottom line of some firm. Basic research could suffer, not because these corporate research grants are bad in and of themselves, but because they might displace research on more fundamental issues. Thus, there is an argument for more general gifts to a university's foundation, which will build the endowment and provide for a perpetual source of revenues.

Gifts do not need to be made to a foundation, however. They can be given to the university for more general purposes on an annual basis. Why should a corporation, which intends to last in perpetuity anyway, give money to a foundation? The foundation will then dole out the money in perpetuity, which is something the corporation could do through annual gifts rather than a large lump-sum amount. In some cases, such as with the Carnegie and Rockefeller foundations, the donors might have such sizable wealth that they would prefer to establish a more organized group to determine how the money can best be used. But in other cases, tax laws push corporations (and individuals) to make large gifts to foundations rather than spread the gifts over time. For one thing, a gift can be made of an asset on which the donor has an unrealized capital gain, providing a tax deduction and avoiding the capital gains tax. Few people relish sending their money to the IRS, so making a donation of appreciated property may be preferable for tax reasons to selling the property and giving the proceeds to a cause a little at a time. Even when capital gains are not an issue, giving money sooner rather than later enables a tax deduction for a charitable contribution to be taken sooner, providing a tax advantage. Thus, despite the greater accountability inherent in a steady stream of donations, the provisions of the tax code encourage giving endowments.

For this reason, an inquiry into the way in which tax laws affect the activities of foundations is relevant from a policy perspective. There may be a tendency among those committed to the idea of laissez faire to argue that what donors want to do with their money is their business. They earned the money, so let them spend it as they like. However, when their disposition of their assets is influenced by tax law, there may be public policy reasons to alter the tax advantages to particular types of activities. As this section demonstrates, corporate philanthropy, even when the corporation has its narrow interests in mind, creates much more accountability than donations to foundations. Even when corporate philanthropy furthers the interests of the corporate donor, the activities funded by corporate philanthropy must be in the best interest of the recipient, or the money would not be accepted.

Corporate donors recognize the concept of enlightened self-interest, and see that it is to their advantage to engage in charitable activities.[9] One would not want to discourage the charitable impulses of corporations, but at the same time one must question whether changes in the tax code or other laws governing foundations and, more generally, charitable activity, would make those donations work more for the public interest.

Congressional Questions about Foundation Accountability

Congressional questions about the activities of foundations began early in the twentieth century. Beginning in 1910 Rockefeller tried to get Congress to charter his Rockefeller Foundation.[10] To the general public, it appeared that Rockefeller wanted to use the foundation to soften the public's unfavorable opinion of him. Rockefeller was willing to turn control of the foundation over to Congress and other outside individuals to ensure that his private interests were separate from the foundation's activities, but even this appeared suspicious at a time when Standard Oil was in the process of being dismantled by the government for antitrust violations. Meanwhile, the Hearst newspapers discovered that Rockefeller had paid nearly $100,000 to a U.S. senator and had written correspondence suggesting that Congress do something to rein in its antimonopoly legislation, even as President Teddy Roosevelt wore with pride his reputation as a trust-buster. Congress was clearly unwilling to be a party to any of Rockefeller's activities, and finally Rockefeller gave up his quest for a Congressional charter and chartered the foundation in the state of New York in 1913.

Rockefeller lost interest in trying for a Congressional charter, but Congress did not lose interest in Rockefeller's foundation. In 1916 Congress created a Commission on Industrial Relations which concluded that a handful of wealthy individuals, after gaining control over a large segment of the U.S. economy, and pushing for political control of the nation, were using nonprofit foundations to gain control over the nation's educational system, over its health care system, over social services, and other facets of American life. Congress was concerned that despite the use of antitrust laws to control the power of the small group of capitalists that exerted so much control over the economy, they were using foundations as a capitalist tool to further their own interests.[11]

While Congress was concerned about foundations as a tool of capitalism in the teens, its concerns were just the opposite when it formed the House Select Committee to Investigate Tax-Exempt Foundations and Comparable Organizations in 1952. To help gather information, the Committee sent questionnaires to foundations which included the question, "Have foundations supported or assisted persons, organizations, and projects which, if not subversive in the extreme sense of the word, tend to weaken or discredit the capitalistic system as it exists in the United States and favor Marxist socialism?" [12]

Even more serious investigations took place in the 1960s, led by Democratic Representative Wright Patman of Texas, who had served in Congress since 1929 and had long been suspicious of foundations. As chapter 4 reported, several activities of the Ford Foundation particularly upset Patman. The Foundation aided the registration of black voters in Cleveland, which helped Carl Stokes become the first black mayor of a major city, it promoted public school decentralization in New York City, and it provided stipends to some of Robert Kennedy's staff members after Kennedy's assassination in 1968. Many members of Congress became so concerned about the activities of nonprofit foundations that the 1969 Tax Reform Act placed a large number of new regulations on foundations with the intention of keeping foundations out of politics, keeping them from controlling businesses, and making them more accountable and open to the general public.[13]

As the series of Congressional investigations of foundations show, Congress has been concerned about the accountability of foundations throughout the twentieth century. Its main concerns was not that foundations might waste money, or that foundation employees might benefit from tax-free expenditures, but rather that the activities of foundations were antithetical to the public interest.

The Many Dimensions of Accountability

As the discussion in this chapter illustrates, a consideration of the accountability of nonprofit foundations raises the questions of who foundations should be accountable to and what foundations should be accountable for. Should foundations be accountable to their donors, or do donors give up at least some of their oversight by leaving an endowment? Should foundations be accountable to government? Clearly they should be to the degree that they benefit from being favored under the tax laws. The option always exists for foundations to give up their tax-favored status to be treated like any other corporation. These issues will be considered in more detail in the Chapter 10, which discuss policy alternatives for dealing with foundations. But if foundations should be held accountable to someone, what is it that they are accountable for?

Because nonprofit foundations enjoy favorable treatment under the tax laws they should be held accountable for not using their tax-preferred status to avoid paying taxes on activities that ordinarily would be taxed. This would cover the provision of untaxed benefits to donors, employees, trustees, and indeed anyone else. While this is a serious public policy issue, it is beyond the scope of this study. A second area in which foundations might be held accountable regards the wise use of their money. Stories abound about extravagant and wasteful activities of foundations and other charitable organizations.

Often, organizations spend a substantial amount of their income to raise additional funds. For example a Fraternal Order of Police telephone fundraising campaign promised 80 percent of the profits for charity. However, the expenses of fundraising consumed two thirds of the donations, leaving only one third as profits. The promised 80 percent of this one third left only about 27 percent of the donated money for charitable purposes. Few people would be willing to donate to such causes if they realized ahead of time that only a bit more than one quarter of the money they donated would be used for a charitable cause, while those manning the phone banks got most of the money. Even worse is the case of the United Cancer Council, a charity based in Indiana, which raised $5.1 million in 1985 but spent only $20,000 on cancer research.[14]

As noted earlier, a common way to try to avoid scrutiny for excess fundraising expenses is to list as one of the organization's activities public education on an issue. Then, whenever a solicitation letter is mailed or a phone call is made, information is included on the seriousness of the cause for which funds are being solicited. The letter or phone call is then categorized as public education rather than fundraising. Such activities are deceptive, but difficult for the small donor to uncover. Thus, money contributed to foundations may often end up diverted for the benefit of those who run the foundations rather than for those worthy causes that donors believe they are supporting. Foundations that operate entirely from endowments will not face these fundraising issues, but in other areas they are equally unaccountable.

When one thinks of accountability, these are the dimensions of accountability that most readily come to mind. Is the foundation making efficient use of the money at their disposal? Are foundation trustees and employees profiting from money that was intended to go to other causes? Is the foundation set up as a way to avoid the payment of taxes rather than for some public purpose? As important as these aspects of accountability are, they are of only minor importance to the aspect of foundations being considered in this study, which is the types of ideas that are produced by foundations. Yes, the general public has an interest in seeing that foundation money is not being spent fraudulently, or wasted. But beyond that, the general public also has an interest in seeing that foundation programs actually are in the public interest, rather than counter to it. Foundations should be accountable to the general public for the results of their foundation activities, because of their tax-exempt status, but as this chapter has shown, they are not.

Accountability is being considered in a narrow and specific way in this study, then. The issue is, to whom does a foundation answer for the projects it funds, and for the consequences of its programs? Regardless of whether foundation money is wasted or spent fraudulently, another dimension of accountability is holding foundations responsible for funding programs that really are in the public interest. It is this dimension of accountability that is the focus of this book.

Elusive Standards

Ideally, one could come up with some clear standards for judging whether foundations are meeting their public responsibilities. A viola-

tion of public trust is a relatively easy call in cases of fraud or mismanagement, but is more difficult when one is trying to judge whether foundation activities are in the public interest. Ultimately, there are no clear
criteria that can be set out, and it is a matter of using one's judgment.
Congress did that in 1969, and as the debate made apparent, there were
arguments on both sides of the proposed reforms, and the activities
Congress tried to eliminate were defended by some as being in the public
interest.

Appearances are important, for several reasons. Pragmatically, Congress may act again if foundations appear to have violated their public trust. More important for the mission of foundations, when they
are trying to develop and promote ideas, their success ultimately hinges
on having their work taken seriously and accepted as legitimate. Thus,
at least in this regard, the incentives of foundation managers are congruent with the public interest. Whether there are additional regulations or restrictions that could be put on foundations to further ensure
that their activities will correspond to the public interest is a question
that is taken up in more detail in chapters 10 and 11. When we get to
that point, we must recognize that any recommendations must be made
in circumstances where standards for judging the activities of foundations are elusive.

Ideas and Other Foundation Products

Foundations fund many useful projects. The Rockefeller Foundation
has had spectacular successes in funding programs dealing with a number of diseases, including hookworm, typhoid, malaria, hepatitis, and
others. A number of other foundations deal exclusively with health problems, while other foundations have aided education for the poor, have
helped improve housing standards, and have provided benefits in a number of other ways. When foundations help individuals to improve their
lives, the benefits are relatively easily recognized. But when foundations make grants for the purpose of undertaking public policy studies,
developing ideas, or funding intellectual centers and specific educational programs, the degree to which such programs are in the public
interest is less obvious. Ideas can subvert the public interest just as
easily as they can promote it. Thus, there is even more reason to examine the accountability of foundations when they are developing and
promoting ideas.

When ideas are available for sale to the general public, there is direct accountability. Authors who present their ideas in books are accountable to publishers who evaluate their material prior to publication, and publishers are accountable to the book-buying public. Colleges and universities must sell their ideas to prospective students, or those students will go elsewhere. The degree of accountability may be open to debate. Are students (and their parents) really able to judge the quality of education offered by various colleges? Yet colleges do have reputations to uphold, and they are worried about their enrollments. They care not only about the numbers of students they attract, but also about the quality, as indicated by grade point averages and standardized test scores. Likewise, even though readers do not know the contents of a book before they read it, both publishers and authors have reputations that they try to uphold. These market checks on ideas do not exist for the ideas funded by nonprofit foundations, however, because the ideas are funded from the income from foundation endowments. Thus, foundation-funded ideas are free from the accountability that exists for others who produce ideas.

Perhaps it should be this way. There is a difference between good ideas and popular ideas, after all. Perhaps there should be a way for the development of less popular but socially valuable ideas. Foundations can fill a role by financing those ideas that may help improve the condition of mankind, yet do not have a ready market. If this is so, then there must be a way for foundations to identify those ideas that are in the public interest, and the question goes directly back to accountability. How are foundations held accountable for the quality of the ideas they promote? The answer is: they are not. While in the abstract the general public might hope that foundations fund ideas that are in the public interest, there is no mechanism in place to ensure that this happens. Without accountability, foundations fund those programs that its trustees and management want to fund. And while foundations themselves may have missions, it is worth examining, in light of the assertion that foundations work to further the public interest, what the general public can hope to get from foundation funding of ideas. The next chapter takes a step in that direction by looking at the role that foundations can play in the economy.

Notes

1. Joseph C. Goulden, *The Money Givers* (New York: Random House, 1971), pp. 27-28.
2. Goulden, *The Money Givers,* p. 37.
3. Problems such as these are recounted in detail with regard to health charities by James T. Bennett and Thomas J. DiLorenzo, *Unhealthy Charities: Hazardous to Your Health and Wealth* (New York: Basic Books, 1994). See also Robert A. Liston, *The Charity Racket* (Nashville, TN: Thomas Nelson Publishers, 1977).
4. Jerald Schiff, *Charitable Giving and Government Policy: An Economic Analysis* (New York: Greenwood Press, 1990), and Henry Hansmann, "The Role of Nonprofit Enterprise," *Yale Law Journal* 89 (April 1980), pp. 835-901.
5. Adolf A. Berle and Gardiner C. Means, *The Modern Corporation and Private Property* (New York: Macmillan, 1933).
6. A prominent article describing the problem is Michael C. Jensen and William H. Meckling, "Theory of the Firm: Managerial Behavior, Agency Costs and Ownership Structure," *Journal of Financial Economics* 3 (October 1976), pp. 306-360.
7. This list is not meant to be exhaustive. For example, firms also are accountable to their employees, to the community in which they are located, to their suppliers, and to many other groups.
8. Susan Rose-Ackerman, "Ideals versus Dollars: Donors, Charity Managers, and Government Grants," *Journal of Political Economy* 95, No. 4 (August 1987), pp. 810-823.
9. Robert L. Payton, *Philanthropy: Voluntary Action for the Public Good* (New York: Collier Macmillan Publishers, 1988), pp. 199-203, makes a clear case that corporations recognize that they have an enlightened self-interest in philanthropy.
10. The Rockefeller Foundation's Congressional scrutiny is discussed by Goulden, *The Money Givers,* pp. 32-40, and Michael O'Neill, *The Third America: The Emergence of the Nonprofit Sector in the United States* (San Francisco, CA: Jossey-Bass, 1989), pp. 145-146.
11. F. Emerson Andrews, *Patman and Foundations: Review and Assessment* (New York: Foundation Center, 1968), p. 2.
12. O'Neill, *The Third America,* p. 145.
13. O'Neill, *The Third America,* pp. 145-146.
14. These examples are from Robert L. Payton, *Philanthropy,* chapter 1.

9

The Role of Nonprofit Foundations
in the Economy

Economists commonly divide the economy into two sectors: public and private. The public sector is the government, which raises its revenues through taxation and undertakes expenditures, presumably, in the public interest. The private sector consists of households and businesses, exchanging goods and services for money, and acting in their own self-interests. Nonprofit organizations do not fit neatly into either one of these categories, and have sometimes been referred to as the third sector of the economy. Some nonprofit firms, such as hospitals, do exchange fees for services, and so bear closer resemblance to private sector firms, even though they may serve some charitable or public service functions. But many third sector organizations receive their revenues from voluntary contributions, rather than as coerced tax payments, or payments in exchange for goods and services, and undertake expenditures to further public interest goals, as envisioned by the donors, rather than providing essential public goods and services, or goods and services in exchange for payment. This third sector is not like the private sector, where parties to private exchanges expect to receive at least as much value as they give up in exchange, and it is not like the public sector, which forces everyone to contribute and so invites everyone's scrutiny as they evaluate what they get relative to what they give up. Those who finance the third sector do not expect to receive benefits equal to what they pay, reducing both the ability to evaluate an organization's effectiveness and the incentive to do so. Once donors are deceased, as is the case with most of the foundations discussed here, donor oversight is impossible. Without donor oversight, and without accountability to voters or customers, the institutional setting of the third sector leaves it with relatively little accountability.

John D. Rockefeller III referred to this third sector of the economy as "the invisible sector." [1] The third sector is invisible partly because of the activities it undertakes, but also partly because of its lack of accountability. Because of its taxation and regulation, the public sector of the economy can hardly remain invisible, and because of periodic elections, part of the visibility of government goes hand in hand with its accountability. A similar story holds for the private sector of the economy. One's relationship with employers looms large in one's life, and when purchasing goods and services, consumers are acutely aware of the resources they are expending, and are often shopping among competing sellers looking for the best value they can get from private sector vendors. Even though the private sector would have to remain visible because people must interact with it, businesses make it even more visible through continual advertising as they compete for consumer dollars.

Little of this applies to the nonprofit sector. People are not forced to interact with it the way they are with both the public and private sectors. Revenues for many nonprofit institutions come from voluntary contributions rather than from coerced taxes or exchanges of money for goods and services. The activities of many nonprofit institutions remain sheltered from the public view partly because people do not have to interact with them, and partly because the bulk of nonprofit organizations undertake their activities with little fanfare and only occasional advertising, and often even with the intention of remaining relatively anonymous in the activities they are undertaking.

Foundations and the Third Sector

What role do nonprofit institutions play in an economy, and how do the nonprofit foundations that are the subject of this study fit into the third sector? The nonprofit sector of the economy is much larger than the general purpose foundations that are the present subject of study, but the larger third sector is of relevance to nonprofit foundations because the public perception of foundations is linked with other charitable activity that is undertaken by the third sector. About half of the nonprofit sector is involved with health care. That includes nonprofit hospitals, churches, research organizations, and philanthropic organizations that assist in the financing of health care for those in need. Most private educational institutions are nonprofit organizations, as are fraternities, trade associations, credit unions, and chambers of commerce. As this partial list indicates, a substantial share of the nonprofit sector is not philanthropic in nature, but the foundations that are of interest to this study fall into the category of philanthropies.

The philanthropic segment of the nonprofit sector is defined by Section 501(c)(3) of the Internal Revenue Code as including those organizations that operate exclusively for charitable, religious, scientific, educational, or literary purposes, as long as no part of the organization's activities benefit any private shareholder or individual, and as long as the organization does not attempt to influence legislation, carry on propaganda, or aid any political campaigns on behalf of those running for public office. Chapter 4 examined the tax laws and their effects on foundations, showing that foundations are treated differently from other nonprofit organizations for tax purposes, but nonprofit foundations have something in common with charitable organizations, and indeed are likely to be thought of that way. While many large foundations operate entirely from income earned on their endowments, contributions made to others that may carry on similar activities are deductible expenses for federal income tax purposes. Donations to churches differ from those made to the United Way, which differ from those made to the American Cancer Society, which differ from those made to the local symphony orchestra, which differ from those made to a nonprofit think tank. What they have in common, however, is that they are all considered charitable contributions for tax purposes.

This places nonprofit foundations on high moral ground, and indeed there is the expectation that the standard of conduct to which such organizations are held is higher than, for example, those dealing in market exchanges.[2] The perception of high moral ground comes from the association of nonprofit foundations with other charitable nonprofit organizations, but this perception is also based on the reality that the nonprofit foundations have gained their tax-preferred status based on the idea that they are acting in the public interest. Their tax-preferred status comes at a cost to the Treasury, and Congress should agree that the nation should bear this cost only if the gain to the general public is sufficient to compensate the nation for the loss in tax revenues. Thus, the tax treatment of nonprofit foundations is closely linked to the idea that they further the public interest in a manner similar to other charitable organizations like churches, the Salvation Army, medical research organizations, and symphony orchestras.

The list of organizations that are given tax preferences under the federal tax laws is diverse enough that it is reasonable to question how they work for the public good. This chapter considers the public benefits that are produced, and that could be produced, by nonprofit foundations. It suggests that there is a role for such organizations, but that their niche is shrinking because an expanding public sector is undertaking activities at the end of the twentieth century that would have been the province of foundations at the beginning of the century.

What Public Purpose Do Foundations Serve?

At first the answer to the question posed by this section head might seem almost too obvious to answer, especially in light of the preceding chapters that have described the many activities foundations have funded. A simple listing of all of the programs and accomplishments of nonprofit foundations shows the many ways in which they have served the public interest. From a public policy standpoint, however, the question must be examined a little differently. Nonprofit foundations are given preferential tax treatment under the federal tax laws in exchange for their public benefits, so one must ask what benefits the third sector brings that could not be generated from the private and public sectors of the economy. The private sector produces substantial benefits to all Americans, so much so that we tend to take them for granted most of the time. The nation has an abundance of food, clothing, and shelter for its citizens, and even most of those classified as living in poverty own automobiles, live in dwellings with indoor plumbing, and have electricity, telephones, and television sets. Surely one would not want to minimize the plight of those least fortunate in American society, but it is a tribute to the private sector that the most common nutritional problem of Americans below the poverty line is obesity.[3]

The private firms that build our homes and stores, the firms that provide us with automobiles and the gasoline to drive them, the farmers who produce our food, the entertainers who give us movies, music, and theme parks all contribute to the public good, albeit because they view that it is in their private interest to do so. More than two centuries ago, Adam Smith, who published *The Wealth of Nations* in 1776 marveled that a market economy channels the efforts of individuals so that each individual, pursuing his own self-interest, is led by an invisible hand to further the best interest of the whole society. The point is: the private sector of the economy contributes substantially to the public interest. Even when government redistribution programs aid in the care of those least fortunate, it is the private sector that produces the income that the government taxes to provide its benefits. Thus, the private sector of the economy is essential to the contribution to the public welfare made by the public sector, while the third sector of the economy is exempt from having to make this contribution.

The benefits produced by the public sector are substantial also. Public roads and parks, educational institutions, public health programs, aid to the elderly and to the poor, and the funding of scientific research are but a few of the benefits that Americans receive through the public sector. Thus, it is reasonable to question why public policy should allow a third sector to pursue activities in the public interest, untaxed, when private sector organizations that further the public interest also are taxed to produce public sector benefits. Whether the third sector produces benefits that are in the public interest is really beside the point. The private and public sectors do, so the real question is whether the additional benefits that are the result of the tax-preferred status of nonprofit foundations are worth the cost in terms of foregone tax revenues.

The Provision of Public Goods

The types of activities that tend to be financed by the grants of nonprofit foundations fall under the heading of what economists refer to as public goods. The economist's definition of public goods differs somewhat from the way in which the term might be used in common conversation, so it is worth considering in some detail how economists use the term. By so doing, this can help identify the niche in the economy that might be beneficially occupied by nonprofit foundations. Economists classify goods as public goods if they have one or both of the following two characteristics: jointness in consumption, and nonexcludability. Jointness in consumption means that once a good is produced, additional consumers can consume the good without reducing the amount consumed by existing consumers. Nonexcludability means that once a good is produced, the producer cannot prevent consumers from consuming it.[4]

Before considering these two public goods characteristics in more detail, note that despite the name, the definition does not imply in which sector of the economy public goods should be produced, or are produced. Some later examples will show that public goods are successfully produced in the public sector, in the private sector, and in the nonprofit sector. There may be a reason to prefer one sector over another for certain public goods, and indeed the purpose of this chapter is to see how the theory of public goods provides an economic rationale for the tax-preferred status of the nonprofit sector.[5]

Jointness in Consumption

The first characteristic of a public good, jointness in consumption, means that once the public good is produced additional users can consume it without reducing the consumption of others. Most goods that come to mind do not have this characteristic. If I drink a soft drink, then nobody else can have it, so it is not a joint consumption good. If I own a pair of shoes, that is one less pair that someone else can own, so again this is not a joint consumption good. But if a television station broadcasts a football game and I turn on my TV to watch, my neighbor down the street, or across town, can turn on his TV to watch too, and I am not deprived of watching the game. Once the game is being broadcast for one consumer, anyone else in the station's reception area can turn on his television to watch, without any existing consumer having to miss the game. The television broadcast signal is a joint consumption good. Another example that economists commonly use is national defense. If people in a particular area are being defended by a nation's armed forces, another person can move to that area and enjoy the protection of the military without any existing person having to give up that protection. As the examples of national defense and television broadcasting show, goods that are joint in consumption can be produced successfully in the public and the private sector.

Nonexcludability

Nonexcludability means that once a good is produced it is difficult for the producer to keep individuals from consuming the good. Why is this a problem? Because goods cost money to produce, and if consumers can consume the good without paying, the producer is going to have a difficult time making any money producing the good. Thus few producers will have an incentive to produce a nonexcludable good, so nonexcludable goods will be underproduced in the economy.

Two examples of nonexcludable goods are television broadcasts and national defense, the same examples used to illustrate jointness in consumption. How do they overcome the nonexcludability problem? With national defense, the government forces people to pay their taxes, and then produces national defense at no direct charge to the consumer. With television broadcasts, the broadcasters do not sell the ability to view programs directly to the viewer, but rather charge advertisers for the right to broadcast their messages along with the broadcaster's other programming. Thus, both the public and the private sector have means for dealing with the nonexcludability problem.

Note that the two characteristics of publicness do not necessarily have to be found in the same good. For example, movies share the characteristic of jointness in consumption, because one the expense of making the movie has been made, additional viewers can view the movie without preventing other viewers from seeing it. If I drink a soft drink, nobody else can drink it. If I watch a movie, lots of other people can see the same movie, either with me, or at another time. Movies can be successfully produced in the private sector because although they are joint in consumption, they are excludable. Movie theaters charge admission, and keep those who do not pay from watching.

Similarly, goods can be nonexcludable without being joint in consumption. Water in a river can provide an example. When there is plenty of water, the nonexcludable nature of the water may not make much difference, but where water is scarce, as in the American West, there are constant battles over water rights. The problem is that it is difficult to keep upstream users from taking water that downstream users want to use. Even when there is water in abundance, upstream users can pollute the water making it unusable, or even harmful, to downstream users, and again, it is difficult to exclude upstream users. Many environmental problems occur because of aspects of the environment that are not joint consumption goods, but that are nonexcludable goods.

Problems with Private Sector Provision

Why not just let the private sector produce all public goods, like it does with television broadcasts? In many cases this is the best solution, but there are problems with the private sector production of both joint consumption goods and nonexcludable goods. If a good is nonexcludable, then it will be difficult for the producer to get consumers to pay. Why should they pay when they can consume the good for free? Television broadcasters have dealt with this problem by selling advertising along with programs, and as the theory suggests, consumers of the programs do not pay for them. With modern technology it is feasible to scramble signals, but then there is the added cost of coding and decoding signals. With cable television, the cable companies can exclude nonpayers, so cable television does not fit the example. To see the problems with nonexcludability, one need only imagine turning national defense over to the private sector and asking for voluntary payment from those who want to be defended. Because there would be no way to exclude a nonpaying individual when the individual's next-door neighbor is paying for defense, people would not have the incentive to contribute, and the nation would spend less on national defense than almost everyone, payers and nonpayers alike, would prefer to spend.

The problem with nonexcludability, then, is that too few consumers will pay for the good, so too little of the good will be produced. Thus, the argument goes, there is a role for government to finance the good using revenues collected from taxes. That way, people cannot avoid paying, and the democratic decision-making process can decide how much we all should pay. Obviously, there is also a potential role for the nonprofit sector. Through the generosity of donors, foundations could finance the production of nonexcludable goods.

Jointness in consumption presents a different kind of problem to the private sector. If the good is excludable, then like the movie theater, the private sector can exclude consumers and charge for the good in order to produce it. The problem is that because it costs nothing to allow an additional consumer to consume the good, if some consumers want to consume it but do not because of the price, we could enhance social welfare by allowing them to consume it.

Consider, for example, a movie theater with many empty seats, charging a price of $6 to see a movie. (I can relate well to this example because almost every time I go to see a movie, there are only a few other people in the theater. Are movies always this way, or is this a reflection on my taste in movies, the times I go to see them, or both?) With empty seats in the theater, what if another viewer wanted to see the movie, but was only willing to pay three dollars to see it? No existing viewer would have to give up her seat to allow the additional viewer to see the movie, so if the additional viewer were allowed to see the movie, it would add three dollars to the total value of the movie. Theater operators will be reluctant to lower the price, however, because they have no good way to distinguish viewers who value the viewing experience at three dollars from those who would pay six dollars, so they would have to lower the price for everybody, losing revenue in the process.

If this argument that it would be socially optimal to admit the viewer who values the movie at only three dollars is accepted, the same argument would apply to other viewers who would only be willing to pay two dollars, or one dollar, or twenty-five cents to see the movie. Taken to its logical conclusion, the optimal price to charge for the movie is zero, but then the movie could not be produced in the private sector because there would be no revenues to offset the costs of the movie. Thus, the argument goes, the good should be produced in the public sector, financed through tax dollars, so that all potential consumers can have access to the good.

This is done for a number of goods with this jointness in consumption characteristic, using this rationale. Public roads, public parks, and public radio provide good examples. Once again, if donors can be found, there is a potential role for the third sector to provide joint consumption goods so that all consumers can have free access.

Video Rental Stores and Libraries

To examine the public goods issue in more detail, consider two similar institutions in contemporary society, video rental stores and libraries. Both circulate goods that have substantial joint consumption characteristics. While it is true that two people cannot read the same book at the same time, or that two households cannot watch the same videotape at the same time, one can use the good after another is finished, and with both books and videos, while one might want to watch or read a second time, most of the value of the good comes from the first exposure. Furthermore, unlike private consumption goods like shoes or soft drinks, consumption of the good does not use it up, so it is available for additional new consumers to receive the same value as earlier consumers. Both video rental stores and libraries are in the business of circulating goods that are joint in consumption, but excludable. A video rental store might be characterized as a for-profit library of videos.

The major difference is that video rental stores charge customers for the videotapes they see. As with the movie theater, this excludes some consumers from the good. Those who might like to watch a video, but who do not want to pay the rental fee, will not consume it, so the total social value of the video will be reduced. Libraries that lend books at no charge allow everyone to use the book as long as it has some positive value. For readers who value the reading experience at six dollars, they can read the book, as can those who place a value of three dollars, two dollars, one dollar, or even twenty-five cents on the experience. Yet because most libraries are run in the public sector, they allow free access and so enhance the value of their collection to the general public when compared to a regime where they might rent books and thereby exclude those who would like to read them, but not at the price that is being asked.

Should video stores be turned into public video libraries, like the public libraries that make books available to patrons at no charge? There may be other differences, and many would argue that the public good is better advanced by citizens who are reading than citizens who are watching television. Nevertheless, the public goods principle applies to both types of organizations. This example also shows the possible role for the nonprofit sector. Andrew Carnegie established more than 2,500 public libraries as a part of his philanthropic activity, and this chapter shows that from the standpoint of economic theory, he was producing a public good that would tend to be underproduced if left to the private sector.

Problems with Public Sector Provision

Economic theory shows that there are problems with the production of public goods in the private sector, and that those problems will lead to the underprovision of public goods. The standard public goods argument is that therefore the government needs to step in to correct this failure of the market to allocate resources optimally. This theory that the market's inability to efficiently produce public goods leads to the implication that the government should produce them was eloquently developed by Paul Samuelson, a respected Nobel laureate in economics, in a pair of articles he published in the middle 1950s,[6] and was integrated into a broader economic theory on the problems that markets can face in producing certain types of goods.[7] One needs to think carefully about the logic here, and another Nobel laureate in economics,

James Buchanan, has noted that just because the market may not allocate resources perfectly when measured against some ideal standard does not mean that the government can do any better.[8]

Public sector provision of a public good can overcome the problems of jointness in consumption and nonexcludability by paying for the public good through tax revenues which people are forced to pay, and then distributing the good at no charge to those who want to consume it. However, this results in other problems that may be at least as great.

If a good is nonexcludable but is not a joint consumption good, then the good must somehow be rationed. But if the good is nonexcludable, it is difficult to ration it, meaning that it will either become inefficiently congested, or that an inefficiently large amount of the good will be produced. An example can illustrate. Consider a highway, which can have the characteristics of a joint consumption good if it is not congested. Additional travelers can use the road at no cost to additional users. Many rural roads and even interstate highways in isolated areas fit this description. If the road is congested, however, as might be the case during rush hour in an urban area, additional users do reduce the consumption available to others, and in very congested roads, another user cannot get on the road until an existing user gets off. The road is like a private consumption good. One solution would be to ration the road, perhaps by making it a toll road, but for many downtown streets this may not be feasible. Another solution is to build more capacity, but because drivers do not have to pay for entering a congested road, the road will have to be inefficiently large in order to accommodate all of the traffic that would like to use it for free. Thus, government provision of a public good will entail some inefficiency unless the good is completely joint in consumption.

Even for a pure joint consumption good, allowing access without charge entails some inefficiency because unless a charge is made for a good, there is no way to tell how much it is worth to consumers. Without having an adequate gauge of a good's value, there is no good indicator of how much of the good should be produced, or of what the optimal characteristics of the good are. Consider the option of charging viewers to watch individual television shows versus allowing them to view government-produced television at no charge. People who watch free television simply indicate that they value the show more than nothing, but when people pay to watch, they give a better indication of the value to them. Similarly, someone who drives on a free road simply indicates that it is more valuable to him than not driving, but if someone chooses a toll road, he provides market evidence of the value of the road.[9]

Payment for the public good does not make much difference to the public goods currently produced, but it does give a tangible indication of the value of the goods, so it provides a guide to future producers of public goods. They can use the information they get in order to produce goods that are more valuable to consumers in the future. For example, government-produced free television gives no indication to the government as to which programs are more valued to viewers than the others, so the government has no market evidence on which to decide what types of shows to produce more of, and which should be curtailed in the future. American television broadcasts are a little better because advertisers have an incentive to determine the relative popularities of shows, and will pay more to advertise on more popular shows. Even better is the market for movies to be shown in theaters, because the box office receipts for each movie can be determined. Thus, if viewers place a high value on a particular type of film, that type will make more money, which will encourage studios to produce more of what viewers like.

Even with pure joint consumption goods, then, exclusion and rationing by requiring consumers to pay a price can help to make future production more efficient.[10] Market provision of public goods may entail some efficiency problems, but there are similar problems with government provision of public goods. Whereas the problems of market provision start with an abstract theory of public goods, the problems with government provision are more directly related to the subject matter of the previous chapter, which is the lack of accountability. When the government pays for public goods with tax payments, it is not accountable for the value of government output that is returned to consumers. In the private sector, consumers will not pay unless the value they receive is greater than the price they are asked to pay. In the public sector, however, taxpayers have to pay regardless of whether they think they are getting good value for their tax dollars. Similarly, because the government typically gives its output away at no charge, there is no accountability for the value of the output from the ultimate consumers either. If they consume government output, one can be confident that they value it more than nothing, but there is no way that the government can be held accountable for showing that the output it produces is worth more than it costs to produce.

Foundations Versus Government

Few observers of the past two centuries of economic progress would deny that the market system is a great mechanism for producing improved standards of living, yet in some areas the market may not produce goods as efficiently as would be ideally possible. The preceding sections of this chapter have shown that when goods are joint in consumption, or are nonexcludable, the private sector will have a tendency to underproduce them. While some have taken that as an argument for government production, the chapter has shown why government production may also be inefficient. While government will not necessarily underproduce public goods, it may overproduce them, it may produce them inefficiently, and it may not produce the optimal mix of public goods. Economists have focused heavily on the public and private sectors in their analysis of public goods, and have largely ignored production from the nonprofit sector.

The nonprofit sector offers several important advantages over the public sector in the production of public goods. Most clearly, when compared to the public sector, payments into the nonprofit sector are voluntary. When the nonprofit sector is considered in the broadest sense, much revenue arrives in the form of market payments in nonprofit organizations such as hospitals and schools. When considering nonprofit foundations, payments are made as voluntary donations rather than the most likely alternative: tax payments. The voluntary nature of contributions offers several advantages of the nonprofit sector over the public sector. First, in a free society, freedom is a basic value, and coercive taxation, while perhaps a necessary evil to preserve freedom, is at the same time antithetical to the principles of freedom. Any time an activity can be financed through voluntary contributions rather than coerced tax payments, that alone provides a substantial advantage.

Another advantage of voluntary contributions over coerced taxation is that donors must be sold on the value of the activities that they are going to finance. As chapter 2 illustrated, there may be a myriad of motivations for establishing a foundation or contributing to an existing one, but the bottom line is that whatever motivations donors have, they will be looking for causes that can use their money productively. This provides some degree of accountability at the outset that does not exist when coercive taxation is used as a source of revenues.

Yet another advantage of relying on voluntary contributions is that it allows donors to act in a virtuous manner, and to feel a sense of pride because of the good they do for others. This aspect of philanthropy is woefully neglected by economists who have devoted attention to charitable activities. One can donate money to the Salvation Army to help feed and shelter those who are down on their luck, although all taxpayers are also helping that group of people through their financing of the substantial array of programs that are undertaken by governments at all levels. Even if the public sector and the nonprofit sector are equally effective (and there is no indication that they are), donors to charities are actively deciding to do something good with their money, whereas they have no choice when they pay their taxes. Indeed, the same people who are so generous to charitable organizations employ attorneys and accountants to help them keep their tax bills to a minimum. There is virtue in voluntarily contributing to worthy causes; there is no virtue in paying taxes.

This argument goes beyond just the good feelings that are generated by those who contribute to worthy causes. By moving an increasing share of America's programs to help those in need from the nonprofit sector into the public sector, we are designing a society that works less by the virtue of its citizens and more through the compulsion of its government. Do we want to have a society that operates through coercion or through virtue? Do we want to have a society that relies more on government or more on the nonprofit sector? This issue of virtue versus coercion puts foundations in the most positive light as an alternative to government.

Philanthropy and Public Goods

There are clear advantages to relying on the third sector rather than government when that is feasible. Philanthropy can play a role specifically related to public goods because the problem with the market provision of public goods is that they tend to be underproduced. With regard to joint consumption goods, the fact that the market must charge for them rations them and keeps them from being as widely consumed as would be possible. With regard to nonexcludable goods, market production is problematic because it is difficult to charge for goods when people can consume them without paying. In both cases the solution is to provide public goods to consumers at no charge. Philanthropies are in a position to do this by financing public goods with the contributions of their donors.

The problems with public sector provision of public goods revolve around the coercive nature of tax payments and the problems of a lack of consumer feedback on the value of the goods. Again, while philanthropies are not in a position to completely overcome these problems, they overcome them to a substantial degree because they receive their revenues through voluntary donations rather than through coercive tax payments. Thus, it is apparent that many of the problems that both the public and private sectors have with regard to the provision of public goods are overcome by provision through philanthropies.

Just because philanthropies can overcome these problems that the public and private sectors have in the production of public goods does not mean that they actually will overcome these problems. As chapter 8 has shown, the accountability problems that exist with nonprofit foundations may be severe, and certainly mitigate some of the advantages that have been discussed in this chapter. Nevertheless, the theory of public goods provides a clear-cut rationale for philanthropic activity in an economy, to overcome problems in the public and private sectors.

The Problem of Free Riders

Philanthropies have a problem of their own, which is that individuals may not have a sufficient incentive to contribute to them. The product of philanthropy is often like a nonexcludable good, and as in the case of a nonexcludable good, that may give people an insufficient incentive to contribute. Individuals who benefit but do not contribute are referred to as free riders.

The free rider problem arises because the real motivation of donors is not to give their money away, but rather to solve some problem that people face. Donors want to relieve hunger, to stave off disease, to create a more peaceful international atmosphere, or create some other public good. Thus, if others donate their money to help solve these problems, that provides as much of a benefit for the donor as if the donor had contributed money. The donor's goal is to make the world a better place to live, not to reduce her own wealth.

Because all potential donors benefit whenever any of them contributes to a worthy cause, there is the incentive for each of them to donate less and free ride on the benefits generated by the donations of the others. Because all donors face the same incentives, all donors have a reduced incentive to give, so there will be too little philanthropic activity in the aggregate. This provides one justification for government involvement in redistributive activity.[11] Everyone will be better off—even the donors—if the government forces people to give. The reason this could be true is that while many people want to see the results of philanthropic activity, donors may be reluctant to give if they are the only ones, and others ride free off their donations. Therefore, they would like to strike an agreement among all of the potential donors saying, "I'll give if you will too." But with a nation full of potential donors, it would be very difficult for everyone to get together to make this agreement, so the government forces everyone to go along. Essentially, people could agree to be forced to give if everyone else were forced to give too.

As persuasive as this argument might sound, there are some problems with it. For one thing, it is a justification for government coercion, but stripped of the fancy rhetoric, government taxation remains coercive.[12] All of the problems cited earlier regarding the government provision of public goods remain. For another thing, the free rider problem may not be as severe as economists often envision it. If the economist's argument is to be taken at face value, nobody would ever have an incentive to engage in any philanthropic activity, yet despite a government that is very active in social causes, there is still a substantial amount of private philanthropy. Along with this observation comes an interesting body of theoretical work suggesting that it really is optimal in the long run for people to act cooperatively rather than in their own narrow self-interests.[13]

Furthermore, the free rider problem is unlikely to apply to the really large foundations that are the topic of this study. While most people might figure that their contributions will make little difference, and that it would not be noticed if they shirked in their philanthropic activities, those arguments do not apply to those who have very large fortunes. Recall that Andrew Carnegie discussed in his "Gospel of Wealth" the disgrace of dying rich. Furthermore, people with such large fortunes also realize that their own individual contributions can make a difference for mankind. Rockefeller certainly saw that in his lifetime as several of his projects—such as his hookworm project—showed dramatic tangible results. One cannot deny the potential for the free rider problem in philanthropy, but regardless of how broadly it applies, there is still every reason to encourage private philanthropy to go as far as it can before government programs address these problems.

The Free Rider Problem and the Tax Code

Why should philanthropic contributions be given tax preferences in the tax code? The previous several sections suggest an answer. For many reasons private philanthropy provides a desirable alternative to the public and private sectors for the provision of public goods, but because of the free rider problem, people may not have sufficient incentive to engage in philanthropic activity. By allowing contributions to be made tax free, and by allowing foundations a tax-preferred status, this entices additional money into the third sector and allows the third sector to expend more than otherwise it would. Many of the problems addressed by the third sector, from health problems to social problems to problems of international cooperation, are problems that will be left to the government if they are not handled elsewhere, and because they tend to be public goods, the private sector will not be able to deal with them in an optimal manner either. Are foundations a better solution? Chapter 8 has discussed the accountability problems that exist with foundations that may compromise their ability to work in the public interest, but the work of voluntary contributions in the third sector remains in intriguing alternative to the work financed by coerced taxation. Thus, a major policy question becomes, are there changes in the laws governing the operation of the third sector, and more specifically governing nonprofit foundations, that might enable them to produce results that are more in the public interest?

Can Nonprofit Foundations Produce Ideas?

Many of the arguments that have been developed in this chapter apply generally to the public goods produced in the nonprofit sector of the economy. While one might question whether some of the output produced in the third sector fits the economist's definition of a public good, ideas certainly qualify. Once ideas are produced, additional people can use those ideas without diminishing their availability to anyone else. Furthermore, once an idea becomes known, it is difficult to exclude people from using it. These arguments are often put forward as justifications for the government production of basic research. Few people, or businesses, have the incentive to engage in basic research because once the ideas are developed, their competitors can use them just as readily as they can. Furthermore, basic knowledge is most valuable when it is widely disseminated, and if private firms develop knowledge they are likely to keep it proprietary. Publicly funded knowledge can be used by everyone.

Faculty jobs at major research universities are often described with the slogan, "publish or perish." Indeed, universities do evaluate their faculty productivity in large degree by looking at their research output, and they often judge their research output by the amount that they publish. This is not the place to debate the wisdom of the practice of emphasizing faculty research and publication so heavily, but it does fit in with the production of ideas, and especially basic as opposed to applied research, as public goods. If research results are public goods, there is little incentive for private organizations to produce them, and the results produced by private organizations will be likely to be kept proprietary. This type of research can be most effectively produced if public organizations produce them, and if those who produce them are actively encouraged to publish them and have them disseminated widely.

The public organizations do not necessarily have to be in the public sector, however. They can be nonprofit organizations, as are many universities and many medical research organizations. And they can receive their funding through foundation grants. The question then becomes one of evaluating whether these nonprofit foundations have the incentives to channel their resources into the most promising areas, and whether they have the incentive to work for the public interest. Indeed, it may be that despite the potential for the production of ideas through nonprofit foundations, their lack of accountability, coupled with an institutional structure that is not oriented toward the public interest, means that foundation-sponsored research does little good, or maybe even a little harm.

The advantages of funding the production of ideas through grants from nonprofit foundations are potentially great, as this chapter has shown. The problems arise because of lack of accountability, and because ideas funded through foundations are sheltered from any market test of their validity or efficacy. As the previous chapter has argued, while foundations themselves are accountable to nobody for their activities, the output financed by foundation grants is directly accountable to the foundations, and ultimately to the foundation trustees. This creates a problem with perception and credibility, because foundation-funded ideas can appear to be no more than the work of hired hands to further the agenda of the foundation's trustees. The real problem is that the perception of bias is solidly grounded in the realities of foundation activities. By the very nature of foundations, the more ideological the content of the foundation's activities, the greater skepticism it deserves.

The Influence of Tax Laws on Nonprofit Foundations

From a policy standpoint, this discussion on the production of ideas, as public goods, through the funding of nonprofit foundations would be largely academic were it not for the fact that foundations are given tax-preferred status in several dimensions. In a free country, the general public might be interested in knowing how wealthy individuals dispose of their fortunes, but in a truly free country, if they made their money honestly, they should be allowed to determine how their wealth is spent. If the tax laws did not favor foundations, that would be the end of the story, but the tax benefits given to foundations are substantial, so the revenue cost to the Treasury is substantial. For starters, the initial contributions that created the foundations are made tax free, so the inheritance taxes that might normally be paid are foregone. While one could debate the fairness of inheritance taxes, that is beside the point. Bequests to foundations are treated differently from bequests to the family and friends of the deceased. There must be some public interest justification for this preferred treatment.

Then, once the foundation is operating, it is again treated preferentially in comparison to other businesses. If the foundation were taxed like any business, then observers could hardly be critical of the businesses engaged in by foundations. Because they operate in a tax-favored environment, however, the general public has a legitimate reason to expect that the tax revenues foregone by the Treasury because of the tax preferences to foundations are more than compensated for by the public benefits that foundations produce. This chapter has shown that there is a potential role for foundations to play in the production of public goods. How nonprofit foundations fill this role is a question that has been asked throughout the twentieth century.

Public policy toward foundations is implemented through tax law. The tax laws influence the activities of foundations in a number of ways, because foundations must meet the conditions set by Congress and the Internal Revenue Service in order to retain their tax-preferred status. These laws set conditions on foundation investments, on the amount that foundations must disburse from their assets, and on the types of activities in which foundations engage. Are the tax laws stringent enough to optimally constrain foundation activities? Are they too stringent, preventing foundations from taking advantage of opportunities to serve the public interest? Do they allow foundations too much leeway to act against the public interest? The next chapter considers a number of public policy issues related to the creation and operation of foundations.

Notes

1. Michael O'Neill, *The Third America: The Emergence of the Nonprofit Sector in the United States* (San Francisco, CA: Jossey-Bass Publishers, 1989), p. 1.
2. John W. Nason, *Trustees and the Future of Foundations* (New York: Council on Foundations, 1977), p. 79.
3. Randall G. Holcombe, *Public Policy and the Quality of Life: Market Incentives Versus Government Planning* (Westport, CT: Greenwood Press, 1995), p. 6.
4. The Economist's definition of public goods is discussed in more detail in Randall G. Holcombe, *Public Finance: Government Revenues and Expenditures in the United States Economy* (Minneapolis/St. Paul, MN: West Publishing Company, 1996), ch. 5.
5. Henry Hansmann, "Economic Theories of Nonprofit Organization," chap 2 in Walter W. Powell, ed., *The Nonprofit Sector* (New Haven, CT: Yale University Press, 1987), considers the public good justification for nonprofit organizations, and finds it wanting. However, he does not consider foundations specifically, where the theory may have more validity.
6. Samuelson's influential articles are "A Diagrammatic Exposition of a Theory of Public Expenditure," *Review of Economics and Statistics* 37 (November 1955), pp. 350-356, and "The Pure Theory of Public Expenditure," *Review of Economics and Statistics* 36 (November 1954), pp. 387-389.
7. A good statement of this theory is found in Francis M. Bator, "The Anatomy of Market Failure," *Quarterly Journal of Economics* 72 (August 1958), pp. 351-379.
8. James M. Buchanan, "Public Finance and Public Choice," *National Tax Journal* 28 (December 1975), pp. 383-394.
9. This theory is developed by Jora R. Minasian, "Television Pricing and the Theory of Public Goods," *Journal of Law & Economics* 7 (October 1964), pp. 71-80.
10. The efficiency of the price system in allocating resources is eloquently expressed in Friedrich A. Hayek, "The Use of Knowledge in Society," *American Economic Review* 35, No. 4 (September 1945), pp. 519-530.
11. The argument is more fully developed in Harold M. Hochman and James D. Rogers, "Pareto Optimal Redistribution," *American Economic Review* 59 (September 1969), pp. 542-547.
12. Leland B. Yeager, "Rights, Contract, and Utility in Policy Espousal," *Cato Journal* 5, No. 1 (Summer 1985), pp. 259-294.
13. Robert Axelrod, *The Evolution of Cooperation* (New York: Basic Books, 1984).

10

Policy Issues

Nonprofit foundations have funded, and continue to fund, a wide range of socially beneficial activities in the United States. Should the nation tamper with these institutions that have done so much good for the nation and the world? The shortcomings of foundation activities have been readily acknowledged by those in the third sector, who want to protect foundations from policy changes that might hamper the future activities of the organizations. Other organizations have provided substantial benefits to the nation as well, however, and policy alternatives to improve their operations are often considered. Many activities of government contribute to the well-being of the nation, yet laws are passed, policies for reform are instituted, and constitutions are even amended in order to make governments function more effectively. In the same spirit, government is also ready to enact public policy changes to improve the functioning of business. Even while recognizing the social contributions of nonprofit foundations, public policy toward them should be periodically reconsidered with the idea that the third sector, like the first and second, might be able to operate more effectively, and more for the public good, if policy changes were made.

There are two good reasons why nonprofit foundations deserve more scrutiny from a public policy standpoint than either business or government. First, they are given a privileged status through the tax laws, so it is reasonable to periodically evaluate whether the favored treatment they receive as a matter of public policy is generating a sufficient social return to justify that treatment. Second, nonprofit foundations are allowed their privileged status because they are created with the intention of furthering the public interest. Thus, it is reasonable to consider both whether taxpayers are getting their money's worth from tax-preferred foundations, and even if they are, whether public policy changes might be able to more successfully direct the energies of foundations toward the interests of the public. Private sector firms are established for private purposes, and although the public interest is served as private interests are served, the primary purpose of private business is to further the goals of the entrepreneurs and generate income for the owners. This is accomplished by simultaneously satisfying the goals of the customers of business. But the mission of business is to satisfy the private interests of those who transact, rather than to fulfill some public purpose. Foundations are set up explicitly for some public purpose.

More than two centuries ago Adam Smith observed in *The Wealth of Nations* that individuals undertaking exchanges in a market economy, while pursuing their own self-interests, are led by an invisible hand to pursue the best interest of the entire society. But as fond as Smith was of the market economy, he was just as suspicious of the third sector, and warned that the effect of endowments was to reduce the incentive to act in the public interest, because of the lack of accountability created by endowments.[1] The preceding chapters have documented the problems and speculated on their causes. This chapter discusses some policy alternatives that address those problems.

Policy Alternatives and the Creation of Foundations

Before examining specific policy issues, consider more generally the policy alternatives that might be applied to nonprofit grant-making foundations. The context within which foundations are created is an important element in dealing with the policy issues. While many foundations are established by living donors, in most cases the life of the foundation extends beyond the life of the donor, which is where many of the interesting policy issues begin. Present tax laws allow individuals to deduct their charitable contributions from their taxable incomes. Andrew Carnegie intended to give away the bulk of his fortune before he died, but found it impossible to do so because his fortune was so large. The sole purpose of Carnegie's foundation was to allow him to continue giving away his fortune after his death. Fundamentally, foundations are a conduit that allow people to continue to make charitable contributions beyond their lifetimes.

The tax laws that allow charitable deductions also impose inheritance taxes, and this is the first place where tax policy is relevant to foundations. Perhaps foundation endowments should be subject to inheritance taxes before the money goes to the foundation. This would treat bequests to foundations just like any other bequests. There is a certain logic to it, especially if one dislikes the idea of the dead exercising control over aspects of a society long after they have departed. Subjecting bequests to foundations to the inheritance tax would provide a tax advantage for giving during an individual's lifetime rather than waiting until death. While this would reduce the influence of the deceased, it has two drawbacks. The first, which would occur in cases like Carnegie's, is that some people have such large fortunes that the money might better be spread over a number of years extending beyond the lifetime of the giver. The second, which would be more relevant for smaller bequests, is that because there are uncertainties regarding the length of a person's life and the expenses one might incur late in life, charitable bequests might be a residual for many donors. The recipient of the charitable bequest would end up receiving less, and there would seem to be no good reason why recipients should be penalized for receiving bequests rather than donations from living donors.

There are potential problems with taxing charitable bequests when charitable contributions are deductible from taxable income. This implies that charitable donations from income should be treated in the same way as charitable bequests, which might be done by adjusting the inheritance tax, the income tax, or both. Most proposals for a flat rate income tax that have been made in the 1980s and 1990s have been based on the structure advocated by economists Robert Hall and Alvin Rabushka,[2] and their proposal would disallow deductions for charitable contributions so that they would be taxed as any other expenditure out of income. To make a parallel adjustment in estate taxation would mean either to tax bequests to foundations as any other bequest is taxed, or to eliminate taxation on all bequests. Thus, one possible route to reform would be to undertake a more major tax reform, of which the tax treatment of foundations would be only a part. This chapter will focus on policy changes that would be aimed directly at foundations, deferring until the next chapter a consideration of the effects on foundations of more general reforms of the tax structure.

Foundations provide conduits through which the public interest can be served, but the nonprofit grant-making foundations that are the subject of this book are not the only organizations that receive income from endowments. Harvard University's endowment in 1992 was $5.1 billion, for example, which placed it just behind the third largest grant-making foundation. The Ford Foundation, the largest foundation, with assets of $6.5 billion in 1992, was only slightly larger than Harvard's endowment. While this book has focused on grant-making foundations, any public policies regarding endowments would presumably have some implications for universities, churches, and other organizations that earn income from endowments. If grant-making foundations were singled out, donors could give directly to these other types of organizations. Churches do undertake a wide variety of charitable activities that might be viewed as similar to those of grant-making foundations, and if bequests to foundations were more heavily taxed, churches might become more like foundations.

From a policy perspective, it is worth considering extreme policies, such as preventing the formation of new foundations, draining the resources from existing foundations, or subjecting bequests to foundations to inheritance taxation. In a free country, such policies would be ill-advised. People should be able to do what they want with their wealth, as long as they are not causing direct harm to others. Considering the options for disposition of wealth, leaving it to a foundation for the purpose of enhancing the public good seems as public-spirited as any other possibility. Even the alternative of taxing bequests into foundations does not appear attractive when we recognize that charitable contributions can be given tax-free during the donor's lifetime. Extreme ideas that would limit the ability of individuals to create foundations would not appear to further the public interest. Nevertheless, the tax system currently provides an incentive for the creation of foundations, and an ideal policy would have a neutral effect, especially considering the resource allocation problems associated with foundations. There is no reason for tax laws to favor the creation of foundations. The next chapter considers more general tax reforms and their potential effects on foundations, leaving this chapter to consider policies that would affect foundation activities directly.

Policy Alternatives and the Operation of Foundations

Most of the policy issues considered in previous chapters have had to do with the way that foundations are operated, and naturally so because that is where the problems appear. The questions of accountability and remaining committed to donor intentions fall under this heading. Perhaps foundations would better further the public interest if they had limited lifetimes. Perhaps there is a better way to choose trustees, or to manage foundations. Perhaps the activities foundations can pursue should be further limited, or subject to more government oversight. If we rule out the more extreme policies that would limit the formation of foundations, the real policy issues revolve around the tax laws, because the tax laws convey to foundations their status. If the reasoning of the previous section is accepted, then there should be no problem with somebody creating a for-profit foundation, using after-tax money for an endowment and paying taxes on the foundation's operations. Thus, nonprofit foundations exchange their tax-preferred status for an agreement to work within certain parameters that help ensure that the foundation's activities actually further the public interest. Those parameters include the types of activities the foundation undertakes and the way that the foundation is managed.

This volume has examined one aspect of foundation activities: their promotion of ideas and public policies. The previous chapters have shown that over the twentieth century foundations have exhibited biases in their promotion of ideas and that they have sometimes acted irresponsibly by interjecting their private resources into public policy debates. The same might be true about individuals who spend their own money in their own lifetimes. The presidential candidacies of Ross Perot in 1992 and Steve Forbes in 1996 are examples of how private fortunes might be used to influence public policy. Would the public interest have been better served if Perot and Forbes had saved their money to establish foundations that might endure beyond their lifetimes? If leaving bequests to foundations becomes less attractive, one would expect some potential future foundation resources to be diverted to this type of political activity. Which is more in the public interest is only peripherally relevant, however, because in a free society we try to give great latitude to people like Perot, Forbes, Rockefeller, Ford, and MacArthur, to dispose of the money they earned as they see fit.

In order to evaluate the impact of foundations on the promotion of ideas and on the course of public policy, the next section places foundation activity in a larger context.

Foundations and the Promotion of Ideas

The degree to which foundations use their resources to promote ideas is debatable, partly because of data limitations and partly because there is not a clear dividing line that delineates the production of ideas. With more than 5,000 grant-making foundations, a complete picture could be painted only by looking at every grant made by every foundation. Studies in medical and agricultural areas could potentially have a substantial amount of ideological content, for example, that could only be seen by reading the study. Medical studies might consider issues like population growth and fertility rates, which could touch on issues of birth control and abortion, and some studies on AIDS could be considered to have an ideological slant. Agricultural studies might include an analysis of agricultural policies and farm management that might be viewed as ideologically oriented. Field work is more problematic because it would be necessary to travel to the location where the work is being done to monitor the degree to which workers are promoting ideas and ideologies.[3]

In one sense every foundation grant is ideologically driven, because trustees are trying to spend their resources in order to maximize the public welfare. Any educational activity must be involved in the promotion of ideas, because that is the nature of education. The building of libraries, as Andrew Carnegie did during his lifetime, was driven by his belief in the social value of reading, but this generally shared view does not fall neatly into any place on the political left-to-right spectrum. Educational grants to minority students, or those who study social work, have more ideological content. Grants to particular universities have some ideological content. Grants to finance the writing of books like Gunnar Myrdal's *An American Dilemma* or Charles Murray's *Losing Ground* are more clearly ideological. The purpose of the foundation grants that financed those works was explicitly to promote ideas. There is a continuum between extreme cases like these where foundation grants are designed to promote ideas and cases like Rockefeller's hookworm project that are more charitable than ideological.

While one might be wary of drawing a clear line, and while most grants do have an ideological component, if only because the purpose of the grant is to improve social welfare as envisioned by foundation trustees, when a narrow definition is used it is clear that most foundation money does not go toward the promotion of ideas. For example, in 1993 only 2.7 percent of total foundation grants went specifically targeted toward social science, but another 23.8 percent went to education. With more than one quarter of foundation money going toward education and social science, the promotion of ideas could be viewed as the major activity of foundations. But 18.2 percent of foundation grants go toward health programs, and another 14.6 percent to human services, where the promotion of ideas will tend to be secondary to the improvement of individual well-being.[4] Thus, in a chapter that looks at the policy issues one must be cautious about drawing overly broad conclusions about foundations in a book that has focused on only a small part of foundation activities. Proposals that might be beneficial when looked at only from the perspective of improving the quality of ideas promoted by foundations might have more generally detrimental effects if applied to all foundation activity.

Think Tanks and Corporate Philanthropy

Foundations have a long history of supporting think tanks that produce public policy ideas. Influential think tanks such as the Brookings Institution, the American Enterprise Institute, and the Heritage Foundation have all received substantial foundation support. However, increasingly the financial support for such organizations comes from corporate and private donors rather than from foundation grants. The number of "third sector" think tanks and other nonprofit organizations, such as environmental groups and legal defense groups, has been increasing substantially over the years, and with this increase has come more support from the private sector relative to nonprofit foundations. In 1993 foundation grants for all purposes totaled about $9.2 billion, while corporate philanthropy totaled $5.9 billion.[5] Foundation grants are almost one and a half times as great as corporate gifts, but this figure shows that corporate philanthropy is an important source of revenues for the third sector.

When considering any bias in foundation promotion of ideas, one might also take into account the effects of corporate philanthropy, and the liberal bias noted in chapters 4 and 5 with regard to foundations seems to be just as pervasive—and perhaps more so—in corporate philanthropy. A recent study done by Stuart Nolan and Gregory P. Conko indicates that corporations give overwhelmingly to liberal rather than conservative causes, and often donate to organizations that directly oppose their own interests.[6] For example, in 1991 Exxon donated $112,500 and Mobil donated $4,500 to the Audubon Society. Thanks to donors like Exxon and Mobil, the Audubon Society was able to successfully lobby to expand the Arctic National Wildlife Refuge in order to prevent oil exploration there. The Environmental Law Institute, which assisted Congress to develop legal mechanisms to penalize oil companies for harming the environment, received grants of $5,000 from Exxon, $5,000 from Texaco, and $2,500 from Phillips Petroleum. The Environmental Law Institute was instrumental in developing the legal analysis that led up to criminal charges against Exxon for the Valdez oil spill. Texaco and Ashland Oil contributed to the Alliance to Save Energy, which advocates adding fifty cents per gallon to gasoline taxes. As Nolan and Conko demonstrate in their study, corporate philanthropy continues to have a substantial liberal bias in the 1990s.

One might argue, as Nolan and Conko do, that corporations are making contributions that work against their own self-interests, but the public policy issues with regard to corporate philanthropy are different from those related to nonprofit foundations. Corporations give away the money they earned, and if there is a problem, it is that stockholder interests are not sufficiently represented by management. Foundations, in contrast, have no accountability to anyone, and because they receive tax-favored status, their activities are more an issue of public policy. Nonetheless, one could not argue that the liberal bias in foundation grants would be eliminated if foundation grants were made more in line with corporate philanthropy.

The Big Picture

When looking at the ideas promoted by foundation grants as a part of a bigger picture, one must take account of the fact that foundations do much else besides promote ideas, and that ideas are promoted with the use of corporate philanthropic dollars as well. But both of these sources of philanthropy pale beside philanthropic contributions by individuals. Table 10.1 shows the sources of private philanthropic funds for 1993, and total foundation grants of $9.2 billion were overwhelmed by individual contributions of $102.6 billion. Individual philanthropy made up 81.3 percent of the total, compared to 7.3 percent of total philanthropy that came from foundation grants. Bequests were nearly as great a source of philanthropy as foundation grants, and as already noted, corporate philanthropy is also significant. As table 10.1 shows, despite the substantial size of foundation grants, individual and corporate giving, along with private bequests, make up 92.7 percent of total non-governmental philanthropy.

TABLE 10.1

Sources of Private Philanthropic Funds, 1993

Source	Billions of Dollars	Percent of Total
Individuals	$102.6	81.3
Foundations	$9.2	7.3
Corporations	$5.9	4.7
Bequests	$8.5	6.7
TOTAL	$126.2	100.0

Source: *Statistical Abstract of the United States,* 1995 ed., p. 393.

When considering the economy as a whole, public sector activity should also be included in the total. In 1992 the federal, state, and local governments in the United States spent $202 billion on public welfare, which is about twice as much as total non-governmental philanthropy. Much private philanthropic activity contributes to education, and government spent $354 billion on education. Governmental health expenditures, another major target of private giving, were $119 billion. Thus, looking only at these major areas of government expenditures, government spent $675 billion—more than three times the amount spent by all non-governmental philanthropy. Adding these government expenditures to total private philanthropy gives $801 billion, of which the $9.2 billion in grants from nonprofit foundations makes up less than one and a half percent of the total.

One might make the argument that foundations do not devote very much of their total resources to the promotion of ideas.[7] As we have seen, this depends upon how broadly one wants to define the promotion of ideas. But one surely could make the argument that foundation grants are a relatively insignificant source of philanthropy. When only private philanthropy is considered their contribution is a noticeable, yet small, 7.3 percent of the total. When the public sector is added, their contribution is less than one and a half percent. These statistics say much about the changing role of foundations over the course of the twentieth century. At the turn of the century, when government was relatively small, foundations could play a major role in education, public health, and aid to the poor. As government has increasingly taken over these activities, foundations play a less significant role. To fully assess public policy issues that relate to foundations, one must take account of how foundations fit into the larger economy, which includes the public sector. Within that framework, consider some of the policy issues that have come up in the preceding chapters.

Government Oversight

One possible avenue through which public policy toward nonprofit foundations might be altered would be to mandate increased government oversight over the activities of foundations. Government oversight could take a number of forms. Early in the twentieth century, Britain placed its foundations under the complete supervision of a board of Charity Commissioners.[8] The commissioners are charged with determining whether a foundation is using its resources in the best way possible to further the public interest, and have the power to make changes when they judge that the public interest is not being served. They can modify the stated purposes for which endowment funds are to be used, they have the power to combine or divide endowments to better serve the public interest, and they can change the investment powers of foundations. When they believe that funds are not being expended to serve the public interest, they even have the power to direct endowment funds to applications that they believe are more appropriate.

A move in this direction has been proposed for the United States by the Union Institute in Washington, D.C. In their 1992 publication, *The Nonprofit Policy Agenda: Recommendations for State and Local Action,*[9] the Union Institute advocates establishing government commissions that could address the policy concerns of the nonprofit sector and enable the third sector to speak with a more unified voice. The Union Institute advocates government funding in order to enable the third sector to be more independent of the desires of private donors. The Union Institute believes it is undesirable for nonprofits to have to continually justify their role in the economy, and sees government oversight as a way to enable the third sector to become more independent.

In a critique of the Union Institute's report, Thomas DiLorenzo argues that if their recommendations were adopted, the third sector would in effect be merged with government, greatly reducing the independence of the third sector by subjecting all nonprofits to the oversight of a new bureaucracy.[10] No matter which side of the argument one looks at, it is apparent that negative consequences would result from increased government oversight of the type recommended by the Union Institute. By creating a unified voice for the third sector, donor intent would be even less relevant than it is today, because with government oversight the activities of the third sector would have to become more homogeneous. Those with a major voice in the oversight, which probably would mean those foundations with the largest endowments, might end up with more power, but diversity of opinion and purpose surely would be sacrificed in the process. If the third sector really did become more independent of donor intent, as the Union Institute would like it to be, then the lack of accountability, which already is a problem in the third sector, would increase.

When one looks specifically at grant-making foundations, it is easy to see how increased government oversight would act to make foundations more like an extension of the public sector. Increased homogeneity would work against the funding of innovative ideas. The notion that foundations could speak with one voice would obviously be counterproductive in the context of creating a public dialog to evaluate the creation of new ideas through foundation grants. Ideally, foundations should operate more like the private sector, where innovation and initiative are rewarded. Thus, from a policy standpoint, while it makes good sense to evaluate what conditions foundations should meet in order to retain their tax-favored status, to increase government oversight over the activities of foundations would be counterproductive.

The Union Institute proposal involves creating some kind of general government oversight with a vaguely defined mission and a substantial ability to use its power in arbitrary and poorly defined ways. If there were some kind of more specific proposal for increased government oversight, such as an improved method for screening foundation activities to enforce the prohibition against political activities, or even a proposal for restricting even further the types of activities foundations could finance, it might be worth evaluating to weigh the costs against the benefits. In effect, this is what Congress did in 1969 when it placed a number of additional restrictions on foundations. Policy changes in some specific areas are considered later in this chapter. Additional oversight of a more general nature that might direct foundation policy in unspecified ways would not be desirable, however, because it would make the third sector more like the public sector, and government dollars already far outnumber foundation dollars, as the figures earlier in the chapter have illustrated. For the same reasons that one would not want to restrict the formation of foundations, one also would not want to create some type of general oversight or policymaking organization with the power to direct ways in which foundation resources can be used.

Tax-Favored Status

If increased government oversight is not a potentially productive avenue for improving the performance of nonprofit foundations, then the public policy question becomes, what criteria should foundations have to meet in order to retain their tax-favored status? In American society, the tax laws determine how much of an individual's income and wealth can be directed as its owner desires and how much goes to the government, via tax payments, for public purposes. Donors have decided to take some of the wealth the tax laws have left them for private purposes and turn that too toward public purposes, and it is the public interest nature of the foundation that justifies tax-favored status as a public policy. This is why the real public policy issue is the conditions foundations should have to meet in order to be favored under the tax laws.

Consider the extreme alternative where the tax-favored status of foundations was eliminated entirely. In this case, foundations would be treated as businesses under the tax law. In this hypothetical situation, the only tax preference that would be retained for foundations is that they be allowed to deduct charitable contributions from their before-tax income for tax purposes. They would be taxed on their income, but would be allowed to deduct charitable contributions before calculating their taxable incomes. Consider a foundation under this alternative that earns income from investments, but spends its entire income on grants to qualified tax-exempt organizations, which might include universities, tax-exempt think tanks, churches, and medical charities. Because the foundation's charitable contributions equaled its income, it would owe no taxes. Thus, foundations are not as tax-favored as they first appear, especially considering the fact that the individuals endowing the foundations could have made tax-free charitable contributions throughout their lifetimes. If foundations undertook their own projects, by underwriting studies, organizing conferences, and so forth, those might be considered business expenses, and so could also be deductible, although the IRS frowns on businesses that consistently lose money. Perhaps such expenses would better be treated as expenses that a hobbyist incurs when the hobby returns some income (like the photographer who sells some photos, but who consistently has more expenses than income from photography).

One can imagine a situation where subjecting foundations to tax laws similar to those faced by other businesses would place relatively little burden on them, but might free them from their awkward position in which they are not really a charity, not really a business, and not really a part of the public sector. But while such a change would raise a little more tax revenue, and so would limit somewhat the resources available to foundations, it would not fundamentally alter the problems cited in earlier chapters: the lack of accountability, the separation of foundation activities from the intentions of the donors, and so forth. Foundations are helped by the tax laws, but the real problems cited about foundations are due directly to the fact that people have left fortunes to establish foundations that can exist in perpetuity to try to further the public interest. Perhaps the existing requirements are not so bad after all.

When considering treating foundations like businesses for tax purposes, one would have to look at other possible effects of such a move. For example, under the tax structure in effect in 1997 capital gains are subject to taxation when realized, which gives holders of appreciated assets an incentive not to sell them. If foundations live in perpetuity, they would have a strong incentive not to sell appreciated assets, which might cause potential problems. The current laws restricting the amount of any company that a foundation can own might mitigate that to a degree, but one could imagine a situation in which a few foundations own more than half of a corporation under current tax laws, and if the stock they owned consisted mostly of unrealized capital gains, the corporation would find itself in a different situation from more broadly held firms. On the one hand, it would be insulated to a degree from market pressures, but on the other hand it might be pressured by its third sector owners (to increase dividends, for example).

If increased government oversight is accepted as a poor alternative for improving the performance of the third sector, then the issue comes down to what criteria foundations should have to meet to retain their tax-favored status. Some problems that have previously been considered as policy issues can be reviewed at this point.

The Elite Causes Supported by Foundations

One criticism of nonprofit foundations is that while they do engage in charitable causes that benefit the less fortunate, they also heavily support causes that benefit the wealthy. They support opera halls and art galleries, and give money to elite educational institutions.[11] The charge of elitism has a ring of truth to it, especially when one realizes that grants to provide health care pay the salaries of doctors, and grants to universities pay the salaries of professors. Still, one must question how those who are outside the elite would benefit if contributions to foundations were more limited, or if tax benefits were restricted. Perhaps in lieu of charitable activity the potential donors would spend the money directly for the benefit of themselves, their families, and friends. Policy issues are clouded when analysts argue that the rich get benefits from a policy rather than showing how those less well off suffer. Thus, any arguments that foundations support elite causes must be extended to show how, if some policy were changed, those outside the elite would fare better as a result.

The donors who endowed foundations were themselves members of an elite, so it is hard to argue that the money they earned should not be allocated toward causes with which they would have approved. Furthermore, while one might debate whether money might better serve the public interest if it went to support a symphony or a children's health clinic, unless the symphony actually works against the public interest, one could hardly object to its being funded by an endowment from elite individuals. The elitism argument loses much of its force once one considers not how much better off elite individuals might be due to the expenditure, but rather whether those outside the elite are negatively affected by it.

Self-Perpetuating Boards of Trustees

One feature of many nonprofit foundations that aggravates the lack of accountability is the practice of having self-perpetuating boards of trustees. When trustees leave the board, the remaining board members appoint a replacement. The issue is closely related to the accusation of elitism just considered, because a foundation's trustees will originally be constituted following the instructions of the donor, which will almost always result in an elite group of trustees, and candidates considered after the original board is constituted will have to at least meet the approval of this elite group, inevitably perpetuating an elite group that will in all likelihood be drawn from among a small circle of individuals.

Surely such elitism would be objected to in government, where public dollars fund programs intended to further the public interest, but that same type of elitism is accepted with regard to corporate directors for companies that are owned only by those who choose to buy the stock. Are foundation trustees more like government officials, in which case there should be more of an open competition for trustees, or more like corporate directors, in which case selection from an elite group is acceptable? Furthermore, if it is acceptable to select from an elite group, is it nevertheless unacceptable to have the existing trustees doing the selection?

Foundations are established with private money freely donated, so they differ from government, and are similar to corporations, in that important respect. On that ground, the wishes of the donor should be paramount. Another issue arises because corporations, in order to be ongoing enterprises, must continue to earn profits, whereas there is little accountability for foundation trustees. In effect, an elite and self-selected group of individuals is able to determine how foundation resources are spent with very little oversight. The advantage of such a selection procedure is that the existing trustees are in a good position to know what would make a good trustee, so may be able to do a better job of selecting a qualified trustee than some outside group. The only qualification to this advantage is that there is little penalty to be paid by trustees if they select underqualified replacements, because there is no accountability. But this same qualifier comes with any other method of appointing trustees.

Some biases are likely to come with self-perpetuating boards, but those biases will favor picking qualified individuals who fit into the status quo operations of their foundations. This may impart a certain conservatism to foundations, in the sense that they will be slow to change (rather than in the political sense), but if the alternative is a more democratic method of selection, the risk there is that while trustees may be more representative, they may not be as qualified for the position. Changing the method of trustee selection also would violate the principle of donor intent. Because foundation endowments have their origins in the private donations of their creators, there seems to be little reason to tamper with self-perpetuating boards of trustees where they exist. Foundations are not an extension of the political system, and this issue is best addressed by foundations themselves rather than by government policy.

Diversity Among Trustees

Trustees themselves have pushed this as an issue, and one can hardly object when a board of trustees wants to see more diversity within their ranks. However, if the concept of self-perpetuating boards of trustees is accepted, one can hardly object to a lack of diversity among trustees from a public policy standpoint. The question from a policy perspective is not whether more diversity would be beneficial, but rather whether any public policy action should be taken to try to encourage diversity. Foundations are not representative governments, and there seems to be little reason for public policy to address the issue. More diversity may be valuable, and it may be worthwhile for foundation trustees themselves to push the issue, but there is no good reason for it to be addressed in public policy toward foundations.

Should Trustees be Compensated?

For the most part, foundation trustees receive little or no compensation for their activities, and this limits the group of individuals who would be eligible to serve as trustees. Sufficient compensation would allow individuals to be employed as trustees, and so would vastly increase the numbers of individuals who might be chosen as trustees. But not everybody is qualified, and an argument could be made that if the organization is really philanthropic, those who direct the organization's operations should have motives that are primarily philanthropic. Thus, there is an argument against compensation. On this issue, as with other policy issues, foundations themselves, and individuals who are inclined to create new foundations, should consider them seriously in order to try to create as effective a foundation as possible. New foundations could learn from the experiences of existing foundations. Identifying items as important issues for foundation policy does not necessarily make them important issues for public policy, however. On pragmatic grounds, there seems no good reason not to leave the status quo as it is. Following this line of reasoning, those who create new foundations should be able to choose the compensation rules they believe would be most effective.

Family Members as Trustees

The argument against allowing family members to serve as trustees is that the foundation can become a method whereby the family can pass control of the family's wealth down through generations, avoiding the inheritance tax. Because of restrictions on the activities of foundations, however, the foundation's funds will be used for philanthropic activities, broadly defined, and it seems reasonable to allow the heirs of a donor to help determine the disposition of the donor's assets after the donor has passed away. Yes, the family will have power over the disposition of the funds, but the family earned them in the first place. Furthermore, family members may have more of an incentive to see that the money is productively spent if it is spent in the name of the family. In addition, over time those immediately associated with the donor will pass away, further eroding the donor's ties to trustees. Again, on pragmatic grounds, there seems to be no good reason for objecting to the appointment of family members as trustees.

Networks and Accountability

Because foundation trustees come from a small elite group, there is considerable overlap among foundation boards of trustees, and perhaps more significantly, there is overlap between foundation trustees and the boards of organizations that are the recipients of foundation grants. How much of a problem this is depends upon how concerned one is about elitism in foundation activities. While it is true that foundations often share trustees with recipient organizations, in some cases, such as the Brookings Institution and the National Bureau of Economic Research, foundations were instrumental in creating the organizations. The organizations then act as extensions of the foundation. Seen in this way, foundations either could fund their own projects, or they could contract out to other organizations that have the same general orientation they have in order to do a more competent and, perhaps, objective job. When a think tank does the work, the final product may appear more objective than if a foundation did the work in house, and the possibility of deception may be a problem, but at the same time, if a foundation views its mission as furthering the public interest, one cannot expect the foundation to be objective in the sense of giving all ideas an equal hearing. The foundation ought to be biased toward its trustees' conception of the public interest.

If this is the case, then any overlap between foundations and organizations receiving foundation grants can be seen as a way for ensuring that the grantor and the recipient have similar ideas as to how the money is to be spent. This will produce bias in the sense that what is produced with foundation grants is biased toward the views of foundation trustees, but one should have little problem with the idea that foundation trustees try to spend the foundation's money in a way that they think worthwhile. If there is a problem here, it is with bias in the trustees, not in any overlap among boards.

Restrictions on Foundation Activities

Thus far, most of the specific policy issues discussed have revolved around the trustees. Another broad area of policy questions revolves around whether foundations should be more restricted in the types of grants that they give. This was an issue that was discussed extensively in 1969, and that resulted in restrictions being placed on the political activities of foundations.

In 1969 the primary issue was the political activities of foundations, but another issue to consider is that foundation activities might compete with activities undertaken by for-profit organizations. Agricultural and medical research might fall under this heading, and directly related to the topic of this volume, the publication of books, research reports, and other activities intended to disseminate ideas. Many foundations publish a substantial number of books to disseminate the results of foundation-funded research. The Russell Sage Foundation is a case in point, and as a matter of policy wants to publish under its own name the results of research it funds. Should such activities that directly compete with private sector producers (book publishers, in this case) be sheltered from taxation? The evidence is that where tax advantages exist, there is a substantial crowding out of for-profit activity,[12] and given the lack of accountability of nonprofit foundations when compared to for-profit firms, one might want to either limit the role of foundations, or subject some of their activities to taxation.

Foundations are created to further the public interest, and are given tax benefits in exchange for doing so. Thus, restrictions on the scope of activities allowed by nonprofit foundations seems reasonable as a condition of their retention of nonprofit status, and it further seems reasonable to periodically reconsider whether the existing restrictions are appropriate. In 1969 Congress created additional restrictions, and despite the anticipation that those restrictions would sharply curtail foundation activities in a number of areas, in fact they have had relatively little impact. Overtly political activities have been limited, but public policy work that is sometimes directly related to pending legislation is financed by foundations, accompanied by the disclaimer that the work is not intended to "aid or hinder the passage of any legislation." Should restrictions on foundation activity be further tightened? The argument for further restrictions does not seem to be overly compelling at this time, but the arguments of those who would want to argue otherwise do not seem unreasonable.[13]

As a matter of principle, foundations accept restrictions in exchange for their tax-preferred status. That status is granted to allow foundations to further the public interest. Thus, in principle the restrictions on foundation activity should be subject to continual reexamination to see if they can be modified to more closely direct foundation activities to serve the public interest. Thus, there is no reason to rule out further restrictions in principle.

In practice, my judgment (which may not be shared by everyone) is that the 1969 limits provide acceptable current boundaries for foundation activity, but my conclusion is based on pragmatism rather than principle. The principle is that the boundaries are open to reevaluation at any time, and my pragmatic conclusion is that they are satisfactory at the present time. My conclusion is made in light of the biases of foundation programs I have discussed in previous chapters, and does not mean that I would endorse current foundation activities as serving the public interest as much as might be possible.

Despite my belief that foundations could better use their resources to further the public interest, I am willing to allow foundations additional latitude for three main reasons. First, the trustees who control foundations are vested with the power to direct foundation resources, and I am willing to let them use that power to make what might appear to me to be bad decisions. Second, because by allowing foundations to pursue a number of different courses, some of which might turn out to squander resources, it is possible that some innovative and nonobvious programs will be funded as well, which will work for the public interest in unforeseen ways.[14] Foundations should be free to use their resources for programs that have a high probability of failure, but that would have high payoffs if they worked. This can best be done by preserving foundation autonomy. Third, because foundations are privately endowed, they deserve more latitude than government, which is funded by compulsory payments from its citizens.

In principle, the tax-preferred status of nonprofit foundations warrants restrictions on their activities. They are already restricted, and in my view, these restrictions are adequate at the present time. However, the principle opens the possibility of revising these restrictions at any time that they do not appear to be serving the public interest, because either they are too restrictive or are not restrictive enough.

Should Foundations Live Forever?

Perhaps the most crucial policy question regarding nonprofit foundations is whether they should last in perpetuity. Governments have potentially unlimited lives, as do corporations. Why should foundations not have the same potential life-span in the third sector as institutions in the other two sectors? Possible answers to that question have already been considered. Nonprofit foundations do not have the same level of accountability to the general public as do businesses and government. Furthermore, as time passes, donor intent of necessity will become more remote in a foundation's activities. How can people of one generation be in a position to divine how their money can be best spent to further the interests of those generations into the future? A number of examples in chapter 6 showed the kinds of problems that can arise when attempting to remain true to a donor's intent over a period of generations. John Stuart Mill thought it completely irrational that the perpetual nature of a foundation could transform "a dead man's intentions for a single day [into] a rule for subsequent centuries." [15]

Julius Rosenwald, who established a $25 million foundation for the education of blacks in the South in 1917, gave a clear argument against allowing foundations to last in perpetuity. He said,

> I unqualifiedly disapprove of the efforts made by certain benevolent trusts and foundations to perpetuate themselves by restricting their enterprises and expenditures to the interest on the invested capital, and not only leaving the principal untouched but even adding from time to time to it from unused income. I am opposed to the principle of storing up large sums of money for philanthropic uses centuries hence for two reasons: First, it directly implies a certain lack of confidence with regard to the future, which I do not share. I feel confident that the generations that will follow us will be every bit as humane and enlightened, energetic and able, as we are, and that the needs of the future can safely be left to be met by generations of the future. Second, I am against any program that would inject the great fortunes of today into the affairs of the nation 500 or 1000 years hence. [16]

Rosenwald's arguments have some force. Whatever good the Carnegie and Rockefeller foundations are doing today, Americans (and citizens of the world) are much better off at the end of the twentieth century than they were at the beginning. Unless one doubts the march of progress in the future, would not those fortunes have been put to better use if they were completely spent decades ago? That also would help to preserve donor intent. Furthermore, as Rosenwald argues, why should men that lived a century ago continue to have an influence over public affairs today?

The questions that Rosenwald raised early in the twentieth century are still raised at the end of the twentieth century. Writing in the periodical *Philanthropy*, which is aimed at philanthropic organizations, James Payne questions the wisdom of perpetual foundations on several grounds, but most forcefully argues that the financial security that comes with an endowment can cause foundations to lose touch with indicators that they are using foundation resources for the public good. Payne draws an analogy: "What kind of cars would Ford be making today if the company had been able to ignore customers and coast along on an endowment? The Edsel, popular with Ford executives, would probably be their leading model." [7] Having to seek contributions creates the accountability that Payne sees as desirable.

Yet another argument against giving foundations perpetual life is that the foundation trustees and management can become preoccupied with managing the foundation's portfolio rather than spending the foundation's assets to further the public interest. There is a considerable amount of prestige that goes along with being a trustee of a large foundation, which gives trustees an incentive to maintain the size of their foundation, perhaps taking some attention away from the foundation's programs.

The argument in favor of allowing foundations to survive in perpetuity rests primarily on the principle of donor intent. The donor intended to establish a foundation that would last in perpetuity, and because it is the donor's money, the donor's wishes should be followed. Other possible arguments are that less money would go into foundations if they could not last in perpetuity, and as a counterargument to Rosenwald's optimism argument, things may not be as good in the future as they are today.

If foundations did not last in perpetuity there would be a greater turnover of foundations, but over the long run it might not make much difference in the number of foundation dollars spent. The fact that the Carnegie and Rockefeller foundations might already be gone would be countered by the more rapid rate of expenditures of the Ford and MacArthur foundations. New foundations could learn from the experiences of the old ones, rather than perpetuating the old ones that are stuck with antiquated charters. Experience might count for something too, however. The pragmatic arguments swing both ways on the question of whether foundations should live in perpetuity.

In principle, if bequests are allowed in our society (as they always have been), then those leaving them ought to be able to determine the conditions, including setting up foundations that will last in perpetuity. However, if they want those bequests to receive some tax-favored status, it is then reasonable to place restrictions on them. If inheritance taxes are paid on the endowment before it goes into a foundation, then there should be no objection to allowing foundations to exist in perpetuity. Because the bequests pass tax free, placing a limited life on the tax-preferred status of a foundation so endowed may be a reasonable condition. The arguments in favor of limiting the tax-preferred life of foundations are persuasive, and perhaps after a certain period, such as the forty years that was discussed in 1969, foundations should lose their tax-preferred status. In practice, allowing foundations to exist in perpetuity does not appear to have harmed the public interest in any significant way in the twentieth century, so I would see no reason to alter the status quo. In principle it might be altered if conditions changed, but if it was, the appropriate policy change would be to eliminate the tax-preferred status of foundations after a certain number of years.

Without confiscating the wealth left by the donor, there would be no way to actually terminate a foundation, so even if a foundation's nonprofit status were removed, a foundation still could remain in perpetuity without its nonprofit status. The foundation's ability to make grants would be reduced by any taxes that it owed, and future donors might be less inclined to create foundations. Existing foundations would still be able to function much as they currently do, however, with no tax preferences. While it would be relatively easy to remove the tax benefits foundations enjoy after a certain number of years, it would be more difficult to prevent them from existing in perpetuity.

Conclusion

The first nine chapters examined facts about foundations, and found that there are a number of reasons why foundations tend to allocate resources in ways that may not further the public interest. The institutional environment within which they operate plays a big role, because those who decide how foundation resources are allocated are spending money that is not theirs, and are accountable to nobody for their decisions. These problems with the institutional environment have tended to manifest themselves in the types of ideas and public policies foundations have promoted. After examining the facts, this chapter has shifted gears and examined possible public policy changes that could be made to enhance the operation of the third sector, especially with regard to its promoting; if ideas and public policies. Major reforms were undertaken in 1969, and for the most part those reforms were warranted. Several decades later those reforms seem to have served their purpose, and at the end of the twentieth century public policy toward foundations strikes the appropriate balance between foundation independence and government control.

This does not imply that foundation activities always further the public interest, or that foundations could not be run more efficiently, or more for the benefit of the public interest. Rather, it says that foundations were established with private funds in order to further public purposes, and a structure was put in place by the donors to select trustees to determine how those foundation funds could best further the public interest. Foundations have, indeed, exhibited biases in the past, and these biases may be inherent in the process by which trustees are selected for most foundations. Those who want to establish foundations in the future have a chance to learn from this, and if they do not like the direction of current foundations, they can design their foundations to take a different direction. With hindsight one might conjecture that Carnegie, Rockefeller, Ford, and others might feel some distress at the ways their money has been used after they died. The fortunes that they had an opportunity to make because of the productivity of the market economy have, in many instances, been used to oppose those very market institutions that produced the wealth that endowed their foundations.

This history of foundations might provide some guidance to those considering forming foundations in the future. With self-perpetuating boards, one could attempt to select trustees with particular biases and hope that those biases would perpetuate themselves. And because donor intent becomes increasingly remote over time, and perhaps less relevant, individuals who create foundations should give serious consideration to giving them limited lives rather than allowing them to exist in perpetuity. Donors might also consider less general mandates than the very broad mission statements that guide foundations like Carnegie's and Rockefeller's. These are policy questions for individual foundations, however, rather than public policy questions. The fundamental public policy question is whether additional government restrictions and oversight will serve the public interest. Further restrictions and oversight would make foundations more homogeneous, would lessen their abilities to innovate (although for the most part they do not seem very innovative now), and would have the potential to make them more an extension of the public sector at a time when the public sector is already very large by historical standards.

In addition, one would have to have a great deal of confidence in the government to think that additional governmental restrictions and oversight would improve the performance of nonprofit foundations. At the end of the twentieth century, citizens are suspicious of government power and seem to doubt the efficacy of governmental solutions to nongovernmental problems. This is yet another reason to weigh the options seriously before tinkering with the status quo.

Because of the tax benefits nonprofit foundations receive, government restrictions on their activities should be expected in exchange. Furthermore, their special status should hold them to higher standards of conduct than individuals engaged in private sector activities, and foundation activities should expect to be scrutinized by the public and by the government. Because of the perception of problems in the 1960s additional restrictions were placed on foundations in 1969. With several decades of hindsight they appear to have served their purpose, but foundations should expect continuing scrutiny and additional restrictions if in the future there are additional questions regarding whether foundation activities serve the public interest. The major problems with the resource allocation decisions made by foundations are unlikely to be solved by tinkering with policies dealing with regulation and oversight. Indeed, more regulation and oversight would probably be harmful. Policy options that would improve the performance of the third sector are more likely to be more broad and general changes in the tax structure that would have implications well beyond foundations. In the 1990s many serious suggestions for major tax reform have been put forward, and the next chapter considers how more major changes might affect foundation formation and operation.

Notes

1. Adam Smith, *The Wealth of Nations* (New York: Modern Library, 1937, orig. 1776), pp. 716-722. Smith's discussion, which deals with university endowments, is more generally applicable.
2. Robert E. Hall and Alvin Rabushka, *The Flat Tax* (Stanford, CA: Hoover Institution Press, 1985).
3. See, for example, Elinor Ostrom, *Crafting Institutions for Self-Governing Irrigation Systems* (San Francisco, CA: Institute for Contemporary Studies, 1992), who examines irrigation systems funded by grants (not always foundation grants), and finds that how successful they are depends mostly on the institutions created for governing them rather than the technological characteristics of the systems. Thus, Ostrom finds that the social science aspect of such projects is more important than the engineering aspect.
4. *Statistical Abstract of the United States,* 1995 ed., p. 394.
5. *Statistical Abstract of the United States,* 1994 ed., p. 390.
6. Stuart Nolan and Gregory P. Conko, *Patterns of Corporate Philanthropy: Executive Hypocrisy* (Washington, DC: Capital Research Center, 1993).
7. See Brian O'Connell, *Philanthropy in Action* (New York: Foundation Center, 1987) for a review of the good causes foundations have supported, by someone active in the business of philanthropy.
8. Horace Coon, *Money to Burn* (London: Longmans, Green and Co., 1938), p. 17.
9. Deborah Koch, Project Coordinator, *The Nonprofit Policy Agenda: Recommendations for State and Local Action* (Washington, DC: Union Institute, May 1992).
10. Thomas J. DiLorenzo, *Hidden Politics: "Progressive" Nonprofits Target the States* (Washington, D.C.: Capital Research Center, 1993).
11. Teresa Odendahl, *Charity Begins at Home: Generosity and Self-Interest Among the Philanthropic Elite* (New York: Basic Books, 1990).
12. Henry Hansmann, "The Effect of Tax Exemption and Other Factors on the Market Share of Nonprofit Versus For-Profit Firms, *National Tax Journal* 40, No. 1 (March 1987), pp. 71-82.
13. Indeed, some observers believe that policy advocacy is a socially beneficial activity of foundations. See J. Craig Jenkins, "Nonprofit Organizations and Policy Advocacy," chap. 17 in Walter W. Powell, ed., *The Nonprofit Sector* (New Haven, CT: Yale University Press, 1987).
14. Friedrich A. Hayek's article, "The Use of Knowledge in Society," *American Economic Review* 35, No. 4 (September 1945), pp. 519-530, eloquently expresses the ways in which the individual knowledge of everyone can be better harnessed in a decentralized system, rather than relying on the central planning of even the most competent and knowledgeable individuals. This argues for allowing substantial variety in foundation activities.
15. Quoted in Francine Ostrower, "Donor Control and Perpetual Trusts: Does

Anything Last Forever?" chapter 15 in Richard Magat, ed., *Philanthropic Giving: Studies in Varieties and Goals* (New York: Oxford University Press, 1989).

16. William H. Rudy, *The Foundations: Their Use and Abuse* (Washington, DC: Public Affairs Press, 1970), pp. 31-32.
17. James L. Payne, "The Voluntary Ideal: Should Charities Live Forever?" *Philanthropy* 9, No. 4 (Fall 1995), p. 16.

11

Conclusion

The ideas that are promoted with foundation money have been controversial throughout the twentieth century. When the Carnegie and Rockefeller foundations were created prior to World War I critics charged that capitalist robber barons were not content only to control American business. Rather, through the reach of their foundations they wanted to control our educational institutions, our social services, and even our governments. Foundations were viewed as a mechanism through which the worst features of capitalism would extend themselves throughout our society. After World War II the fears of foundation power came from the other end of the political spectrum as Congress was concerned that foundations were financing a left-wing political agenda with their huge fortunes, unaccountable to anyone for their activities. The social and political agenda was being turned away from the concepts of limited government and laissez-faire economics, using fortunes that were made within the very system that foundations set out to attack.

This volume has focused on how tax laws affect the ideas that are financed by nonprofit foundations. The tax laws allow foundations to be established with tax-free donations and bequests, and then allow foundations to operate as nonprofit organizations. Because they are granted nonprofit status, their activities are restricted through tax laws, which is the main way that foundations are regulated. Requirements for retaining nonprofit status in turn affect foundation activities and so affect the ideas and public policies that foundations promote. The influence of the tax laws that govern foundations is a key element because it is through the tax laws that public policy toward foundations is designed. If one wants to consider policy changes toward foundations, tax policy must play a prominent role.

In exchange for tax-preferred status, it is reasonable to expect foundations to meet some requirements. In addition, foundations are created to promote the public interest, so again, it is reasonable to evaluate what changes might be made to the requirements placed on foundations that might further enhance the public good. Throughout the twentieth century, foundation activities have been scrutinized by the general public and by Congress, and in 1969 major reforms were made that limited the activities foundations could pursue. Part of the motivation of the 1969 tax reforms was to limit fraud and abuse, and to try to prevent foundations from being used as a mechanism for the avoidance of tax payments. But a major part of those reforms was also designed to limit the influence of foundations over public policy issues.

In principle, it is easy to accept the idea that foundations established to further the public interest, and given tax breaks in order to do so, should have some restrictions placed on their activities in order to ensure that their activities actually do promote the public good. With several decades of hindsight, this volume has evaluated the results of the 1969 tax reform and concluded that at the end of the twentieth century, the 1969 reforms seem to have accomplished what they intended. They have limited fraud and abuse, and have kept foundations from pursuing overtly political agendas, but without preventing them from remaining involved in the analysis of public policy issues. In too many instances, however, foundations still give the impression of pursuing a political agenda rather than undertaking activities that are less tied to ideology and that are more obviously in the public interest. The 1969 tax reforms were intended to curb abuses of foundations in several areas, and they succeeded. At the same time more fundamental problems with the way that foundations allocate resources remain. The remaining problems have more to do with the incentive structure of foundations, which gives an elite group of individuals the power to allocate resources which are not theirs and which they did not earn, with almost no oversight or accountability.

The previous chapter discussed a number of possible reforms that have been considered to improve the performance of foundations, but concluded that none of those reforms showed much potential for improving the performance of foundations, and indeed that many proposed reforms would make matters worse. One might hope that foundations would devote fewer resources to projects with strong ideological content, and one might recognize the persistent liberal bias in foundation activities. Nevertheless, additional government control over foundations would in many ways be counterproductive. The possibility of additional government oversight must be viewed cautiously, especially by individuals who are concerned about ideological bias in foundation activities, because government programs tend to have ideological biases too. In short, additional regulation is not the way to improve the performance of foundations.

If one steps back to look at foundations and tax policy in a larger context, it is apparent that foundations were not created due to incentives designed specifically to encourage them, but rather through the indirect effect of allowing charitable contributions, including bequests to create foundations, to be made tax free. As income and inheritance tax rates rose throughout the twentieth century the creation of foundations became increasingly popular as a way to avoid inheritance taxes. High inheritance taxes coupled with the opportunity to pass money into foundations tax free has encouraged the formation of foundations as a side effect of treating the creation of a foundation as a charitable activity. Charity has not always been the sole motive for creating foundations, however. Donors have used foundations to maintain family control of corporations, to aggrandize their family names, and to pass power and status on to their heirs by placing them on foundation boards. Foundation activities have been controlled by regulations aimed directly at the foundations themselves, but the formation and operation of foundations have also been influenced by the tax code more generally. Thus, it is reasonable to consider how more general tax reforms might affect foundations.

One would not want to recommend general changes in the tax code for the sole purpose of affecting foundation activity specifically, but at the same time, when general changes are proposed it is reasonable to consider how foundations are affected. For example, in the 1980s and 1990s a number of major tax reform proposals have been put forward. A move to a flat rate income tax has been proposed by a number of economists and politicians, as has some more direct type of consumption tax like a value added tax or national sales tax.

Charitable Contributions and Foundations

One of the characteristics of many tax reform proposals is that they would eliminate the tax deductibility of charitable contributions. The flat tax proposal of Robert Hall and Alvin Rabushka has provided the framework for a number of flat tax proposals in the 1980s and 1990s, and their proposal would allow no deductions for charitable contributions.[1] Value added taxes would treat charitable contributions almost identically to other expenditure items, assuming that charitable organizations would not be rebated for value added taxes already levied on their purchases, so with regard to foundations there is a similarity between value added taxation and many flat tax proposals. Sales taxes can be (and typically are) designed to exempt charitable organizations, so, like the current income tax, would treat charitable organizations more favorably. Nobody has proposed levying sales taxes on people's contributions to charity. While charitable contributions might be treated in a number of ways, the Hall and Rabushka flat tax policy of treating charitable contributions like any other expenditure is a good policy to use as a benchmark for analysis, both because it has received serious political consideration and because the policy stands in solid contrast to the current one of allowing deductibility of charitable contributions.

The evidence suggests that the level of charitable contributions is affected relatively little by its tax deductibility,[2] but the timing of contributions is affected as taxpayers try to minimize their taxes, and the allocation among possible recipients is also affected. Worthy causes abound, and people who make substantial contributions make them in such a way as to maximize the tax benefits. For example, few donors would give $1,000 to the Salvation Army bell ringer at Christmas, leaving no evidence for the IRS of a charitable contribution, when they could mail them a check instead and be assured of a tax deduction. Likewise, institutional gifts to organizations that help the needy, like the Salvation Army, are encouraged over directly providing personal help to people in need, because personal gifts to individuals are not deductible.

The tax deductibility of contributions to qualified charities clearly affects the nature of charitable activity and makes it more impersonal. It also places tax-exempt organizations like art museums and symphony orchestras, which provide benefits primarily to upper-income people, on an equal footing with organizations that help the needy. Ironically, one can take a tax deduction for a charitable contribution to a symphony orchestra, but not for a meal that one buys for a needy family that has fallen on hard times. If charitable contributions were not tax deductible the evidence suggests that the total level of philanthropy would be affected relatively little, but people would be freer to allocate their philanthropic dollars in ways that they believed were beneficial, without having to consider the tax consequences. The case for eliminating the deductibility of charitable contributions has been made by those who propose a flat tax along the lines of that proposed by Hall and Rabushka. If the tax deductibility of charitable contributions were eliminated, how would that affect foundations?

The largest foundations are established through bequests rather than charitable contributions, but they are affected by the deductibility of charitable contributions because they provide an alternative way to avoid taxation. The creation of a foundation does not pass wealth on to one's heirs directly, but it may do so indirectly, through benefits like trusteeships and other family associations with the foundation. Currently endowments to foundations are treated in a manner similar to charitable contributions under the income tax, and if the deductibility of charitable contributions were eliminated, as would be the case under a true flat tax, that would tilt the balance toward foundations. Without the deductibility of charitable contributions, major donors would have the incentive to forego charitable contributions and instead endow foundations, assuming that inheritance tax laws remained unchanged. Given the problems with foundations, there would be a strong argument for maintaining the balance between charitable contributions for income tax purposes and charitable bequests under the inheritance tax, either by taxing endowments like other bequests, or by eliminating taxes on all bequests.

A persistent theme in American politics is equality of opportunity, so if a choice is to be made between taxing all bequests, including those to establish foundations, or eliminating inheritance taxes entirely, most people's initial reaction would surely be to tax all bequests. The argument is not so clear cut, however, and after some analysis the idea of eliminating all inheritance taxes has some appeal.

Inheritance and Bequests

The taxation of bequests as it exists in the United States at the end of the twentieth century is based on questionable motivations. The general idea behind it is that by taxing large inheritances, it helps to level the playing field. It does so in an odd way, though, by imposing substantial costs on some, but providing little if any benefit to the general public. In 1995 estate tax revenues made up only 1.1 percent of total federal revenues, so spreading that money across the general population would provide relatively little general benefit. Even that is likely to be an overestimate. One study of inheritance taxation concludes that on net the estate tax costs the government revenue because people take tax-deductible charitable contributions during their lifetimes to avoid inheritance taxes, thereby reducing income tax collections by more than the total amount of revenue raised by inheritance taxes.[3] If inheritance taxes do level the playing field, they do so by lowering those on top rather than by benefiting those on the bottom.

There is no doubt that those who are born into wealthy families have advantages that last throughout their lifetimes, and that those who are born wealthy are much more likely to remain wealthy. The evidence suggests that only a small part of this advantage is due to the inheritance of wealth, however, and that the bulk of the advantage comes from the opportunity for a better education along with the upbringing, connections, and interpersonal relationships that come with wealth.[4] Even a confiscatory tax on bequests would not eliminate most of the advantages of being born wealthy, because the education, upbringing, and connections associated with wealth have a bigger effect than the money inherited by the children of the wealthy. As a result, inheritance taxation can have only the most modest of equalizing effects. What one inherits from one's parents is much more than a monetary bequest, and the ability of the inheritance tax to equalize wealth is very limited.

The inheritance tax does little to provide equality of either wealth or opportunity, and what it does do is a result of bringing those at the upper end of the wealth scale down a bit rather than providing any benefit to those at the lower range of the scale. Meanwhile it has the negative effect of distorting economic choices by pushing people to look for ways to avoid the tax. There are many ways that this can be done by passing benefits on to heirs untaxed, such as by providing gifts to them during their lifetimes, by providing benefits like education and travel opportunities, and even by purchasing tangible assets like art and gold that can, perhaps, be passed along to heirs undetected by the tax system. The inheritance tax distorts choices in another way as well: it encourages people to leave money in ways that will be untaxed, including leaving money to endow foundations.

If the inheritance tax produces little in the way of real advantages, it does have some real disadvantages. If one considers only its effect on foundations, there is a good argument for making bequests to foundations have the same tax status as other bequests. As the tax system is currently designed, there is a tax advantage to leaving money for the creation of foundations, and the problems with allocating resources through foundations have been discussed at length. In theory, there are problems with trusting the responsibility for foundation assets to trustees who are accountable to nobody, and in practice the resulting problems have attracted enough attention to prompt major public policy changes. In a free society, if people want to endow foundations with their fortunes, there is no good argument for trying to prevent them, but there are good arguments against encouraging them to do so, as is the case with the current tax laws. One option would be to tax bequests into foundations, but the inheritance tax itself creates many inefficiencies and few benefits. A better option would be to eliminate inheritance taxation altogether.

Poverty and Equality

Inheritance tax policy is a part of a broader issue of how public policy should address disparities in income and wealth. There is a tendency for people to equate policies that help those in poverty with policies that create more income equality, but there are major differences between the potential policy goals of helping those in poverty and creating more income equality.[5] By looking around the world one can see that those at the bottom end of the income distribution fare best in prosperous economies. In the United States most people below the poverty line have indoor plumbing, telephones, and television sets—amenities that are considered luxuries in many parts of the world. In the United States the most common nutritional problem of those below the poverty line is obesity. This says a great deal about the merits of a society that is wealthy enough to overfeed even its poorest citizens. This is not meant to minimize the plight of those at the bottom end of the income distribution, but rather to point toward the types of public policies that can help those who are the least fortunate.

There is a great deal of wisdom in Henry Ford's idea that the best thing he could have done to enhance the welfare of mankind was to invest his profits in his business in order to provide more people with good jobs. This helps in three ways. First, it provides better incomes to workers, improving their welfare; second, higher incomes lead to more charitable activity to help the disadvantaged; and third, it provides a larger tax base from which to fund redistributional programs. More investment is likely to come from wealthy people, so an unequal distribution of income can help raise the welfare of those at the low end of the income distribution.

The goal of equality would be most easily achieved by lowering the incomes of those at the top end of the income distribution. It is hard to bring the incomes of those at the bottom of the income scale up, as three decades of the "war on poverty" in the United States has shown. By contrast, it is relatively easy to appropriate the incomes of those at the top end of the income distribution. Many people who claim to favor income equality do so because they imagine that it will come about by lowering the incomes of those at the top and raising the incomes of those at the bottom. Such an outcome would not only further equality, but also would help those in poverty. Someone who really favored equality as a goal would have to be willing to trade off some harm to those at the bottom in exchange for more equality. In other words, if equality is accepted as a goal in itself, rather than as a means to the end of helping those who are least fortunate, one would have to be willing to endorse some policies that would make everyone worse off, if at the same time they harmed those at the top more than those at the bottom, so created a more equal result. If one would always refuse to endorse any policy that produced more equality by harming everybody, then the real end of that person would be helping the least fortunate, rather than pursuing equality per se.[6]

If equality of income and wealth itself is not held as a goal, then the question becomes what types of tax and redistribution policies would best help those at the low end of the income distribution? Economists who are sympathetic with the idea of using the tax system as a redistributive tool have concluded that those at the bottom of the income distribution are helped most by tax systems that do little in the way of redistribution, because the those who are worst off are helped most by a tax system that provides an incentive for upper income people to earn more income as opposed to a tax system that transfers substantial portions of their incomes.[7] If the overriding public policy goal with regard to the income distribution is helping out those at the bottom, rather than creating more equality even if it harms those at the bottom, then the way to achieve that goal is to promote the growth of national income rather than to try to redistribute the income that is being produced. Taken in this context, the elimination of inheritance taxes altogether is a reasonable policy.

Charitable Contributions, Inheritance Taxes, and Foundations

When considering all of the effects of tax policy on the American economy, its effect on foundations is a small part of the total story indeed, and one could hardly recommend abolishing inheritance taxes based solely on an analysis of foundations. However, in the context of public policy debate, a number of serious proposals have been forwarded to eliminate the tax preference given to charitable contributions, and the economic research done on the topic suggests that charities themselves would see little if any adverse impact. Such a move would eliminate the current equating (for tax purposes) of public policy organizations with the charities that help the least fortunate members of our society, and this would likely to be beneficial. Given the resource allocation problems associated with foundations, one would also want to eliminate the encouragement the tax system now gives people to establish foundations. That could be done either by taxing bequests to foundations, which would push people toward other tax shelters, or by eliminating inheritance taxation altogether. Because inheritance taxation creates incentives that harm the productivity of the economy, and because in any event inheritance taxation provides little if any benefit to those at the bottom of the income distribution, the argument for keeping it is tenuous.

While one could not recommend abolishing inheritance taxation based on a study of foundations, it is clear that if the inheritance tax were abolished the bias toward the creation of foundations and its attendant resource allocation problems would be eliminated. Thus, when evaluating potential tax reforms, this analysis of nonprofit foundations finds additional support for proposals like the Hall-Rabushka flat tax that eliminate the tax-preferred treatment of charitable contributions, and an elimination of inheritance taxation. Those are bold recommendations from a study of foundations, but as this analysis has shown, inefficiencies in the allocation of foundation resources are substantial, and are inherent in the structure of the foundation sector. After major reforms in 1969, however, additional tinkering with minor reforms and regulations of the sector would be likely to make matters worse. If one really wants to make public policy changes to enhance the performance of foundations, major changes to the tax structure must be undertaken.

Major Issues: Accountability and Donor Intent

In this concluding chapter, it is worth briefly recapping the importance of the major issues of accountability and donor intent to emphasize the fundamental causes of resource misallocations in the foundation sector. Foundations operate from the incomes of their endowments, so they do not need to satisfy customers, and they do not need to raise any additional funds. As a result, the trustees who run foundations are accountable to nobody. They decide, within the very wide parameters of the law, how they can best use foundation resources to promote the public interest.

The clear disadvantage of such lack of accountability is that there is no penalty for foundations to pay when their activities run counter to the public interest, or even when they are not as much in the public interest as would be possible. They will not lose customers, because they have none, and they will not lose donations, because they solicit none. Yet this lack of accountability was viewed as an advantage of foundations by Rod MacArthur, who was for a time a trustee of the MacArthur Foundation. MacArthur argued that the lack of accountability allowed foundations the latitude to experiment with high-risk programs that might pay off with public interest benefits, but that would be infeasible in either the public or private sectors. MacArthur's point must be conceded, although at the close of the twentieth century foundations appear to be following more traditional paths rather than taking risks. Lack of accountability offers potential advantages, although the potential disadvantages are at least as apparent.

The concept of donor intent also raises some interesting questions. Some foundations have a very narrow statement of donor intent, which has resulted in an obvious waste of resources in cases where donors could not anticipate that the needs that were so real when they were alive would vanish decades, or centuries, down the road. For the present study, however, the more important cases involve foundations that have a very general statement of donor intent. If a foundation is charged only with improving the welfare of mankind, or some similarly vague charge, then any specific intentions of the donor can be pushed aside by the priorities of the trustees. The Carnegie Corporation is a clear case where, despite the very general wording of Andrew Carnegie's charter, his own philanthropic activities give a clear indication of what he thought was in the public interest. After Carnegie's death, his foundation's activities deviated significantly from the course he had steered during his lifetime.

One might argue against adhering to the intentions of the donor. Why should the dead be able to influence public policy from beyond the grave? In fact, donor intent is not a major issue for the largest foundations, which were created with very general missions to further the public interest. The issue of donor intent really becomes an extension of the accountability issue, then.

Lack of accountability is an issue that should keep the scrutiny of the general public on foundations. Elected officials are accountable at the ballot box. In the private sector, firms must satisfy their customers to remain in business. Foundation trustees answer to nobody. Because of this, and because their mission is to further the public interest, the public has a right to expect that foundations will maintain the highest standards and avoid any activities that might appear to be questionable. In light of the environment within which foundations operate, they should be carefully scrutinized, and it is reasonable to expect that public policy toward foundations would change in response to foundation activities that would appear to violate the public trust that is placed in them.

Institutional Incentives

The lack of accountability of foundations is a feature of the institutional structure within which they operate. They can take risks that would be unacceptable for either private sector firms or public sector governments precisely because they do not have to justify their actions to anyone, as Rod MacArthur pointed out. The wide latitude given foundation managers also allows them to waste money, and to indulge themselves in furthering their own views of the public interest, especially where public policy issues are concerned. The 1990s saw presidential candidates Ross Perot and Steve Forbes spend millions of their own dollars to have their policy views heard, and both, after the fact, said they thought it was money well spent. Foundation trustees are explicitly prohibited from using foundation money for political campaigns, but they can still spend foundation money on ideologically charged policy studies, conferences, and the like. Unlike Perot and Forbes, the money they spend is not their own. Money could be wasted on foundation programs that ultimately have little impact, or even that work counter to the public interest. The lack of accountability for foundation trustees almost guarantees that this will be the case.

Foundations do many good things, however, and at their best fill a void by financing activities that would not be undertaken by either the public or private sectors. Foundations can fill this void precisely because they do not have to justify their activities to anyone. Along with this comes inevitable inefficiency and waste, but this inefficiency and waste may best be viewed as one of the costs of allowing foundations to operate. There is a difference, however, between allowing foundations to operate and creating incentives that favor foundations over other ways to dispose of one's income. The tax treatment of foundations could be improved if the tax system was neutral toward foundations, rather than encouraging the formation of foundations as it does now.

Economist William Niskanen has studied government bureaucracies extensively and concluded that the incentive structure of the public sector leads government bureaucracies to be inefficiently large, wasting taxpayer dollars when compared to a measure of ideal economic efficiency.[8] Yet some activities can only be carried out by government. Most people would not want to give up government production of national defense, police protection, courts, roads, or even welfare programs. This is true despite the fact that the general public perceives a substantial amount of waste and inefficiency in all these areas. If we are going to have a public sector, then some inefficiency is inevitable because of the nature of public sector institutions.[9] The same argument applies to foundations. They can contribute to the public good in ways the public and private sectors cannot because they do not have to answer to anybody, but this lack of accountability brings with it inevitable inefficiencies and abuses. We would like to control the problems as much as possible, but we do not want to eliminate the benefits of foundations as a by-product of trying to control their inefficiencies. Regrettably, one by-product of the wide latitude given foundation trustees is that they can indulge their ideological biases when making grants.

Foundation Biases

Chapters 3, 4, and 5 examined the ideas supported by foundation funding, and showed that there has been a clear liberal bias in foundation funding throughout the twentieth century. While early in the century some feared that foundation money would be used in order to extend the control of capitalists beyond their businesses and into social and political issues, in fact the opposite has happened. The fortunes that have been earned through successes in the capitalist system have been used to oppose the system that created those fortunes. The biases have arisen because foundation trustees tend not to be as committed to the market system as the individuals who have earned the fortunes that created the foundations. Sometimes the descendants of those who earned the fortunes have become trustees, but these individuals did not have the experience of earning the wealth, and may feel a bit guilty because they were lucky enough to have been born into a rich family. They have attended good schools, but in the process have acquired some of the anticapitalist bias that has been associated with American universities in the twentieth century. Other times trustees come directly from academia or government, again with antimarket biases.

While one can recognize this bias, and while those who in the future may establish foundations might want to factor it into their plans, it is unclear that there is any reason for public policy to respond to it. The foundations were established according to the donors' wishes, and it is in fact hard for those donors to control current activities from the grave. Thus, foundations proceed, steeped in their liberal biases, and accountable to nobody.

Two factors might mitigate this liberal bias. First, because it has been recognized, conservative organizations have been established to counter it. Second, the liberal bias in foundations may have been a product of the times. The twentieth century, because of wars, economic depression, and social unrest, created a liberal academic atmosphere that has spilled over into government, into popular opinion, and into foundations. At the end of the twentieth century the trend of ideas is in the other direction. The ideas of Karl Marx and John Maynard Keynes are being countered by the ideas of Friedrich Hayek and Milton Friedman.

Whether in fact the trends of the twentieth century will reverse themselves in the twenty-first century remains to be seen, but it does appear that the intellectual pendulum is swinging the other way.

It is one thing to recognize this liberal bias, but quite another to advocate public policies to do something about it. There are several arguments that can be made from a conservative point of view against taking any action. First, foundations are fundamentally private arrangements, created with private money. The government should not interfere with such private arrangements. Second, given the liberal biases of those in government, any government influence over foundation activities is likely to reinforce any liberal bias that now exists in foundations. While it is true that the last two decades of the twentieth century have seen a turn toward conservatism in the federal government, civil servants are likely to remain more liberal than the general public, simply because they have chosen to work for government.

While some liberal observers of foundations agree with my assessment of the liberal biases of foundations, and approve of their liberal agendas,[10] others see a conservative bias, especially since 1970.[11] Yet the same arguments against government intervention still apply. Would liberals want to turn foundations over to the control of increasingly conservative politicians? In a free country, should individuals still not be able to allocate philanthropic dollars as they see fit? Regardless of how one evaluates the biases of foundations, there are still reasons for being cautious about turning foundation activities more over to government control.

Public Policy Possibilities

The principle that foundation activities should be controlled to a degree by government in exchange for the tax benefits they receive has already been discussed. What types of public policies might be initiated to control the effect of foundation programs on the promotion of ideas and public policies? The previous chapter examined a number of possibilities in detail. This section summarizes those possibilities to reinforce the conclusion that while there are well-recognized problems with the way that foundations allocate their resources, public policy measures to address those problems are likely to do more harm than good. The public policy possibilities fall into five general categories. (1) Create additional government restrictions on foundation activities;

(2) Establish more government oversight; (3) Tax foundations; (4) Mandate changes in the way that trustees are selected; and (5) Change the tax system to be neutral toward the formation of foundations.

Additional Restrictions

Additional government restrictions were created in 1969 in response to perceived problems with foundations. Even supporters of foundations saw some justification for additional restrictions at that time, and the restrictions that were placed on foundations then seem to have served their purpose. There appears to be no compelling reason in the 1990s to further restrict foundation activities, but additional restrictions should be viewed as an option if problems are perceived in the future. Because of the special status of foundations and their charge to further the public interest, even the perception of problems might warrant action. Foundations should be held to high standards of propriety.

Additional Government Oversight

Oversight of a general nature, such as the creation of a government office of foundations, or an evaluation of the merits of specific foundation activities, would likely be counterproductive. Foundations would become more homogeneous, more limited in their activities, and most significantly, more like the government itself. Because the government already is a major presence in the economy, foundations should be encouraged to operate outside the umbrella of government, undertaking activities that the government is not well-equipped to do. Further accountability to government would work in the opposite direction.

Tax Foundations

Perhaps the tax-preferred status of foundations should be removed altogether. When one reflects on the problems with foundations, which go back to the issues of donor intent and lack of accountability, one can see that taxing foundations will have relatively little impact. It would reduce the amount of money that foundations would have available to spend, but at the same time it would remove them from the government oversight created by the tax laws. Foundations would continue to exist, and could continue to live in perpetuity, taxed or not. Foundation assets could be confiscated to enforce a limited life on foundations, but as the previous chapter argued, confiscation of foundation assets would also be counterproductive. While at first taxation might seem like a good policy option, on deeper examination, taxation would not attack the fundamental issues, and would merely transfer resources from foundations to the government.

Change the Method of Trustee Selection

Perhaps the problem lies with foundation management, and foundation boards should not be self-perpetuating. Perhaps trustees should be selected more democratically. Who, then, would select foundation trustees? One should be leery of having elected officials do the selection, or indeed any government official, because foundations would then move closer toward being an arm of the government. Because foundations are established with private resources, the previous chapter argued that there is no good reason not to allow the donor to specify the manner in which trustees would be selected. While it is true that the current methods of trustee selection skews foundation activities toward that elite group that manages foundations, it is hard to see that another method of selection would be more in the public interest. Even if it is, this is probably an area better left to the determination of the foundations themselves, rather than a public policy issue.

Tax Neutrality

By making bequests to endow foundations exempt from inheritance taxation, the tax system encourages the formation of foundations. As argued earlier in the chapter, while one would not want to discourage people from using their incomes in this way, there is not a good argument for using the tax system to encourage the formation of foundations either. An elimination of inheritance taxation would create neutrality.

When the public policy possibilities were examined, one could see in principle that there is a role for public policy to control the activities of foundations, but after the 1969 reforms, additional reforms are likely to be counterproductive. The real problem is not an underregulation of foundations but rather a tax system that encourages people to create them. This bias in the tax system should be eliminated, so the policy implications point not toward policies aimed specifically at foundations, but toward biases in the tax system more generally.

The Social Roles of Government and Foundations

In the nineteenth century, foundations were established primarily to improve the well-being of those least well off in society, but throughout the twentieth century, as foundations have branched out from their original missions, government has moved in as the guardian of the welfare of society's least fortunate. Indeed, one of the reasons that foundations see less reason to cater to the needy is that government has taken such a large redistributive role in the twentieth century. As large as foundations are, their annual expenditures pale beside those of government, so there is little reason for them to spend in areas where government has a substantial presence. To have an impact, foundations should be doing something different from governments.

Some observers applaud the movement of government transfers into areas that formerly were the province of private charities.[12] By professionalizing social services and providing a guaranteed source of revenues through taxation, the safety net is much more secure than it would have been if voluntary support had been relied upon. At the same time, the growing government that has crowded out private philanthropies has made the third sector less relevant to the well-being of society. At one time, Andrew Carnegie built libraries for people. Now government builds libraries. At one time philanthropies provided hospitals and health care to those in need. Now government provides that health care far more comprehensively than private philanthropies could ever hope to. Because of the increased role of government, foundations are less relevant to social welfare than they were earlier in the century, and public policy toward foundations is much less important to the overall social well-being of the nation than if government programs were less pervasive.

A related development is the increased willingness of third sector organizations to look toward government grants as a source of funding. Foundations, operating from endowments, do not apply for government funding, but the government acts as an alternative revenue source for grant recipients, and some programs are run with a combination of government and foundation funds. Thus, developments in the public sector have pushed it to take on more of the role traditionally undertaken by the nonprofit sector.[13] As the nonprofit sector is forced to coexist with the public sector as their roles increasingly overlap, the voluntary sector is in danger of becoming crowded out by the compulsory sector.[14]

Government programs, financed through taxation, have the advantage that funding is assured. They have the disadvantage that the taxpayers who fund the programs have little direct oversight or control over the programs they fund. An even larger disadvantage, however, is that the virtues of private initiative and individual sacrifice for the common good are lost when government coercion replaces private cooperation. Contributing money for the public interest is a virtuous activity; paying taxes is an obligation that people try to minimize. The same people who donate fortunes to private foundations hire tax attorneys and accountants to help them discover ways to minimize their tax bills. There is virtue in philanthropy; there is no virtue in paying taxes.

Michael Novak states, "One of the most overlooked characteristics of the free society is the principle that it is not necessary—it is even dangerous—to serve public needs soley [sic] through the state." [15] Foundations would have a more significant role to play in the modern economy if government were not so big. At the end of the twentieth century, government has taken over the most significant roles that foundations held at the beginning of the century. This is, undoubtedly, one of the factors that has pushed foundations more toward supporting the production of ideas and the promotion of public policies.

Foundations and the Production of Ideas

Foundation funding of the production of ideas has had a recognizable influence over the course of American society and over the direction of public policy. Gunnar Myrdal's book, *The American Dilemma,*[16] and Charles Murray's book, *Losing Ground,*[17] are two prominent examples, but countless other books, reports, and conferences have also had their input into American life. At the same time, foundation-sponsored studies must be viewed as sharing the biases of the sponsoring foundations, so ideas promoted by foundations lose some of their effectiveness. The researchers who receive foundation grants are undoubtedly doing work they believe in, but they were selected by a biased procedure whereby foundations support researchers who promote the foundation's point of view. The bias lies with the types of ideas that foundations fund, rather than with those to whom funding goes.

As the twentieth century has progressed, foundations have become increasingly involved with the production of ideas, and foundation-sponsored work has become increasingly ideologically oriented. Rather than supporting basic education programs, or giving general support to educational institutions, funding has moved toward conferences, studies, and other projects that have a clear ideological point of view. Individual works such as the two just cited may have a substantial amount of influence, yet observers recognize that the aggregate amount of work supporting any particular point of view has as much to do with the ideological orientation of those who fund the production of ideas as with the merit of the ideas themselves. It is easy to write off the production of foundation-funded ideas as a product of the biases of the foundations themselves.

The biases go in both directions, and the steadfast liberalism of the Carnegie Corporation is offset to a degree by the conservatism of the Adolph Coors Foundation. Foundations with a liberal orientation tend to be larger than those with a conservative orientation; in 1992 the Carnegie Corporation had over $1 billion in assets, compared to the Adolph Coors Foundation's asset base of $125 million, but the balance could be tipped as new foundations are created. While the direction of bias might be of interest, what is more relevant to the impact of foundation funding is that there is the perception that foundation funding is subject to ideological bias. This recognition lowers the impact of foundation ideas.

The twentieth-century foundation foray into the production of ideas has several causes. One is the idea that foundation funding is potentially more productive when it helps create an environment in which everyone can be productive, so that problems can be avoided, rather than trying to respond after the fact to problems that have arisen. Another is that government is playing an increasingly large role in activities that were at one time the province of private charitable activity. The effect of government's role has been two-fold. First, it has crowded foundations out of some areas. Second, because government policy is so important, it has provided the incentive for those who run foundations to try to influence government policy in order to further the public interest rather than undertaking programs more directly. The idea that foundations can help illuminate a productive course for the public sector goes back to the early part of the century, when the Rockefeller

Foundation and others would undertake demonstration projects with the hope that governments would support them once their efficacy was demonstrated. Foundations have shifted increasingly away from demonstration projects, however, and toward studies and conferences as methods of persuasion.

The promotion of ideas by foundations, and their biases on both the political left and right, are assisted by tax laws that give nonprofit foundations favorable treatment. Even so, there is not much to gain by changing the tax laws as they relate to the operation of foundations. Major reforms were undertaken in 1969, and they have served the limited purpose of curbing the most egregious abuses of foundations. If future abuses become apparent, future changes would be warranted. Meanwhile, critics must recognize that additional government oversight and restrictions would serve to further homogenize foundations and make them more an extension of the public sector. Because the public sector is so large relative to foundations at the end of the twentieth century, the extent that foundations have a contribution to make to the quality of life must rest with their ability to undertake activities that are unsuitable for either the public or private sectors. That means keeping them independent of government.

Foundation grants are dwarfed by both private philanthropy and by government expenditures. Even in the promotion of ideas, think tanks funded by private contributions and government-sponsored projects temper any impact that foundation-sponsored research has. Because foundations have the recognized potential for bias in the ideas they promote, this further blunts the impact of foundation-sponsored work. Foundations are free to run with their biases because they are accountable to nobody for their activities. There seems to be no good way to get around the lack of accountability of foundations, and the associated problems have been noted at least since Adam Smith wrote on the subject in 1776. Foundations should be more adventuresome than they are and, as Rod MacArthur suggested, take advantage of their lack of accountability to undertake high-risk projects with potentially high payoffs. Too often, they tend to support projects that fit too predictably into the mold of their past activities.

What is true of one foundation is not necessarily true of them all, and what is true of most foundations today will not necessarily be true of foundations in the future. Foundation trustees can be criticized for their actions, but undoubtedly they are trying to further what they believe is the public interest. With little accountability, they are in a good position to change course if that would seem appropriate. Government tends to be monolithic. At the federal level there is only one, but even at the state level governments are constrained by federal regulations and by voters who are wary of major changes. There are thousands of foundations that do thousands of different things and that are in a position to experiment and to take chances, even when recognizing that many failures are likely along with a few successes. While they have not always lived up to their potential, foundations do have the opportunity to accomplish things that are beyond the reach of the public and private sectors.

At the beginning of the twentieth century, when government was small, the virtuous and charitable acts of philanthropists had large impacts on the quality of life. Carnegie's libraries and Rockefeller's health programs helped large groups of people to get more out of life and at the same time set examples so that others might be inspired to do some part to help promote the public good. At the end of the twentieth century governments build libraries and are major health care providers. With the government taking over, the virtues of private initiative are sacrificed and the public good is financed through compulsory taxation rather than voluntary contributions. With big government there is less of a role for foundations to play, making public policy toward foundations less relevant from a public interest standpoint.

Foundations have become more ideologically oriented over the course of the twentieth century, beyond a doubt. The liberal bias of many of the largest foundations has been countered to a degree by a conservative bias on the part of some others, but regardless of the direction of bias, its existence is well-enough recognized that it is easy to write off the ideas produced by foundation funding as an extension of the biases of foundation trustees. Thus, foundations are less effective as supporters of public policy ideas than they are in the production of goods and services for the public interest—a role that has increasingly been crowded out by government. Favorable tax treatment subsidizes the increasingly ideological activities of foundations, allowing donors to write off their contributions to foundations for tax purposes. Foundation resources could be more effectively spent, but so could our tax dollars. In both cases, the problems occur because of the incentive structure implied in the institutional structures of both the public sector and the third sector.

Foundations do have one big advantage over the public sector—their resources come from the voluntary contributions of donors rather than from coerced payments from taxpayers. The lack of accountability inherent in the system that gives trustees the power to spend other people's money without having to answer to those other people also gives foundations the potential to further the public interest in ways that would not be possible for organizations that do have to be accountable for the way they spend their resources. The general public might hope for more from foundation trustees, but at the same time would not want to eliminate the opportunity that foundations have to further the public interest using private contributions. Foundation grants are already small when compared to private philanthropic contributions, and are even smaller when compared to public sector expenditures. Additional taxation of foundations would transfer resources from foundations to an already much larger public sector, so would do little to alter the balance, and additional regulation would make foundations more an extension of the public sector which, again, would seem to serve little public purpose.

In principle there is solid justification for regulating foundations in exchange for their tax-preferred status. Reforms undertaken in 1969 have curbed the most egregious abuses, and seem to be adequate at the end of the twentieth century. Foundations are chartered to further the public interest, and the general public should hope for more innovative and productive activities from America's foundations. At the same time we must recognize the limits of organizations that have little accountability. The best way to improve the accountability of foundations is to let them know we are watching them; but in fact we are not, and we have little incentive to. Yet in the aftermath of 1969 foundation management does know that if their activities appear too far out of line, they can expect additional regulations. We should hope for better performance from foundation trustees and management, but at this point additional government restrictions would be more likely to harm rather than help promote the public interest.

Notes

1. Robert E. Hall and Alvin Rabushka, *The Flat Tax* (Stanford, CA: Hoover Institution Press, 1985).
2. Charles T. Clotfelter, *Federal Tax Policy and Charitable Giving* (Chicago: University of Chicago Press, 1985), William C. Randolph, "Dynamic Income, Progressive Taxes, and the Timing of Charitable Contributions,"

Journal of Political Economy 103, No. 4 (August 1995), pp. 709-738, Rebecca Schaefer, "So, What Gives? How Tax Policies Affect Charitable Donations," *Issue Analysis* No. 19 (December 20, 1995), Washington, D.C.: Citizens for a Sound Economy Foundation, and Jerald Schiff, *Charitable Giving and Government Policy: An Economic Analysis* (New York: Greenwood Press, 1990).

3. B. Douglas Bernheim, *Does the Estate Tax Raise Revenue?* (Cambridge, MA: National Bureau of Economic Research, 1986).

4. John A. Brittain, *The Inheritance of Economic Status* (Washington, DC: Brookings Institution, 1977) provides evidence, as does Francine D. Blau and John W. Graham, "Black-White Differences in Wealth and Asset Composition," *Quarterly Journal of Economics* 105, No. 2 (May 1990), pp. 321-339. Douglas Holtz-Eakin, David Joulfaian, and Harvey S. Rosen, "The Carnegie Conjecture: Some Empirical Evidence," *Quarterly Journal of Economics* 108, No. 2 (May 1993), pp. 413-435 suggest some disadvantages of inherited wealth.

5. This point is emphasized by Edgar K. Browning, "Inequality and Poverty," *Southern Economic Journal* 55, No. 4 (April 1989), pp. 819-830.

6. Philosopher John Rawls, in his *A Theory of Justice* (Cambridge, MA: Belknap, 1971) provides an example of someone who views equality only as a potential means to the end of enhancing the welfare of those least well off. Rawls' work has had a significant impact in the social sciences.

7. A substantial literature on the topic is based on the seminal work by Peter A. Diamond and James A. Mirrlees, "Optimal Taxation and Public Production: I and II," *American Economic Review* 81 (March 1971), pp. 8-27, and (June 1971), pp. 261-278.

8. Niskanen's most prominent works on bureaucracy are *Bureaucracy and Representative Government* (Chicago: Aldine-Atherton, 1971), "Bureaucrats and Politicians," *Journal of Law & Economics* 18 (December 1975), pp. 617-643, and "The Peculiar Economics of Bureaucracy," *American Economic Review* 58 (May 1968), pp. 293-305.

9. This point was made by Earl A. Thompson, "Review of Niskanen's *Bureaucracy and Representative Government*," *Journal of Economic Literature* 11 (September 1973), pp. 133-140.

10. Ellen Condliffe Lagemann, *The Politics of Knowledge: The Carnegie Corporation, Philanthropy, and Public Policy* (Middletown, CT: Wesleyan University Press, 1989).

11. Mary Anna Culleton Colwell, *Private Foundations and Public Policy: The Political Role of Philanthropy* (New York: Garland Publishing, Inc., 1993).

12. Philip Klein, *From Philanthropy to Social Welfare: An American Cultural Perspective* (San Francisco: Jossey-Bass, 1968).

13. Waldemar A. Nielsen, *The Endangered Sector* (New York: Columbia University Press, 1979), ch. 8.

14. Not everybody sees government entry into the traditional domains of private philanthropy as a threat. James W. Harvey and Kevin F. McCrohan, "Changing Conditions for Fund Raising and Philanthropy," Chapter 3 in

Jon Van Til and Associates, *Critical Issues in American Philanthropy* (San Francisco: Jossey-Bass Publishers, 1990), list twenty-one threats to philanthropy, but do not include this one among them.

15. Michael Novak, "An Essay on 'Public' and 'Private,'" pp. 11-25 in Robert Payton, Michael Novak, Brian O'Connell, and Peter Dobkin Hall, *Philanthropy: Four Views* (New Brunswick: Transaction Books, 1988).

16. Gunnar Myrdal, with Richard Sterner and Arnold Rose, *An American Dilemma: The Negro Problem and American Democracy,* 2 vols. (New York: Harper & Brothers, 1944).

17. Charles Murray, *Losing Ground: American Social Policy, 1950-1980* (New York: Basic Books, 1984).

References

Alchon, Guy, *The Invisible Hand of Planning: Capitalism, Social Science, and the State in the 1920s.* Princeton, NJ: Princeton University Press, 1985.

The American Assembly, *The Future of Foundations.* Englewood Cliffs, NJ: Prentice-Hall, 1973.

Andrews, F. Emerson, *Patman and Foundations: Review and Assessment.* New York: Foundation Center, 1968.

Arnove, Robert F., ed., *Philanthropy and Cultural Imperialism: The Foundations at Home and Abroad.* Boston: G.K. Hall, 1980.

Arthur Andersen & Co., *Tax Economics of Charitable Giving,* 8th ed. Chicago, 1983.

Asch, Peter, *Economic Theory and the Antitrust Dilemma.* New York: John Wiley & Sons, 1970.

Axelrod, Robert, *The Evolution of Cooperation.* New York: Basic Books, 1984.

Bator, Francis M., "The Anatomy of Market Failure," *Quarterly Journal of Economics* 72 (August 1958), pp. 351-379.

Beard, Charles A., and William Beard, *The American Leviathan: The Republic in the Machine Age.* New York: Macmillan, 1930.

Beardsley, Tim, "Resisting Resistance: Experts Worldwide Mobilize Against Drug-Resistant Germs," *Scientific American* 274, No. 1 (January 1996), p. 26.

Bennett, James T., and Thomas J. DiLorenzo, *Unhealthy Charities: Hazardous to Your Health and Wealth.* New York: Basic Books, 1994.

Berle, Adolf A., and Gardiner C. Means, *The Modern Corporation and Private Property.* New York: Macmillan, 1933.

Berman, Edward H., *The Influence of the Carnegie, Ford, and Rockefeller Foundations on American Foreign Policy: The Ideology of Philanthropy.* Albany: State University of New York Press, 1983.

Bernheim, B. Douglas, *Does the Estate Tax Raise Revenue?* Cambridge, MA: National Bureau of Economic Research, 1986.

Blau, Francine D., and John W. Graham, "Black-White Differences in Wealth and Asset Composition," *Quarterly Journal of Economics* 105, No. 2 (May 1990), pp. 321-339.

Bolton, Sarah Knowles, *Famous Givers and Their Gifts.* Freeport, NY: Books For Libraries Press, 1971, reprint of 1896 ed.

Bremner, Robert H., *Philanthropy,* 2nd ed. Chicago: University of Chicago Press, 1988.

Browning, Edgar K., "Inequality and Poverty," *Southern Economic Journal* 55, No. 4 (April 1989), pp. 819-830.

Brittain, John A., *The Inheritance of Economic Status.* Washington, DC: Brookings Institution, 1977.

Buchanan, James M., "Public Finance and Public Choice," *National Tax Journal* 28 (December 1975), pp. 383-394.

Buchanan, James M., and Richard E. Wagner, *Democracy in Deficit: The Political Legacy of Lord Keynes.* New York: Academic Press, 1977.

Chambers, M.M., *Charters of Philanthropies: A Study of Selected Trust Instruments, Charters, By-Laws, and Court Decisions.* Boston: D.B. Updike, 1948.

Clarkson, Kenneth W., and Donald L. Martin, eds., *The Economics of Nonproprietary Organizations.* Greenwich, CT: JAI Press, 1980.

Clotfelter, Charles T., *Federal Tax Policy and Charitable Giving.* Chicago: University of Chicago Press, 1985.

Colwell, Mary Anna Culleton, "The Foundation Connection: Links Among Foundations and Recipient Organizations," in Robert Arnove, ed., *Philanthropy and Cultural Imperialism.* Boston: G.K. Hall, 1980.

_____, *Private Foundations and Public Policy: The Political Role of Philanthropy.* New York: Garland Publishing, Inc., 1993.

Coombs, Philip, *The Fourth Dimension of Foreign Policy.* New York: Harper & Row, 1964.

Coon, Horace, *Money to Burn: What the Great American Philanthropic Foundations Do with Their Money.* London: Longmans, Green and Co., 1938.

Cowen, Tyler, *In Praise of Commercial Culture.* Cambridge, MA: Harvard University Press, 1998.

Cuninggim, Merrimon, *Private Money and Public Service: The Role of Foundations in American Society.* New York: McGraw-Hill, 1972.

Diamond, Peter A., and James A. Mirrlees, "Optimal Taxation and Public Production: I and II," *American Economic Review* 81 (March 1971), pp. 8-27, and (June 1971), pp. 261-278.

DiLorenzo, Thomas J., *Hidden Politics: "Progressive" Nonprofits Target the States.* Washington, DC: Capital Research Center, 1993.

Drucker, Peter F., *Managing the Non-Profit Organization.* New York: HarperCollins, 1990.

Dye, Thomas R., *Who's Running America? The Conservative Years,* 4th ed. Englewood Cliffs, NJ: Prentice-Hall, 1986.

Elster, Jon, ed., *Local Justice in America.* New York: Russell Sage Foundation, 1995.

Fink, Richard H., "From Ideas to Action: The Roles of Universities, Think Tanks, and Activist Groups," *Philanthropy* 10, No. 1 (Winter 1996), pp. 10-11, 34-35.

Fremont-Smith, Marion R., *Foundations and Government: State and Federal Law and Supervision.* New York: Russell Sage Foundation, 1965.

Ford Foundation, *The Common Good: Social Welfare and the American Future.* New York, 1989.

Foundation Center, *The Foundation Directory, 1994 Edition.* New York: The Foundation Center, 1994.

_____, *Foundations and the Tax Bill.* New York: Foundation Center, 1969.

Friedman, Milton, *Capitalism and Freedom.* Chicago: University of Chicago Press, 1962.

Friedman, Milton and Rose, *Free to Choose.* New York: Harcourt Brace Jovanovich, 1980.

Goulden, Joseph C., *The Money Givers.* New York: Random House, 1971.

Hall, Peter Dobkin, "Dilemmas of Criticism," *Philanthropy Monthly* 23 (June 1990), pp. 23-27.

Hall, Robert E., and Alvin Rabushka, *The Flat Tax.* Stanford, CA: Hoover Institution Press, 1985.

Hansmann, Henry, "The Effect of Tax Exemption and Other Factors on the Market Share of Nonprofit Versus For-Profit Firms, *National Tax Journal* 40, No. 1 (March 1987), pp. 71-82.

_____, "The Role of Nonprofit Enterprise," *Yale Law Journal* 89 (April 1980), pp. 835-901.

Harrar, J. George, Alan Pifer, and David Freeman, "Effect of the Tax as Seen by Foundations," in *Foundations and the Tax Bill* (New York: The Foundation Center, 1969), pp. 53-67.

Harvey, James W., and Kevin F. McCrohan, "Changing Conditions for Fund Raising and Philanthropy," chapter 3 in Jon Van Til and Associates, *Critical Issues in American Philanthropy.* San Francisco, CA: Jossey-Bass Publishers, 1990.

Hayek, Friedrich A., *The Road to Serfdom.* Chicago: University of Chicago Press, 1944.

_____, "The Use of Knowledge in Society," *American Economic Review* 35, No. 4 (September 1945), pp. 519-530.

Heiser, Victor, *An American Doctor's Odyssey.* New York: W.W. Norton and Co., 1936.

Herrnstein, Richard J., and Charles Murray, *The Bell Curve: Intelligence and Class Structure in American Life.* New York: The Free Press, 1994.

Hochman, Harold M., and James D. Rogers, "Pareto Optimal Redistribution," *American Economic Review* 59 (September 1969), pp. 542-547.

Holcombe, Randall G. *Public Finance: Government Revenues and Expenditures in the United States Economy.* Minneapolis/St. Paul, MN: West Publishing Company, 1996.

_____, *Public Policy and the Quality of Life: Market Incentives Versus Government Planning.* Westport, CT: Greenwood Press, 1995.

Holtz-Eakin, Douglas, David Joulfaian, and Harvey S. Rosen, "The Carnegie Conjecture: Some Empirical Evidence," *Quarterly Journal of Economics* 108, No. 2 (May 1993), pp. 413-435.

Hopkins, Bruce R., *Charitable Giving and Tax-Exempt Organizations* New York: John Wiley & Sons, 1982.

Hunter, T. Willard, *The Tax Climate for Philanthropy.* Washington, DC: American College Public Relations Association, 1968.

Jeffrey Hart, "Foundations and Social Activism: A Critical View," in The American Assembly, *The Future of Foundations* (Englewood Cliffs, NJ: Prentice-Hall, 1973), pp. 43-57.

Jensen, Michael C., and William H. Meckling, "Theory of the Firm: Managerial Behavior, Agency Costs and Ownership Structure," *Journal of Financial Economics* 3 (October 1976), pp. 306-360.

Karl, Barry D., and Stanley N. Katz, "The American Private Philanthropic Foundation and the Public Sphere: 1890-1930," *Minerva* 19, No. 2 (Summer 1981), pp. 236-270.

_____, and _____, "Foundations and Ruling Class Elites," *Daedalus* 116, No. 1 (Winter 1987), pp. 1-40.

Keynes, John Maynard, *The General Theory of Employment, Interest, and Money.* New York: Harcourt, Brace and Company, 1936.

Klein, Philip, *From Philanthropy to Social Welfare: An American Cultural Perspective.* San Francisco, CA: Jossey-Bass, 1968.

Koch, Deborah, Project Coordinator, *The Nonprofit Policy Agenda: Recommendations for State and Local Action.* Washington, DC: Union Institute, May 1992.

Labovitz, John R., "The 1969 Tax Reforms Reconsidered," in The American Assembly, *The Future of Foundations* (Englewood Cliffs, NJ: Prentice-Hall, 1973, pp. 101-131.

Lagemann, Ellen Condliffe, *The Politics of Knowledge: The Carnegie Corporation, Philanthropy, and Public Policy.* Middletown, CT: Wesleyan University Press, 1989.

Lerner, Abba, *The Economics of Control.* New York: Macmillan, 1944.

Liston, Robert A., *The Charity Racket.* Nashville, TN: Thomas Nelson Publishers, 1977.

Magat Richard, ed., *Philanthropic Giving: Studies in Varieties and Goals.* New York: Oxford University Press, 1989.

Marx, Karl, *Capital.* New York: Modern Library, 1906; originally published in 1867.

McCraw, Thomas K., *The Prophets of Regulation.* Cambridge, MA: Belknap Press, 1984.

Miller, J. Irwin, "The Role of Foundations in American Life," in *Foundations and the Tax Bill.* New York: The Foundation Center, 1969.

Minasian, Jora R., "Television Pricing and the Theory of Public Goods," *Journal of Law & Economics* 7 (October 1964), pp. 71-80.

Mitchell, Wesley Clair, *Business Cycles and Their Causes.* Berkeley: University of California Press, 1913.

Murray, Charles, *Losing Ground: American Social Policy, 1950-1980.* New York: Basic Books, 1984.

Myrdal, Gunnar, with Richard Sterner and Arnold Rose, *An American Dilemma: The Negro Problem and American Democracy,* 2 vols. New York: Harper & Brothers, 1944.

Nason, John W., *Trustees and the Future of Foundations.* New York: Council on Foundations, 1977.

Nielsen, Waldemar A., *The Big Foundations.* New York: Columbia University Press, 1972.

_____, *The Endangered Sector* (New York: Columbia University Press, 1979.

_____, *The Golden Donors: A New Anatormy of the Great Foundations.* New York: Truman Talley Books, 1985.

Niskanen, William A., *Bureaucracy and Representative Government.* Chicago: Aldine-Atherton, 1971.

_____, "Bureaucrats and Politicians," *Journal of Law & Economics* 18 (December 1975), pp. 617-643.

_____, "The Peculiar Economics of Bureaucracy," *American Economic Review* 58 (May 1968), pp. 293-305.

Nolan, Stuart, and Gregory P. Conko, *Patterns of Corporate Philanthropy: Executive Hypocrisy.* Washington, DC: Capital Research Center, 1993.

O'Connell, Brian, *Philanthropy in Action.* New York: Foundation Center, 1987.

Odendahl, Teresa, *Charity Begins at Home: Generosity and Self-Interest Among the Philanthropic Elite.* New York: Basic Books, 1990.

O'Neill, Michael, and Dennis R. Young, eds., *Educating Managers of Nonprofit Organizations.* New York: Praeger, 1988.

Ostrom, Elinor, *Crafting Institutions for Self-Governing Irrigation Systems.* San Francisco, CA: Institute for Contemporary Studies, 1992.

Novak, Michael, "An Essay on 'Public' and 'Private,'" pp. 11-25 in Robert Payton, Michael Novak, Brian O'Connell, and Peter Dobkin Hall, *Philanthropy: Four Views.* New Brunswick: Transaction Publishers, 1988.

O'Neill, Michael, *The Third America: The Emergence of the Nonprofit Sector in the United States.* San Francisco, CA: Jossey-Bass Publishers, 1989.

Ostrower, Francine, "Donor Control and Perpetual Trusts: Does Anything Last Forever?" Chapter 15 in Richard Magat, ed., *Philanthropic Giving: Studies in Varieties and Goals.* New York: Oxford University Press, 1989.

Parrish, Thomas, "The Foundation: 'A Special American Institution,'" in The American Assembly, *The Future of Foundations.* Englewood Cliffs, NJ: Prentice-Hall, 1973, pp. 7-42.

Payne, James L., "The Voluntary Ideal: Should Charities Live Forever?" *Philanthropy* 9, No. 4 (Fall 1995), pp. 16-17.

Payton, Robert L., *Philanthropy: Voluntary Action for the Public Good.* New York: Macmillan Publishers, 1988.

Payton, Robert, Michael Novak, Brian O'Connell, and Peter Dobkin Hall, *Philanthropy: Four Views.* New Brunswick: Transaction Publishers, 1988.

Peschek, Joseph G., *Policy-Planning Organizations: Elite Agendas and America's Rightward Turn.* Philadelphia, PA: Temple University Press, 1987.

Powell, Walter W., ed., *The Nonprofit Sector: A Research Handbook.* New Haven, CT: Yale University Press, 1987.

Rabinowitz, Alan, *Social Change Philanthropy in America.* New York: Quorum Books, 1990.

Randolph, William C., "Dynamic Income, Progressive Taxes, and the Timing of Charitable Contributions," *Journal of Political Economy* 103, No. 4 (August 1995), pp. 709-738.

Rawls, John, *A Theory of Justice.* Cambridge, MA: Belknap, 1971.

The Rockefeller Foundation, *1994 Annual Report.* New York: Rockefeller Foundation, 1995.

Rose-Ackerman, Susan, "Ideals versus Dollars: Donors, Charity Managers, and Government Grants," *Journal of Political Economy* 95, No. 4 (August 1987), pp. 810-823.

Rostow, W.W., *The Stages of Economic Growth: A Non-Communist Manifesto.* Cambridge: Cambridge University Press, 1960.

Rudy, William H., *Foundations: Their Uses and Abuses.* Washington, DC: Public Affairs Press, 1970.

Russell Sage Foundation, *Biennial Report: 1990-1991.* New York: Russell Sage Foundation, 1992.

Samuelson, Paul A., "A Diagrammatic Exposition of a Theory of Public Expenditure," *Review of Economics and Statistics* 37 (November 1955), pp. 350-356.

_____, "The Pure Theory of Public Expenditure," *Review of Economics and Statistics* 36 (November 1954), pp. 387-389.

Schaefer, Rebecca, "So, What Gives? How Tax Policies Affect Charitable Donations," *Issue Analysis* No. 19 (December 20, 1995), Washington, DC: Citizens for a Sound Economy Foundation.

Schiff, Jerald, *Charitable Giving and Government Policy: An Economic Analysis.* New York: Greenwood Press, 1990.

Schultz, Theodore W., "Investment in Human Capital," *American Economic Review* 51, No. 1 (March 1961), pp. 1-17.

Sealander, Judith, *Private Wealth and Public Life: Foundation Philanthropy and the Reshaping of American Social Policy from the Progressive Era to the New Deal.* Baltimore, MD: Johns Hopkins University Press, 1997.

Skowronek, Stephen, *Building a New American State: The Expansion of National Administrative Capabilities, 1877-1920.* New York: Cambridge University Press, 1982.

Smith, Adam, *The Wealth of Nations.* New York: Random House, Modern Library, 1937; orig. 1776.

Surrey, Stanley S., *Pathways to Reform: The Concept of Tax Expenditures.* Cambridge: Harvard University Press, 1973

Tarbell, Ida, *History of the Standard Oil Company.* New York: Macmillan, 1904.

Thompson, Earl A., "Review of Niskanen's *Bureaucracy and Representative Government,*" *Jounral of Economic Literature* 11 (September 1973), pp. 133-140.

Tucker, M. Belinda, and Claudia Mitchell-Kernan, eds., *The Decline in Marriage Among African Americans: Causes, Consequences, and Policy Implications.* New York: Russell Sage Foundation, 1995.

Van Til, Jon and Associates, *Critical Issues in American Philanthropy.* San Francisco, CA: Jossey-Bass Publishers, 1990.

Warner, Amos G., *American Charities: A Study in Philanthropy and Economics.* New York: T.Y. Crowell, 1894.

Weaver, Warren, *U.S. Philanthropic Foundations: Their History, Structure, Management, and Record.* New York: Harper & Row, 1968.

Whitaker, Ben, *The Foundations: An Anatomy of Philanthropy and Society.* London: Eyre Methuen, 1974.

Yeager, Leland B., "Rights, Contract, and Utility in Policy Espousal," *Cato Journal* 5, No. 1 (Summer 1985), pp. 259-294.

Yinger, John, ed., *Closed Doors, Opportunities Lost: The Continuing Costs of Housing Discrimination.* New York: Russell Sage Foundation, 1995.

Zurcher, Arnold J., *The Management of American Foundations: Administration, Policies, and Social Role.* New York: New York University Press, 1972.

Index

275

About the Author

Randall G. Holcombe is the DeVoe Moore Professor of Economics at Florida State University and research fellow at The Independent Institute in Oakland, California. He received his Ph.D. in economics from Virginia Polytechnic Institute and State University, has taught at Auburn University and Texas A & M University, and is the recipient of the Ludwig von Mises Prize and Georgescu-Roegen Prize.

Professor Holcombe has testified before numerous federal and state government committees, and he is the author of studies for the U.S. Department of Energy, U.S. Geological Survey, and Center for Naval Analysis.

In addition to *Writing Off Ideas* from The Independent Institute, he is the author of the books, *Public Finance and the Political Process, An Economic Analysis of Democracy, Public Sector Economics, Economic Models and Methodology, The Economic Foundations of Government, Public Finance,* and *Public Policy and the Quality of Life*. A member of the editorial board of the journal, *Public Finance Review*, he is the author of over one hundred articles and reviews in scholarly journals, and a contributor to eighteen books.